Charles Rogers

Traits and stories of the Scottish people

Charles Rogers

Traits and stories of the Scottish people

ISBN/EAN: 9783337234270

Printed in Europe, USA, Canada, Australia, Japan

Cover: Foto ©Andreas Hilbeck / pixelio.de

More available books at **www.hansebooks.com**

TRAITS AND STORIES

OF THE

SCOTTISH PEOPLE

BY THE

REV. CHARLES ROGERS, LL.D., F.S.A. SCOT.
AUTHOR OF "FAMILIAR ILLUSTRATIONS OF SCOTTISH LIFE,"
EDITOR OF "LYRA BRITANNICA," ETC., ETC.

" Caledonia! thou land of the mountain and rock,
 Of the ocean, the mist, and the wind;
Thou land of the torrent, the pine, and the oak,
 Of the roebuck, the hart, and the hind:
Though bare are thy cliffs, and though barren thy glens,
 Though bleak thy dun islands appear,
Yet kind are the hearts, and undaunted the clans,
 That roam on these mountains so drear!"—HOGG.

LONDON
HOULSTON AND WRIGHT
65, PATERNOSTER ROW
MDCCCLXVII.

INTRODUCTION.

ENCOURAGED by the success of my "Familiar Illustrations of Scottish Life," and at the request of my Publishers, I have prepared the present work. I have been indebted to many sources of information—some rare, others familiar. Possessing a store of Scottish traditions which have been transmitted in my own family, I have used these amply. My friend, Dr. Hugh Barclay, Sheriff Substitute of Perthshire, has again favoured me with a budget of interesting Lore.

The Work may not be unacceptable. A new story adds to the sources of human enjoyment. The Traits and Characteristics of a people are worthy of preservation. The Scots were formerly a most peculiar race. Their domestic habits and social customs differed materially from those of the south. Their legal system and ecclesiastical arrangements still differ; but international prejudices are subsiding. I know of only one living Scotsman who bears a grudge at England and protests against southern supremacy. Scottish grumbling has yielded to

English generosity. The Rose and the Thistle have been intertwined, and grow lovingly together.

In the course of a few generations the distinctive peculiarities of Scotsmen will entirely disappear. During the last half-century there have been changes of a remarkable description. English manners have been penetrating northward. Many northern customs, "more honoured in the breach than the observance," have become obsolete. Domestic comforts have been increasing. Certain obnoxious social practices have disappeared; others have been ameliorated. The superfluous population have, in the mercantile centres of the south, and in our prosperous Colonies, successfully employed their energy and intelligence. The plain fare of brose and bannocks has prepared the Scotsman to endure hardships, and, irrespective of comforts by the way, to press on to the goal of honour and emolument.

In the present Work have been described the Traits and Peculiarities of the Scots during the latter half of the past Century and earlier portion of the present. There are likewise Illustrations of the habits of conspicuous persons at earlier periods, and some Anecdotes relating to men of genius and learning who have lately departed from the scene.

The manners and customs of the peasant population of the Scottish Lowlands were first delineated by Mrs. Elizabeth Hamilton in "The Cottagers of Glenburnie," while Mrs. Grant, of Laggan, in her " Letters from the Mountains," depicted the peculiarities of the Scottish

INTRODUCTION. v

highlander. Sir Walter Scott followed, describing in his own inimitable manner the entire edifice of Caledonian society. He has left nothing undone. Yet the historical inquirer may be interested to discover further illustrations of the evidence, on which the great novelist has founded the Characters in his Fictions.

The deep religious earnestness of the Seventeenth Century considerably waned after the termination of the struggles which ceased at the Revolution. From the middle till the close of the Eighteenth Century, Scotland could lay no claim to religious superiority. The bulk of the people were uncultivated and rude. Licentiousness prevailed among all classes. Riotous excess became the characteristic of a gentleman.

The upper ranks dined early and sat late. When the substantials of dinner were consumed, the gentlewomen were expected to return to the spinet or the distaff. The punch-bowl, now copiously filled, was placed before the host. There was a succession of public and family toasts and numerous sentiments, to all of which a glass of the potent liquor was drained off. The drinking-glasses of the period contained twice as much as those of the present time. Special toasts were drunk with peculiar honours,—each guest mounting upon his chair, and resting his right foot upon the table, quaffed his liquor; he then raised his glass aloft in upturned fashion, and gave nine loud huzzas. On such occasions the overthrow of the table was not an unfrequent occurrence.

When tea or coffee was announced, the host accompanied his guests to the drawing-room. The younger gentlemen tarried with the ladies, but the seniors soon returned to the dining-room to renew their potations. There were instances in which hard drinkers died in their chairs. A West country laird at one of these social meetings was seized with apoplexy and immediately expired. "The laird's looking unco gash," said the host, who had at length remarked the altered appearance of his guest. "'Deed is he," answered a neighbour, "for he's been with his Maker this hour and mair. I didna like to spoil the fun by speaking o't." This anecdote, which is perfectly authentic, presents a shocking picture of the convivial habits of the last century.

Saturday dinner-parties were common; they were protracted till the Sunday had closed. Every guest was expected to drink till he fell under the table. When all had reached this degrading position, the male attendants of the family entered and carried them to their chambers. When the apartments were insufficient for the number of guests, those who were unaccommodated with beds were extended on the floor, and covered, their neckcloths being loosened to prevent the risk of suffocation. The servants expected handsome gratuities from the guests as they departed.

The administrators of the law indulged in copious

libations of brandy and claret. "To be drunk as a judge" was a proverb. The Senators of the College of Justice continued their festivities until morning hours. Circuit dinners terminated by the members of the court sinking under the tables from which they had been feasting.

Synod suppers did not terminate till considerably after midnight. On one occasion, at four a.m., the Moderator of the Synod of Aberdeen requested *Boots*, who is the youngest member of the court, to ring the bell. The waiter appeared. "Is the kettle bilin'?"* inquired the Moderator. "It is, your reverence," responded the attendant. "See, then," added the Moderator, "that ye keep it aye fou † an' aye bilin'."

A distinguished clergyman of the capital was fond of claret. Paying a morning visit to a parishioner, he was entertained with a pint bottle of the liquor, which the host pronounced to be very old. "It's unco sma' o' its age!" said the reverend gentleman, significantly.

When drunkenness abounded, profane swearing was common. Persons of rank distinguished themselves by the grandeur of their oaths. They swore loftily, but were sometimes disconcerted. A landowner in Roxburghshire was a noted swearer. Walking in his demesne one day with a friend he was indulging his habit, when one of the labourers on the estate suddenly presented himself. The hind was known for his piety. "Whisht," said the landowner,

* Boiling. † Full.

"let that fellow pass; I am never free to swear when he is in sight."

Illicit distillation was another practice consequent on the national love of potent beverages. It was lamentably prevalent. The idle highlander planted his still in the remote glen or the mountain corrie, and prepared his usquebaugh* by the light of the moon. He was an incorrigible offender. An Argyleshire highlander was reproved by his minister for engaging in this illegal traffic. "Ye mauna ask me," said the smuggler, "to gie't up, for it supports the family. My faither an' his faither afore him made a drappie. The drink is gude—far better for a bodie than the coorse big-still whusky. Besides, I permit nae swearin' at the still, an' a' is dune dacently an' in order. I dinna see muckle harm in't." The speech contained arguments which were cogent to the utterer, and determined his resolution.

A parish minister in Fifeshire had succeeded in obtaining the modification of a heavy penalty, imposed on a parishioner who had a second time been found guilty of smuggling. The offender had solemnly promised to abandon the practice. When his difficulty was overcome, he waited on the clergyman to thank him for his intercession. "I hope, John," said the pastor, "that, as you have promised, you will carefully avoid everything of this sort for the future." "Surely, sir, surely," said John; but as he was leaving the apartment he shook his benefactor hear-

* The original Gaelic for whisky.

INTRODUCTION.

tily by the hand, and exclaimed, as he made his retreat, "Ye'll get a bottle o' the best o't yet."

Smugglers were generally detected through "informations" communicated to the excise by their neighbours. These received, as a reward, one-half the proceeds of the confiscation, and their names were not publicly divulged. I was informed by an aged supervisor that nearly all his detections were made consequent on the "informations" of neighbours. It is difficult to conceive a state of society more despicable than that in which there obtained such an habitual violation of neighbourly confidence.

Sheepstealing was a common vice of the last century, though hanging was its legal penalty. Many ghost stories had their origin in the sheepstealer throwing a white sheet over his shoulders, for the threefold purpose of concealing his person and his plunder, and of frightening those who might otherwise have guessed his intent, and sought his detection.

Deception largely prevailed. Many of the landed gentry were noted bouncers. They magnified their own importance by practising on the credulity of their retainers. A laird or highland chief, who had once visited London, or had been a few days on the Continent, possessed sufficient materials to astonish his dependants during the remainder of his life. The peasantry were adepts in the art of dissimulation. They generally boasted of their independence, but were ready to obey the laird, both in matters where obedience was due, and where acquiescence in his wishes might more creditably have been resisted.

In small burghs the traders depended chiefly on a few leading persons, to whom they attached themselves. Unlike the highland clansmen, who clung to their landless chiefs with the same ardour of affection as when their hospitalities were administered to a thousand followers, the lowland shopkeeper conserved his personal interest by countenancing only the opulent or those in authority. While Mr. James Guthrie, minister of Stirling, the future martyr, retained public favour, the burgesses flocked to his ministrations. But when he incurred the displeasure of the Court, his parishioners discovered that his prayers lacked unction, and that his discourses were unedifying. The Stirling butchers hounded him with their dogs. His congregation permitted him to be executed without venturing on any petition for his release.

The old Municipal system was tainted with many corruptions. Votes of electors for offices in the Corporation were bought and sold. Bribery at Parliamentary elections was so common that municipal councillors regarded these unlawful gains as the occasional perquisites of office. The rise of certain families in the smaller burghs may be traced to the acceptance of bribes by their founders. There was much contention among municipal rulers for individual ascendency. . They wasted the public funds in interminable litigations. In the course of the last century many of the Burghs were placed under trust. When funds for political purposes were required, burgh magistrates exposed their privileges at public auction to the highest bidder. They sold their Church Patronages. They sold their Landward Superiorities. They bartered the public rights of the burgesses to the neighbouring proprietors for personal advantages. They violated hospital and other charitable trusts. They sold the office of chief magistrate to those who would promise best, but did least, for the public benefit.

This burghal picture was even exceeded in the rural hamlets. There the roads or streets were nearly impassable, the bridges were decayed or broken down, and dungsteads were placed in front of every dwelling. No hind of the last century possessed more than one apartment; his peat fire blazed in the centre, and the smoke, which was intended to find egress by an aperture in the roof, more frequently, after encircling the chamber, escaped by the open door and unglazed windows.

With the commencement of the present century began an era of physical and moral reformation. Agriculture was encouraged; commerce received new impulses. The Clergy were now better educated, and better acquainted with human affairs: they began to exercise a salutary influence on the manners and habits of the people. The farmer now united the

well-cultivated field with the well-kept garden, in
tidy courtyard with the clean fireside. The hin-
procured a better class of dwellings. Streets ae
alleys were threaded with underground sewers, wh:
removed noxious vapours and more noxious diseaa
By a system of thorough drainage, morasses and n-
beds of lakes were converted into fields, producin,
rich cereals and abundant pasture.

The morals of the people have shared in the amelioration of their physical condition. Drunkenness has subsided; illicit distillation has ceased; the old vices have departed, and the national virtues have become more conspicuous.

Scotsmen have ceased to rejoice in national isolation. Though continuing to glory in her independence and ancient liberties, Scotland owns that the proudest day of her history was that of her union with England. The *perfervidum ingenium* remains, but its acrimony has departed. Scotsmen proceed everywhere; and wherever they are found, they are esteemed for their probity and honour, and are characterized by an energy which knows not how to yield, and a determination which is invincible.

C. R.

LONDON, *May* 10, 1867.

CONTENTS.

PAGE

INTRODUCTION 4

CHAPTER I.
THE OLD SCOTTISH CLERGY.

John Knox—George Buchanan—Andrew Melville and James VI.—David Ferguson and James VI.—James Guthrie and Charles II.—Samuel Rutherford and Archbishop Usher—William III. and Principal Carstairs—James VI. and his "Book of Sports"—John M'Vicar—St. Serf—The Laird of Tillicoultry—Peter Beaton—Dean Thomas Forret—John Gray and clerical banking—The Earl of Airlie—Dr. Hugh Blair—Rev. Mr. Gordon and the Duke of Cumberland—Rev. William Veitch and Lord Minto—Alexander Peden—Rev. Robert Shirra—Precentors' announcements—Dr. Ritchie and the landowner—Dr Samuel Charters and the boor—Dr. M'Cubbin and Lord Braxfield—Rev. William Leslie—Dr. Alexander Webster—John Brown of Haddington's Courtship 17

CHAPTER II.
ANECDOTES OF THE POETS.

The Grave of Ossian—The MSS. of Ossian—James I. the originator of Scottish music—James III. and Sir William Rogers—James VI. a Patron of the Poets—The Earl of Stirling—Drummond of Hawthornden—Sir Robert Aytoun—Professor Aytoun—Professor Wilson—Lord Robertson, John Gibson Lockhart, and Sir Walter Scott—Scott and the Ettrick Shepherd—Scott and Robert Burns—Recollections of Robert Burns—"Bruce's Address to his Army"—Lady Nairn and her Songs—Mr. Oliphant of Gask—Lady Anne Barnard—Mrs. Agnes Lyon—Robert Fergusson—Allan Ramsay and his landlord—Thomas Campbell—John Leyden—James Hogg—Allan Cunningham and Cromek—James Grahame—Alexander and John Bethune—Michael Bruce—Robert Pollok—David Gray—Alexander Smith—Hugh Miller—Dr. Thomas Brown—Dr. William Tennant—Robert Tannahill—Robert Allan—Alexander Wilson, and others . . . 54

xiv   CONTENTS.

CHAPTER III.
LAWYERS AND THE LAW.
PAGE

Pertinacity of Scottish suitors—The Stirlingshire lairds and the aged hawthorn—The Dunblane landowner—Andrew Nicol and his *midden heap*—Mr. Campbell of Laguine—Miss Sheddon and her law process—Sir James Campbell and his wife—Lord and Lady Gray—Lawyers' opinions about Law—Erskine of Grange—Lord Monboddo—Dr. John Hunter of St. Andrews—Lord Kames—Kames's Habit of Gossip—Lord Braco—Lord Hermand's Irritability of Temper—Lord Auchinleck—Unpublished Anecdotes of Boswell—Lord Hailes—Sir George Mackenzie and the Earl of Bute—Lord President Dundas — Lord Gardenstone — Lord Braxfield—Lord Eskgrove—Lord Cockburn—Lords Jeffrey and Moncreiff—Lord Chancellor Erskine — Alexander Wedderburn, Earl of Rosslyn—Hon. Henry Erskine—John Clerk, Lord Eldin—John Hagart of Bantaskine— Hugo Arnot—The Advocate and Professor Gregory—The Presbytery of Meigle—Mr. William Roger and John Gunn the Freebooter—Lord Melville and Deacon Webster   97

CHAPTER IV.
ABOUT ROYAL PERSONAGES.

Queen Margaret Atheling—James I. and Richard II.—Jock Howison—James II. and Bishop Kennedy—Remarkable story of James IV. and Margaret Drummond—James V.—James VI. and the Edinburgh professors—Prince Charles Edward—Miss Flora Macdonald—George IV.—The Provost of Leith—Queen Victoria and the farmer—The Queen and the cottar's wife—Pedigree of the Empress of the French—A Sultana—A blacksmith's daughter becoming an Empress   .   . 144

CHAPTER V.
ECCENTRIC CHARACTERS.

Henry David, Earl of Buchan, and Prince Charles Edward—David Stuart, Earl of Buchan—James Boswell—Sir John Dinely—Francis Macnab, of Macnab—Master of Cultoquhey and the Duke of Atholl— Francis Semple and the military commander — James Sibbald — Dr. Walter Anderson and Principal Robertson—Professor Wilkie of St. Andrews—Lord

CONTENTS. xv

Gardenstone—Dr. Adam Smith—Professor Hamilton of Aberdeen—Dr. Thomas Blacklock—John Barclay and his wife—Thomas Coutts—Alexander Cruden—Rev. G. R. Gleig and Calvinistic Theology—Hugh Miller—Durham of Largo—A town-clerk of Stirling and the Earl of Menteith—William, Lord Panmure—The Duke of Gordon as a gaberlunzie—Miss Stirling Graham—Lord Jeffrey taken in—Sir Hugh Lyon Playfair—The "bully" and his conqueror—A curling-match—Neil Gow—Nathaniel Gow and George IV. . . 164

CHAPTER VI.

THE WISE AND THE WEAK.

Rev. John Welch and Louis XIII.—The preservation of the Regalia—Sir William Wallace in female attire—Sir Alexander Boswell and the Burns' monument in Ayrshire—Boswelliana—Story related by old Lord Elcho—Robert Pollok—Dr. Cullen—Lady Wallace and David Hume—Professor Davidson and his students—Andrew Gemmels and the recruiting sergeant—Lord Melville and the barber—Mrs. Glen Gordon and General Hawley—Lady Wallace and the Edinburgh fashions—The Farmer and the Schoolmaster—The Three Porters—The Old Lady and the Mendicant—Blind Alick of Stirling—A Countess of Strathmore—Parsimony of Dr. Glen—Family Register of a Northern Farmer—An Ignorant Examiner of Military Schools—Ignorance of a Scottish Historian—The Cobbler and his Nocturnal Visitor—The Poor Woman and the Sheriff—Scottish Rights . . . 202

CHAPTER VII.

INSCRIPTIONS, RHYMES, AND POPULAR SAYINGS.

Ancient calumnies—Wallace—Robert II.—James III.—Queen Mary—The Earl Marischal and Abbey of Deer—The Regent Mar and Cambuskenneth Abbey — The Lord President Dundas—The Stirling trader—Tombstone inscriptions—Instances of longevity—Sign-boards and finger-posts—Provincial rhymes—Story of Lord Byron—An Earl of Aberdeen—The late Earl of Leven and Craig Clatchart—Rhymes about certain localities — Family characteristics — Rhymes about notable persons — The three Jacobite ladies — A poetical bookseller—The rhyming shopkeepers—Hugo Arnot—Rev. John Ross and his pulpit rhymes 228

CHAPTER VIII.

SOME SCOTTISH ADVENTURERS.

Adventurous spirit of the Scots—Sir Robert Aytoun—Dr. Douglas, Bishop of Salisbury—James Macpherson—Dr. Andrew Bell—Bishop Strachan—Professor Beattie—Sir David Wilkie—Lord Chancellor Campbell—Dr. Robert Watt—Governor Macrae—James Earl of Glencairn—The Earl of Stirling—Robert Menteith—Colonel Edmond—Lieutenant General Anderson—Callander of Craigforth—General Scott—William Forbes of Callander—A Scotsman and the French Revolution—Alexander Selkirk—Scottish smuggling—William IV. and his Scottish courtier 258

CHAPTER IX.

UNFORTUNATE MEN OF GENIUS.

William Ged and the Edinburgh printers—A Scottish minister and the percussion cap—James Watt and the Glasgow hammermen—Dr. James Anderson and his discoveries—James Smith of Deanston—Henry Bell and the Steamboat—William Playfair—Dr. Smollett—Robert Mudie—Dr. Thomas Dick—William Thom—John Younger—Mary Pyper—Andrew Scott—William Nicholson—Isobel Pagan—Stuart Lewis—Thomas Lyle—William Glen—Alexander Hume—Peter Buchan—John Struthers—Elliot Aitchison—Andrew Park—James Macfarlane 288

CHAPTER X.

BIOGRAPHICAL AND HISTORICAL GLEANINGS.

Lord Clyde—David Roberts, R.A.—James Nisbet, the publisher—Dr. James Mounsey and his monument—The Grand Duke Nicholas and the Scottish youth—A prophecy of Alexander Peden—A prototype of Madge Wildfire—Story of Jenny Nettles—The remains of Gil Morice—Johnny Faa and the Countess of Cassilis—Helen of Kirkconnell—Bessy Bell and Mary Gray—Lord Lynedoch—Drummond of Hawthornden—Escape of Lord Ogilvie—The Countess of Strathmore and her groom—Lord Dalmeny's marriage—Chisholm of Cromlix and his confidant—Courtship of Dr. Abernethy—"The Boatie Rows"—David Mallet—Allan Masterton . . . 300

TRAITS AND STORIES

OF THE

SCOTTISH PEOPLE.

CHAPTER I.

THE OLD SCOTTISH CLERGY.

"Along the cool, sequestered vale of life,
They kept the noiseless tenor of their way."
GRAY.

THE cursory reader of Scottish history is apt to form an erroneous estimate of the older clergy. On the surface they appear as gloomy and morose persons wedded to a stern routine of life, and inflexibly opposed to social enjoyment. The truth lies in precisely the opposite direction. Tenacious of sound doctrine, and deeply attached to simple forms of worship, the older clergy were, in private life, distinguished for their generous sentiments and exemplary urbanity. The great reformer, John Knox, was in the council-chamber of Queen Mary bold and uncompromising, because it behoved him there to maintain his right of assembling the lieges for worship. He rebuked the maids of honour, who smiled as they saw him proceed to the Queen's presence, believing, as they did, that he was on his way to ruin. But Knox was in private life abundantly genial. He was a favourite in female society. By pious gentlewomen he was greatly beloved. When, an old man, he married, as his second wife, the daughter of a nobleman, his adversaries said he had obtained the lady's consent by sorcery. He approved of the Geneva system for the government of the Scottish Church, but he did not disapprove of Episcopal forms. He educated his sons at the University of Oxford.

In 1556, Knox was residing at Castle Campbell, Clackmannanshire, with Archibald fourth Earl of Argyle, the first Scottish nobleman who embraced the Protestant doctrines. A small eminence at the castle is pointed out as the scene where the Reformer dispensed the Holy Communion, on one of the first occasions that the ordinance, according to the Reformed method, was celebrated in Scotland. Castle Campbell, which rests upon a ridge of the Ochil hills, is approached through a wooded ravine. In this solitary dell, Knox had one day retired for meditation and prayer. He heard the voices of two young men from an adjoining footpath. They were engaged in animated conversation. Certain words reached the Reformer's ear, which indicated the subject of their colloquy. They were discussing the subject of Popery and Protestantism. One of the youths seemed to have cordially embraced the Reformed doctrines, the other was firmly wedded to the old faith. The debate grew warm. Keen expressions fell on both sides. They were about to be nearly related: the sister of the one in a few days was to become the wife of the other. This consideration did not weigh. The passions of both became excited. They talked loud, and mutually indulged in severe menaces. The Reformer left his retreat, and silently followed them along the footpath. A blow was struck, which was immediately returned. The youths were violently grappling each other when the Reformer stood before them. Subdued by the gravity of his presence, they unlocked their grasps. The stranger counselled forbearance. He knew, he said, the subject of their quarrel. He recommended them to listen to John Knox, who was to preach on the Castle promontory next evening: till then they should part. By some persuasion he secured compliance with his request. The youths separated, to meet again as the stranger had suggested. True to their engagement, they appeared next evening in the congregation. The preacher proved to be the personage who had interrupted their hostilities. They listened with eagerness to his burning words. The Protestant was confirmed in his views; the Catholic was awakened to his errors. At the close of the service, both waited on the Reformer and entreated his blessing. They vowed mutual reconciliation in his presence. The Romanist was received into the

Protestant Church. "A word spoken in due season, how good is it!"

George Buchanan is another of the Scottish Reformers whose name has been associated with violent measures and harsh ways. In reality Buchanan was a good-natured man and a hearty humorist. When he was discharging the duties of preceptor to the young James VI., he discovered his royal pupil's weakness in complying with every request presented to him. One day he handed two papers to the juvenile monarch, which he requested him to sign. James readily attached his name to the documents, without perusing either, or making any particular inquiry as to their contents. In one of the papers, he had formally transferred the royal authority to his tutor for the term of fifteen days. Buchanan now began to assume the state and importance of a sovereign. Being addressed by one of the courtiers with the usual salutation, when the young king was present, he announced that he should expect to be approached with more ceremony, since he had obtained the dignity of the crown. James, who began to suspect that his preceptor had suddenly lost his reason, asked for an explanation. "You are my subject," said Buchanan, "since you have devolved upon me the royal authority for fifteen days. There is the instrument," added he, "by which I have received from you my sovereignty"—placing the document before his pupil. Buchanan improved the occasion by administering to the inexperienced monarch a suitable lecture on his habitual rashness.

When Buchanan was old and beset with infirmities, he received a visit from his friends, Andrew and James Melville. They expected to have found him occupied with his great work, "The History of Scotland," which was then passing through the press. He was employed otherwise. When they entered his chamber, he was teaching his young serving-man to use the letters. "A b, ab; e b, eb," and so on, were the simple lessons which the instructor of the Scottish sovereign condescendingly taught the youth who served him. "You are not idle, sir, I perceive," said Andrew Melville, as he grasped the extended hand of his venerated friend. "Better than stealing sheep or sitting idle, which is as ill," quaintly responded the benevolent sage. A more interesting scene has not been presented in the life-history of any man of learning.

Few persons will be persuaded that Andrew Melville was of other than a saturnine cast of mind. That he was more prone to ebullitions of temper on public occasions than any of the other reformers may be admitted. He was more of a Nathanael than a courtier. The General Assembly had entrusted him to present a remonstrance to the King, representing their want of confidence in some of the royal councillors. Of these the most obnoxious was the Earl of Arran. When Melville was brought to the King's presence at Perth, and the remonstrance which he presented was read, Arran exclaimed, in a tone of menace, "Who dares subscribe these treasonable articles?" "We dare," said Melville, advancing to the table, and there affixing his signature to the document.

At an interview with the Regent Morton, Melville had expressed sentiments adverse to some portion of his public policy. In a moment of irritation, Morton exclaimed, "There will never be quietness in this country till half-a-dozen of you are hanged or banished." "Threaten your courtiers in that manner," said Melville: "it is the same to me whether I rot in the air or in the ground. The earth is the Lord's. I have been ready to give my life when it would not have been half so well expended. I have lived out of your country ten years. Let God be glorified; you cannot hang or exile his truth."

A General Assembly had been held at Cupar-Fife. The two Melvilles were deputed by the meeting to wait on the King at Falkland, to exhort him against acceding to certain measures of his council which were inimical to the Church. James Melville, who had been appointed spokesman, on account of his more courtly manners, began to set forth the object of the deputation. He had not proceeded far when the King, interrupting him, characterized the meeting of the Assembly as illegal and seditious. This was language which Andrew Melville could not tolerate, even from his sovereign. He rose up, and taking hold of the King's sleeve, called him, "God's silly*

* Weak.

vassal." He then sturdily set forth the claims of the Presbyterian Church, concluding,—" There are two kings and two kingdoms in Scotland. There is King James, the head of the commonwealth; and there is Christ Jesus, the head of the Church, whose subject James the Sixth is, and of whose kingdom he is not a king, nor a lord, nor a head, but a member." It is curious to find that from an interview which had a commencement so stormy, the King and Andrew Melville parted good friends.

In his old age, Melville was banished from his native land. He was expatriated on a charge of treason, craftily got up, because of his continued resistance to the royal measures respecting the Scottish Church. It is interesting to remark that the old man composed, in his seventy-fourth year, an ode on the marriage of the daughter of his constant friend, the Duke of Bouillon.

The most witty of the Scottish clergy at the Reformation period was David Ferguson, minister of Dunfermline. He was well known to the King, who, though he did not relish his strong views in favour of Presbyterianism, was otherwise well affected towards him. The Master of Gray had proved an apostate, by abandoning the Protestant doctrines for those of the Romish Church. It was reported among the more zealous Presbyterians that, since his apostasy, his house had often been shaken as by an earthquake. The King, when a boy of fourteen years, asked Mr. Ferguson whether he really believed that

Gray's house was shaken. "Sir," said Ferguson, "why should not the Devil rock his ain bairns?"

Ferguson was appointed by the General Assembly to wait upon the King at Falkland, along with a deputation of the brethren. As James was understood to be extremely displeased by the proceedings of the Assembly, Ferguson commenced the interview by endeavouring to put the monarch in good humour. When the deputation was introduced, the King made an observation on the subject of surnames. "On that matter," said Ferguson, "I can reckon with the best of you in antiquity, for Fergus was the first king of Scotland, and I am Fergus'-son. But as you are an honest man, and have got possession, I will yield you my right." The King laughed heartily, and requested Ferguson to proceed. After hearing the complaint which he presented, James said impatiently, "There is no king in Europe would have endured what I have suffered." "I would not have you, sire," said Ferguson, "like any other king in Europe. Many of them are murderers, but you have differently been brought up." He then proceeded to commend portions of the monarch's metrical translations of the Psalms, and the interview terminated pleasantly.

James Guthrie, minister of Stirling, was a stanch Presbyterian. He was a leader of the Protesters, who denounced all who joined the royal army without subscribing the Covenant. This course was prejudicial to the interests of Charles II., who was then (1651) courting the favour of the Scottish Presbyterians, through whose assistance he hoped to obtain the Crown. With a view to mollify his strong views, Charles paid Guthrie a visit in the manse of Stirling. As the royal visitor entered the apartment, Mrs. Guthrie hastened to hand him a chair. Mr. Guthrie interfered. "Stop, my heart," said he, "the King is a young man, he can get a chair for himself." Charles did not proceed further in making his request. When he came to power, some years after, he hanged Mr. Guthrie.

The celebrated Samuel Rutherford was extremely wedded to Presbyterianism. This is abundantly evident from his published works. His earnest piety and ministerial devotedness secured him a wide reputation among many eminent persons in the sister Church of England, who could only regret the narrowness of his sectarian views. Archbishop Usher was, in the course of a tour, passing through Galloway, and being within a few miles of Rutherford's parish of Anworth, he was seized with a strong desire to proceed thither. He did so, and knocked at Rutherford's door. He was readily admitted. Representing himself as a tourist, he claimed permission to rest himself for a little. It was Saturday evening, and the hospitable minister would not permit the stranger to proceed further on his journey till the Sabbath was past. Rutherford adopted at family worship that evening a method which obtained long afterwards in Scottish households. When he had read a chapter, he put questions to each member of the family on the leading topics which it contained. He likewise questioned the stranger. "How many commandments are there?" said Rutherford to his guest. "Eleven," replied the visitor. "No, you are wrong," said Rutherford; "there are just ten." "Did not our Saviour say," rejoined the stranger, "'A new commandment I give unto you, That ye love one another'?"* Rutherford was struck by the observation, and at once perceived that his visitor was familiar with the Scriptures.

Next morning the pastor of Anworth rose early, and, as was his habit on Sunday mornings, proceeded to a retired part of his glebe to meditate on his discourses. A narrow strip of plantation skirted this portion of the glebe, which was guarded by a sunk fence. From this fence Rutherford heard the voice of prayer. Concealed by the plantation and the upper boundary of the fence, he paused and listened. He recognised the voice of his guest, and remarked that his devotional expressions were singularly felicitous. At length the stranger began to pray fervently for the clergy and people under his care. Rutherford now perceived that he was entertaining a bishop. After breakfast, he repeated to his guest what he had heard, and informed him as to his belief concerning his rank. "I will tell you all," said Usher, who now revealed his name

* John xiii. 34.

and rank, and expressed the satisfaction he experienced in gaining admission to the presence of one whose praise was in all the churches. "I perceive," said the Presbyterian minister, "the grace of God is not confined to the members of any particular denomination. Will you preach for me to-day?" The archbishop readily consented; and adopting the usual Presbyterian forms, preached an admirable discourse, the subject being *the new commandment*. Usher and his host remained attached friends during their mutual lives.

When William III. ascended the throne, at the Revolution, he was chiefly guided in Scottish ecclesiastical affairs by the counsel of Principal Carstairs of Edinburgh. This excellent man, while deeply attached to the Presbyterian system, and though he had experienced personal torture at the hands of those who sought its overthrow, was most kindly disposed towards the deprived Episcopal clergy. One of their number, named Caddell, often called upon him. Observing his clothes to be somewhat shabby, he ordered a suit for a person of his size. When Mr. Caddell next called, Carstairs put on the new garments, and proceeded to censure his tailor for misfitting him. "They are quite useless to me," he said; "they may, however, fit some of my friends. By the way, they are just your size! Try them on." Mr. Caddell complied, and the fit was found to be exact. The poor clergyman reluctantly accepted the suit. When he got home he found the sum of ten pounds in one of the pockets, and on the paper enclosing it was written, "To the Rev. John Caddell, from his friend, William Carstairs."

It is much to be regretted that the liberality of Rutherford and Carstairs has not descended to our own times. We have heard of a dissenting minister —eminent as a divine, and possessing many estimable qualities—who, twenty years after the Disruption of 1843, assured his friends that he had not, since that event, shaken hands with any clergyman of the Established Church.

A late Cameronian minister at Denholm, Roxburghshire, concluded his prayers every Sunday morning by the petition, "Pull down papacy, prelacy, independency, will-worship, and all superstition!"

A more pleasing illustration of the "new commandment" may be related of an English clergyman of our acquaintance, who, in the course of a visit to Scotland a few years ago, preached in pulpits belonging to three different Presbyterian denominations. "Behold, how good and how pleasant it is for brethren to dwell together in unity!"

In the year 1618, James VI. published his "Book of Sports." To render the Presbyterian system less rigid, the monarch commanded that certain sports, which he characterized as "lawful to be observed," should be played in the several churchyards every Sunday, at the close of divine service. John Ross, minister of Blairgowrie, adopted a novel method of withstanding the royal ordinance. He was a strong, athletic man, and seemed much interested in the recreations enjoined by the monarch. Football was selected by the parishioners of Blairgowrie from the list of "the Sunday games." When the services of the church were completed, Mr. Ross appeared among his people in the churchyard, and proceeded to join them in their sport. Throwing his coat on a tombstone, he said,—

> "Lie ye there,
> Minister o' Blair,
> Till I, John Ross,
> Get a game at the ba'."

None of the assemblage kicked more eagerly at the football than did the reverend incumbent. But constant misfortune seemed to attend him, for every kick missed the ball and fell heavily on the ankles of those who stood near. Apologies were promptly tendered, and of course readily received, though every Sunday many of the players returned home halting. At length it was agreed that, on account of the minister's awkwardness, the games should be abandoned. This was the end contemplated by the ingenious divine.

Among the few members of the priesthood who, at the Reformation, espoused the Protestant doctrines, was John M'Vicar, priest of Inverary. He was a person of the mildest disposition, and abundantly tolerant. Unable to induce a considerable portion of his parishioners to embrace the Reformed tenets, he accommodated himself to their prejudices by continuing to administer to them the rites of the Romish Church. There remains at the manse of Inverary an octagonal stone, with two fonts, in one of which Mr. M'Vicar baptized the Protestant members of his flock, while the other contained holy water for the administration of the ordinance to those who adhered to the old faith.

St. Serf, or Servanus, an ecclesiastic of the sixth century, has a traditional celebrity for his piety and virtues. He was prior of a monastery on an islet in Lochleven, which retains his name. He made considerable journeys of a missionary character, in which he was attended by a pet ram, that shared his chamber and lay at his feet like a dog. When the saint was on a visit to Tillicoultry, accompanied by his favourite, the laird of the place, who had conceived an aversion to the churchman, seized the animal, put it to death, and had it prepared for his table. The narrative is thus given by Wyntoun, the metrical chronicler :—

> "This holy man had a ram
> That he had fed up of a lam,
> And usit him to follow aye
> Wherever he passit in his way.
> A thief this sceppe in Ackien stal,
> And ete him up in pieces smal.
> When Sanct Serf his ram had miss'd,
> Wha that it stal was few that wist;
> On presumption, nevirtheless,
> He that it stal arrestit was;
> And till Sanct Serf syne was he broucht.
> That schiepe he said that he stal nocht;

> And tharfor for to sweir an athe
> He said that he walde nocht be laith;
> But sune he blushit rede for schame,
> The schiepe it bletit in his wayme.
> Sa was he detectit schamefullie,
> And at Sanct Serf askit mercie."

The saint was not disposed to pass over the offence lightly. He uttered a prediction, that no heir born to the laird's estate of Tillicoultry should obtain possession of the inheritance. Whatever truth may be bound up in the story, it is sufficiently remarkable that during the course of the last two centuries the estate of Tillicoultry has been possessed by thirteen different families, and that no heir born to it has become the actual owner. In the year 1780 the estate was entailed, a circumstance which seemed likely to discontinue the force of the prophecy, but the validity of the entail being questioned, it was, owing to the want of a single expression, found to be null. The result led to the sale of the property, and the disappointment of the heir-expectant.

There is another priestly legend connected with the hamlet of Tillicoultry. A large stone in the parish churchyard is associated with the following tradition :—The laird of the place had differed with one of the monks of Cambuskenneth Abbey respecting the payment of tithes. In the course of the dispute, the laird smote the holy father with his fist, and laid him prostrate. In process of time the laird died, and was interred in the churchyard.

On the morning after the funeral, the hand of the deceased, which had smitten the monk, projected from the grave, clenched as if in the act of giving a blow. The villagers were horrified by the spectacle; but at length some of them summoned courage to restore the laird's hand to its place in the coffin. But next morning the priest-smiting hand reappeared above the surface, clenched as before. Again was the disjoined arm placed in the coffin, but a third time it appeared above the surface. Some of the villagers had seen a band of evil spirits in the form of monks operating on the grave during the course of the night. A large stone was now placed above the resting-place of the deceased, and the hand was not further disturbed.

In the reign of James II., Peter Beaton, priest of Tullibody, professed an attachment to Martha, daughter of Wishart, laird of Myreton. The maiden, in the hope of his abandoning the monastic life, cordially reciprocated his affection; but the priest, lured by the hope of ecclesiastical preferment, proved insincere, and renounced the fair object of his vows. The maiden died of a broken heart. Shortly before her death she preferred the request that her remains might be enclosed in a stone coffin, to be placed near the door of the chapel by which her false lover entered to the performance of his priestly rites. The unworthy churchman saw the sarcophagus, and, reflecting on his falsehood, became distracted; he died in the ravings of insanity.

The vicar of Dollar, Dean Thomas Forret, was one of the first martyrs who suffered under the régime of Cardinal Beaton. With four others, he was executed at Edinburgh on the 29th February, 1539. At his trial, which was conducted at a council held by the Cardinal, he was accused of preaching to his parishioners—a duty then solely devolving on the friars, of explaining the Scriptures in the vernacular tongue, of instructing his flock in the Decalogue, and of teaching them to repeat the Lord's Prayer in their own language. During his examination, Crichton, bishop of Dunkeld, remonstrated with him on the impropriety of his preaching every Sabbath, as a similar amount of duty might be required of the bishop. Crichton added that he himself had succeeded indifferently well, though he contented himself with his "Portuis" and Pontifical; and that he could thank God he had lived many years and had never read either the Old or New Testaments.

John Gray, who became minister of Dollar after the Revolution, was, on account of his opulence and integrity, entrusted by his parishioners and neighbours with the care of their savings. Owing to some circumstance his credit had become doubtful. Learning that a run was to be made upon him which he felt unable to satisfy, he had recourse to an ingenious device to restore his reputation. Along the wall of his deposit room he arranged a number of pewter pint measures, filled with sand nearly to the brim. Into the small space left at the mouth, he placed a number of gold and silver coins, so that the measures seemed full of the precious metals. A few of them really were filled with coins; and so, when the first applicant requested his deposits, he was told he should have them, and forthwith one of the vessels was emptied on the table. The rustic, seeing such a display of money, confessed that he had been misled by a rumour which he now perceived to be groundless, and he returned his deposits to the minister's keeping. This had the effect of entirely restoring confidence in Mr. Gray.

In smuggling times, the clergyman was often consulted as to the best means of avoiding detection from the officers of excise. "What am I to do, sir, if the gauger comes?" said a smuggler to his minister, "for ilka drap is i' the hoose." "Just tell the truth," said the minister, "and leave the event to Providence." The smuggler consented very reluctantly; "for," said he, "if the gauger tak's the drink, I'm a ruined man." In a few days, as the smuggler had anticipated, an exciseman entered his dwelling, and demanded where he had concealed his contraband merchandise. "Weel, I'll jist tell the plain truth," said the smuggler, "every drap is in a big hole under the bed." "You rascal," said the exciseman; "if it had been there you would not have been so ready in avowing it." So the officer searched the entire premises save the spot indicated, and then left grumbling that he had not effected a detection. Next day the smuggler waited on his minister to express his gratitude for his counsel. "I tauld the truth, sir," said he, "jist as ye required, an' the gauger wadna believe me. Had I dune onything else, nae doubt a' had been deteckit. I shall noo, sir, aye tell the truth, even to the gauger; for it is, as you said, best for a body i' the end."

A clergyman in the North of Scotland was reproving a parishioner for his habits of intemperance. He represented to him that whisky was his greatest enemy. "Are we not told in Scripture to love our enemies," said the irreverent bacchanalian. "Yes, John," responded the minister; "but it is not said we are to swallow them."

The Duke of Queensberry had invited his parish minister to dinner, to meet the Earl of Airlie, who was on a visit to Drumlanrig Castle. The minister was very facetious, and Lord Airlie, who had not met him before, was much interested in his conversation. As it was Saturday evening, the minister begged to be allowed to depart early. But as he rose to leave, the Earl begged he would remain a little longer,—"Just another glass, and then—" said his lordship. He was repeatedly detained with these words, and was only able to accomplish his retreat when the Duke and his guest were unable longer to delay it. The minister was much disgusted by the means taken to prevent his departure and with the excessive convivialities of the castle, and he therefore prepared a discourse for next morning's service on the evils of intemperance. When he had preached half an hour, he requested the precentor to turn the pulpit sand-glass in these words, "Another glass, and then—" The discourse was not lost upon two of his hearers, for whose benefit it was especially intended.

After the deep religious enthusiasm of the seventeenth century had subsided, two parties arose in the Scottish Church. One of these retained the evangelical sentiments of the Reformers, the other upheld a decent conformity to the moral duties as mainly constituting the plan of salvation. Towards the close of last century, the collegiate ministers of the High Church of Edinburgh were leaders of the opposing parties. Dr. Hugh Blair, an eloquent preacher and accomplished rhetorician, set forth in charming words the excellency of virtue, and insisted on strict attention to the requirements of the law of morals. His colleague, Dr. Robert Walker, powerfully set forth the doctrine of the Atonement as the only ground of the sinner's acceptance. One Sunday morning, Dr. Blair preached on his favourite theme —the beauty of virtue, when he used the following apostrophe, "O Virtue, if thou wert embodied, all men would love thee!" The afternoon's service was conducted by Dr. Walker, who, in the course of his sermon, used these words, "Virtue has been embodied. Did all men love her? No, she was despised and rejected of men, who, after defaming, insulting, and scourging her, led her to Calvary, where they crucified her between two thieves."

The Rev. Mr. Gordon, minister of Alvie, harboured

some rebels, who, escaping from the battle of Culloden, threw themselves on his bounty. For the alleged offence, he was brought before the Duke of Cumberland, at Inverness. Mr. Gordon, on being ushered into the Duke's presence, said, "I am straitened, your Royal Highness, between two contrary commands, both proceeding from high authority. My heavenly King's Son commands me to feed the hungry, to clothe the naked, to give meat and drink to my very enemies, and to relieve to the utmost of my power all objects in distress indiscriminately that come in my way. My earthly king's son commands me to drive the houseless wanderer from my door, to shut my bowels of compassion against the cries of the needy, and to withhold from my fellow mortals in distress the relief which is in my power to afford. Pray, which of these commands am I to obey?" "By all means," replied the Duke, "obey the command of your heavenly King's Son. Your character is very different from what it has been represented. Go home in peace, and act conformably to the benevolent spirit of that Gospel which you are professedly employed to preach and to explain."

In his memoir of the Rev. William Veitch, Dr. M'Crie relates the following narrative:—" When Lord Minto visited Dumfries, of which Mr. Veitch was minister, after the Revolution, he always spent some time with his friend, when their conversation often turned upon the perils of their former life. On these occasions his lordship was accustomed facetiously to say, 'Ah! Willie, Willie, had it no been for me the pyots* had been pyking your pate on the Nether Bow port;' to which Veitch replied, 'Ah! Gibbie, Gibbie, had it no been for me ye would hae been yet writing papers for a plack† the page.'" The friends had indeed been good mutual benefactors. Veitch was condemned to die under the tyrannical government of James VII., and the successful efforts of his friend in procuring his freedom tended to his own elevation from the place of an attorney to a seat on the bench as a lord of session.

Mr. Alexander Peden, the famous Covenanter, with some of his adherents, had been hotly pursued by the dragoons of the Government. Nearly exhausted by the rapidity of the flight, Peden ascended a small hill, and prayed thus,—" O Lord, this is the hour and the power of Thine enemies. They may not be idle; but hast Thou no other work for them, than to send them after us? Send them after them to whom Thou wilt gie strength to flee, for our strength is gane. Turn them about the hill, O Lord, and cast the lap o' Thy cloak over puir Saunders, and thir puir things, and save us this ae time, and we will keep it in remembrance, and tell to the commendation of Thy guidness, Thy pity and compassion, what Thou didst for us at sic a time." A cloud of mist arose, which enabled Peden and his party to escape. Meanwhile orders arrived that the dragoons should

---

* "Magpies picking your head."
† A plack is equal to the third part of a penny.

proceed in quest of Renwick and another party of Covenanters.

Mr. Thomas Mitchell, minister of Lamington, adopted a quaint phraseology in his pulpit services. In praying for suitable harvest weather, he expressed himself thus: "O Lord, gie us nane o' your rantin', tantin', tearin' winds, but a thunnerin', dunnerin', dryin' wind.'"

Mr. James Oliphant, minister of Dumbarton, was especially quaint in his public prelections. When reading the Scriptures, he was in the habit of making comments in undertones—on which account seats near the pulpit were much prized, and best filled. It is said, in reading the passage of the possessed swine running into the deep and being there choked, he was heard to mutter, "Oh, that the devil had been choked too!" Again, in the passage as to Peter exclaiming, "We have left all and followed thee!" the remark was, "Aye boasting, Peter, aye bragging; —what had ye to leave but an auld crazy boat and maybe twa or three rotten nets?"

Mr. Robert Shirra, of the Secession Church, Kirkcaldy, was one of the most remarkable of the old school of Scottish divines. With a dignified presence, he combined a vigorous intellect, and a quaintness of speech, which rendered him an extraordinary favourite with the people. Many odd stories have been, without much foundation, associated with his name. Those which follow are unquestionably genuine.

When the first outburst of the first French revolution induced many unsettled and ignorant persons in this country to dream of a universal reign of liberty and equality, several members of Mr. Shirra's congregation waited upon him to obtain an expression of his views. Perceiving that his visitors were carried away by the prevailing sentiments, Mr. Shirra declined to give an immediate reply. The subject he said was so important, that he would study it fully and deliberately before venturing on a deliverance. When his opinion was matured, he would publicly declare it from the pulpit. Probably he might do so on the following Sunday.

The deputation were delighted with the minister's reception, and the kind promise which had been elicited. News of the intended discourse on liberty, equality, and fraternity, spread rapidly in the district. Next Sunday Mr. Shirra's place of worship was densely crowded, hundreds of the working-classes present being full of expectation.

The service proceeded in the usual manner. Having preached an earnest evangelical discourse, Mr. Shirra closed the Bible and spoke as follows:—" My friends, I had a call from some of you the other day, desiring to know my opinion on liberty and equality, when I told you if you came here to-day, I might let you know. Now, since I had your visit, I have travelled in spirit all over the universe, and I shall just tell you what I have seen in my travels. I have travelled over the earth, its frozen and burning zones, mountains and valleys, moist places and dry, fertile lands and sandy deserts, and I have found men and children, big and little, strong and weak, wise and ignorant, good and bad, powerful and helpless, rich and poor. No equality there! I have travelled through the sea, its depths and shoals, rocks and sandbanks, whirlpools and eddies, and I have found monsters and worms, whales and herrings, sharks and shrimps, mackerel and sprats, the strong devouring the weak, and the big swallowing the little. No equality there! I have ascended to heaven with its greater and lesser lights, suns and satellites, and I have found thrones and dominions, principalities and powers, angels and archangels, cherubim and seraphim. No equality there! I have descended into hell, and there I have found Beelzebub, the prince of devils, and his grim counsellors, Moloch and Belial, tyrannizing over the other devils, and all of them over wicked men's souls. No equality there!

"This is what I have seen in my travels, and I think I have travelled far enough; but if any of you are not altogether satisfied with what I have told you, and wish to go in search of liberty and equality yourselves, you may find them somewhere that I have not visited. You need not travel the same road that I have done, for I can tell you positively you will not find what you want on the earth, neither in the sea, neither in heaven, neither in hell. If you think of finding them anywhere else, you may try. Meanwhile I have given you all the information I can. It rests with you to make proper use of it."

Indecorous conduct in church was reproved by Mr. Shirra with a freedom which was characteristic of the earnestness of his character. Seeing a young person asleep in the gallery, he called on those sitting near to arouse him; "For," said he, "should he fall down dead as the young man did in St. Paul's time, he may lie dead for me; I am not able like Paul to raise him to life again." On another occasion, a member of a volunteer corps, who came in rather late, was walking about in search of a seat, and, as Mr. Shirra supposed, to create attention to his new uniform. "Sit down, man," said Mr. Shirra, "we'll see your new breeks when the kirk skails."

Trade had been unusually brisk among the weavers of Kirkcaldy, and they had consequently been in the habit of drinking late on the Saturday evenings— sometimes sallying forth on the Sunday morning, to the great annoyance of the sober and serious inhabitants. In his prayer after sermon one Sunday morning, Mr. Shirra, in allusion to the unhappy custom, spoke thus:—"O Lord, while we recommend to Thy fatherly care and protection all ranks and conditions of men, we in a particular manner pray for the check-and-ticking weavers of Kirkcaldy. In Thy wisdom and mercy be pleased to send them either mair sense or less siller."

For a period the Kirkcaldy fishermen had been suffering from the scarcity of fish. On the return of better times, Mr. Shirra expressed himself thus in his public prayers,—"Oh Lord, we desire to offer our grateful thanks unto Thee for the seasonable relief which Thou hast sent to the poor of this place from Thy inexhaustible storehouse in the great deep, and which every day we have called upon our streets —Fine fresh herrings, sax a penny, sax a penny!"

One Sunday, owing to the sultry state of the weather, several of the congregation exhibited symptoms of drowsiness. After a pause, sufficient to command attention, Mr. Shirra exclaimed, " Hold up your heads, my friends, and mind that neither saints nor sinners are sleeping in the other world." This had the effect of arousing the majority, but one member of the flock was so overpowered that he began to snore. Mr. Shirra again paused, and called out, " John Stewart, this is the second time that I've stopped to wauken you; but I give you fair warning, that if I need to stop a third time, I'll expose you by name to the congregation!"

During the morning service the precentor had intimated that the prayers of the congregation were requested on behalf of David Thomson, a member of the church. " Is David very ill, Henry?" said Mr. Shirra, looking over the pulpit, to the precentor. Having obtained a reply that he was so, he said, " Weel, weel, let's pray for him." He then proceeded to utter in prayer those words of the 132nd Psalm,—" Lord, remember David and all his afflictions."

Expounding the 116th Psalm, when he came to the eleventh verse, " I said in my haste, All men are liars," he quaintly remarked, " Ay, ay, David, you would not have required to make any apology for the speech had you lived in these days; you might have now said it quite at your leisure."

Quoting those words of the 119th Psalm, "I will run the way of Thy commandments, when Thou shalt enlarge my heart," Mr. Shirra proceeded, "Well, David, what is your first resolution? 'I *will run.*' Run away, David, who hinders you? What is your next? 'I will run *the way of Thy commandments.*' Better run yet, David. What is your next? 'I will run the way of Thy commandments, when *Thou shalt enlarge my heart.*' No thanks to you, David; we could all run as well as you with such help."

The reading by the precentor, or leader of psalmody, (hitherto it can scarcely be dignified by the name of *music*) is frequently far from being elegant. It was the custom for him to read the requests for the prayers of the congregation. In fishing villages at certain seasons a usual but very equivocal request ran thus:—"A man going to see (sea) his wife requests the prayers of the congregation." On one occasion a precentor, by a reversion of an ill-written billet astonished the congregation by reading, "A man requests the prayers of this congregation *in great distress.*" So necessary was this introduction to prayer, that in Glasgow for upwards of ten years in all churches on every Sabbath there was announced, "Janet Shaw requests the prayers of the congregation." Janet was long bedridden, and thus formed a stock-piece for the precentor.

A clergyman was preaching in a church where there was a choir who monopolized the psalmody. He listened patiently to a very complex piece of music; when it was finished, he rose and solemnly said, "Now that the *band* have praised *themselves*, let the *congregation* unite with me in *praising* the Lord," and gave out the 100th Psalm, leading the tune himself, in which the congregation heartily joined.

A clergyman was accustomed to make use of scientific terms which his congregation did not understand. He was waited on by a deputation, and requested when he used any such terms in future he would be pleased to add an explanation. On the following Sunday he used the term *hyperbole*, when he added, "As agreed on, I now beg to give an apt illustration of this term. Were I to say that at this moment the whole of my congregation are sound asleep, this certainly would be an hyperbole; but if I say that one-half are in this abject condition, this would be no hyperbole, but the truth." On the following day the deputation returned and begged he would in future abstain from explanations of abstruse terms, which the congregation would endeavour thereafter to obtain from a dictionary.

A rural clergyman who had all his lifetime been a martyr to toothache, in lecturing on the narrative of the fall of man, argued that no more convincing proof could exist of the truth that man sinned and fell by eating the forbidden fruit than that the teeth from infancy to old age were above all the rest of the body the seat of painful disease.

Dr. Ritchie, Professor of Divinity at Edinburgh, was formerly minister of Tarbolton, Ayrshire. In course of his ministrations he happened one Sunday to expatiate on the profanity of using oaths in conversation. A resident landowner who was present was much addicted to the practice, and so conceived that the minister had prepared his discourse purposely to censure him. He sent for Dr. Ritchie to his residence, and accused him of referring to his private habits in the pulpit; adding, that unless the doctor would promise to abstain from such a course, he would not again enter the parish church. Dr. Ritchie calmly replied, "If you took to yourself what I said against swearing, does not your conscience testify as to its truth? You say you will not enter the church till I cease to reprove your sins; if such is your resolution, you cannot enter it again, for which of the commandments have you not broken?" The earnest firmness of the reply subdued the complainer, who thereafter endeavoured to overcome the evil habit which he had acquired.

Dr. Samuel Charters, minister of Wilton, was remarkable for a peculiar *naïveté* in administering reproof or repressing insolence. A boorish parishioner, who had conceived an aversion to him, and so left his church, told him that he had gone to a place of worship where he heard "the true gospel preached." "I am glad to hear," said Dr. Charters, "that one of your stamp goes anywhere."

A minister who was peculiarly dry in his delivery, and therefore little attractive to his congregation, one day was about to be fairly coughed down. At once he stopped, and said, "This position I think I can best illustrate by a beautiful story." The tumultuous cough instantly was hushed. After a pause, the minister proceeded, "I have no story to tell other than I was telling you, and merely wished to find out whether you had the power to stop coughing if you pleased, and now I see you have the power, I proceed with my discourse."

A clergyman who was a hard labourer in his glebe, and when so occupied dressed in a very slovenly manner, was one day engaged in his potato field, when he was surprised by the rapid approach of his patron in an open carriage, with some strange ladies, with all of whom he was to dine in the afternoon. Unable to escape in time, he drew his bonnet over his face, extended his arms covered with his tattered jacket, and passed himself off unnoticed as a potato bogle.*

There was a dinner-party at Douglas Castle, when Lord Douglas had invited Dr. M'Cubbin, his witty parish minister, to meet Lord Braxfield, the noted judge, and some other guests. Braxfield was disappointed to find that there was no claret, and asked his lordship whether he had got any in his cellar.

* Scarecrow.

"There is," said the peer, "but the butler tells me it is unsound." "Let's pree'd," said Braxfield. It was produced and was universally pronounced to be excellent. "I propose," said Braxfield to Dr. M'Cubbin, "since a *fama clamosa* has gone forth against this wine, that you absolve it." "Your lordship is a good judge in civil law," replied the doctor, "but you are not so familiar, I remark, with the laws of the Church. We never absolve till after three several appearances." The claret of the noble host suffered accordingly.

Mr. William Leslie, minister of St. Andrews, Lhanbryde, Morayshire, was addicted to practical jesting. An idle and useless creature in his parish having troubled him for a certificate to enable him to supply the loss of a horse and cow, Mr. Leslie wrote as follows:—"To all his Majesty's loving subjects who can feel for a fellow-sinner in distress. I beg to certify that the bearer, W. I——, is the son of my old bellman, a man well known in this neighbourhood for his honest poverty and excessive sloth; and the son has inherited a full share of the father's poverty, and a double portion of his indolence. I cannot say that the bearer has many active virtues to boast of; but he is not altogether unmindful of scriptural injunctions, having striven, and with no small success, to 'replenish the earth,' though he has done but little to subdue the same. It was his misfortune to lose his cow lately from too little care and too much bere chaff; and that walking skeleton which he calls his 'horse,' having ceased to 'hear the oppressor's voice or dread the tyrant's *load,*' the poor man has now no means of repairing his loss but the skins of the defunct and the generosity of a benevolent public, whom he expects to be stimulated to greater liberality by this testimonial from, thine with respect, &c., WILL. LESLIE."

Dr. Alexander Webster, of Edinburgh, was a person of remarkable merit and corresponding distinction. From a design which he prepared the New Town of Edinburgh was laid out and built. He devised and established the Ministers' Widows' Fund. He procured the first enumeration of the inhabitants of the different parishes. He was leader of the evangelical party in the General Assembly, and was no inconsiderable poet.

Dr. Webster was indebted for his entry into public life under favourable auspices to a prosperous marriage. The circumstances connected with the event are sufficiently interesting. He was originally one of the collegiate ministers of Culross. When discharging the duties of the pastorate in that parish, a young gentleman solicited him to intercede on his behalf with a young lady of the neighbourhood, of whom he had become enamoured, but who had pertinaciously refused his addresses. This young lady was Miss Mary Erskine, daughter of Colonel Erskine of Alva, and a near relative of the Earl of Dundonald. Mr. Webster undertook to intercede for his friend, and on an early day called on the lady for that purpose. His eloquence was fruitless, Miss Erskine assuring him that her determination respecting the object of his mission was unalterable. She added, "Had you spoken as well for yourself, perhaps you might have succeeded better." The hint was not lost. Mr. Webster had acted honestly and pleaded strenuously on behalf of his friend; and he felt himself free, on his next interview with the lady, to speak in his own cause. Miss Erskine, as she had indicated, was "nothing loth" to his new proposals, and afterwards agreed, as her relatives would not yield their consent, that the marriage should be solemnized in private. Several songs were written on the occasion. One on the subject of his courtship, composed by the bridegroom himself, appeared in the *Scots Magazine* in November, 1747. These lines form the first stanza:—

> "O how could I venture to love one like thee?
> And you not despise a poor conquest like me!
> On lords thy admirers could look wi' disdain,
> And knew I was naething, yet pitied my pain.
> You said, while they teased you with nonsense and dress,
> 'When real the passion the vanity's less;'
> You saw through that silence which others despise,
> And while *beaux* were a-talking read love in my eyes."

Dr. Webster was a diligent student, but at the close of the day rejoiced to visit some of his more intimate ministerial friends, and if convenience suited to remain with them to supper. From these suppers he occasionally returned home somewhat late, considerably to the annoyance of his helpmate. He found that he was more readily excused when he had been in the society of his clerical brother, Dr. John Erskine, who was with Mr. Webster a decided favourite. But Dr. Erskine chanced to hear that he had been made a stalking-horse, and so resolved to have a practical joke at his friend's expense. When Dr. Webster next came to supper, Erskine made excuse that he had to go out, but insisted that his friend should remain and take supper with Mrs. Erskine. He proceeded direct to Dr. Webster's residence, and making as it were an incidental evening call, was invited by Mrs. Webster to remain to supper. He accepted the invitation, but took leave of Mrs. Webster long before Dr. Webster's usual hour of returning from the supper-table. On returning to his house he found his friend quite at home, regaling himself over his toddy. When Dr. Webster at last reached his own dwelling he was, as usual, asked by his wife where he had been supping. "I have been down at Dr. Erskine's," was his reply. "Ah! I have found you out at last," said the indignant gentlewoman; "you were not at Dr. Erskine's; and I believe you have never been any of these weary evenings at Dr. Erskine's. I'm a poor deceived woman! The doctor was here, and took supper with me, but left at reasonable hours, as every person of proper conduct ought to do." Fearing that the storm which he had awakened might become serious, Dr. Erskine called at Dr. Webster's early next morning, and explained all. Mrs. Webster would only be reconciled on extracting from her husband the promise, that on every occasion when he supped with Dr. Erskine, he would bring a certificate of the fact.

Dr. Erskine was remarkable for his absence of mind. Meeting his wife in the Meadows, she stopped; he did so too. He bowed, hoped she was well, and again doing obeisance, walked on. When he returned home he informed Mrs. Erskine that he had met a lady in the Meadows, who seemed to know him, but that he could not make out who she was.

A newly appointed clergyman, very critical in his phraseology, had a kirk officer not much learned in philology. One night on leaving the session-house or vestry, John asked the minister if he would "*put out* the candle." "*Put out!*" replied the minister; "never say *put out*, but extinguish the candle." "Then," added the man, "*extinguish* always stands for *put out*." "Always," said the minister. Next Sabbath, one of the dogs forming part of the congregation took umbrage at the length of the exhortation, and began to yelp. John, rising from his official seat, astonished the congregation by the authoritative command, "Some one will be pleased to extinguish that dog!"

The celebrated Mr. John Brown of Haddington had courted a young lady upwards of six years. At length he contrived to overcome his natural diffidence, and spoke to her confidentially. "Janet, my woman, we've been acquainted now for six years," said he, "an'—an' I've never got a kiss yet. D'ye think I may take one, my bonnie lass?" "Just as you like, John," was the lady's answer; "only be becoming and proper wi't." "Surely, Janet," said Mr. Brown; "we'll ask a blessing." The blessing was asked and the kiss taken. "O woman, but it's gude," said the worthy minister; "we'll noo return thanks." In less than six months John and Janet were man and wife.

One clergyman meeting another, the conversation turned on the feeding of swine — no small concern in the economy of the Scottish manse. The one startled the other with the apparently rude remark, "Speaking of swine, how is your wife?" No insult was intended. The gentlewoman was widely famed for swine-culture.

CHAPTER II.

ANECDOTES OF THE POETS.

> "The poet in a golden clime was born,
>   With golden stars above;
>   Dower'd with the hate of hate, the scorn of scorn,
>   The love of love."
>
> TENNYSON.

> "The Poet's eye, in a fine frenzy rolling,
>   Doth glance from heaven to earth, from earth to heaven;
>   And as imagination bodies forth
>   The forms of things unknown, the poet's pen
>   Turns them to shapes, and gives to airy nothing
>   A local habitation and a name."
>
> SHAKESPEARE.

ACCORDING to Macpherson, the Ossianic poems were produced in the third century. There has been a controversy as to whether the son of Fingal was a Highlander or an Irishman. It is undeniable that there are traditions relating to Ossian in both countries, and that strains precisely similar to those which have been gleaned in the Gaelic Highlands have been recovered in those districts of Ireland where the Irish language is still spoken. The Irish confidently claim Ossian, or Oisin, as a native of

Erin. They describe him as the son of Fionn, one of the Fenii, from whom the modern Fenians derive their name. But Scotland claims to have given him, as well as St. Patrick, a burial-place. In the centre of the "Sma' Glen," a stupendous pass of the Grampian Mountains, there is a huge stone of cubical form, designated Clach Ossian, or Ossian's Stone. It is believed to have formed the primitive memorial stone of the great Celtic bard. When General Wade was constructing in 1746 the Highland road which passes through the glen, his men ascertained that Ossian's Stone was resting on four large slab stones placed edgewise. On the removal of the formidable cover a chamber was discovered about two feet square, in which were contained the débris of bones and fragments of coins. The opening of the tomb caused the natives to assemble from vast distances. They took up the slabs, and the relics which they enclosed, and carried them in solemn procession to a sequestered spot among the hills, where they reinterred them amidst the sound of martial music. The spot where the remains were discovered, indicated by the stone, has been celebrated by Wordsworth in these lines :—

> "In this still place, remote from men,
> Sleeps Ossian, in the Narrow Glen;
> In this place, where murmurs on
> But one meek streamlet,*—only one.

    *   *   *   *

---

* The river Almond.

Does then the bard sleep here indeed?
Or is it but a groundless creed?
What matters it? I blame them not
Whose fancy in this lonely spot
Was moved, and in such way exprest
Their notion of its perfect rest.

* * * *

It is not quiet, it is not ease;
But something deeper far than these.
The separation that is here
Is of the grave, and of austere
Yet happy feelings of the dead;
And therefore was it rightly said
That Ossian, last of all his race,
Lies buried in this lonely place."

The banks of the Carron, Stirlingshire, are celebrated in the Ossianic poems. There, according to the bard, Fingal fought with Caracal, son of the King of the World, understood to be Caracalla, son of Severus, the Roman emperor, who, in the year 211, headed an expedition against the Caledonians. The poem of *Comala* contains the following:—" Roll, streamy Carun, roll in joy, the sons of battle fled. The steed is not seen in our fields, and the wings of their pride spread in other lands. The sun will now rise in peace, and the shadows descend in joy. The voice of the chase will be heard, and the shield hang in the hall. Our delight will be in the war of the ocean, and our hands be red in the blood of Lochlin. Roll, streamy Carun, roll in joy, the sons of battle fled." The Irish regard these and similar strains as spurious, maintaining that they are not older than the eleventh or twelfth century.

There is an anecdote in connection with the controversy respecting the authenticity of Ossian's poems which has never been recorded. The father of the writer received the story from his friend, George Dempster, of Dunnichen, the celebrated member of Parliament, who was intimately acquainted with Mr. Macpherson, the accomplished editor of Ossian. Shortly after the publication of Dr. Johnson's "Tour to the Hebrides," in which the authenticity of the Ossianic Poems was so forcibly impugned, the literary world in London was strongly impressed with the conviction that the origin ascribed to the compositions was fabulous. The production of the original MSS. would alone satisfy doubters. The request was an unreasonable one, since the compositions had been recovered from tradition, and the Gaelic had only been a written language within a period comparatively recent. But it was deemed prudent, in order to preserve the popularity of the poems, that a little craft should be practised on southern sceptics. A landowner—one of the Macleods—in the Isle of Skye, gave the loan of old leases and other documents from his charter chest. These were deposited with Messrs. Cadell and Davies, the well-known publishers, and were exhibited at their shop for some months as the originals of Ossian!

The origin of Lowland minstrelsy is as unlikely to be determined as is the age of Ossian. There probably were songs and music in Lowland Scotland in ages prior to the period of written history. The spirit of the national lyre seems to have been evoked during the war of independence, and the ardour of the strain has not diminished since. Wyntoun has preserved a stanza lamenting the death of Alexander III. It is presented here in a modernized form:—

> "When Alexander our king was dead,
> That Scotland held in love and le,*
> Away went sons of ale and bread,
> Of wine and wax, of game and glee.
> Our gold was changèd into lead:
> Christ, born into virginity,
> Succour Scotland, and remeid
> That stands in such perplexity."

Songs were sung by the populace in celebration of the doughty deeds of the brave Wallace. Some minstrel verses were composed in celebration of the victory at Bannockburn.

The first Scottish poet, whose compositions have been preserved otherwise than in scraps and fragments, is James I. He was unquestionably the originator of Scottish music. The elder strains were mere rants, which disappeared on the introduction of proper melodies. James had acquired his musical tastes at the Court of England, where he was fourteen years detained in captivity. By his grandson, James III., the minstrel arts were considerably promoted. He

* Warm regard.

pensioned Henry the Minstrel, cherished the poet Dunbar, and personally composed verses. To the cultivation of music he imparted a decided impulse by pensioning at his court William Roger, or Rogers, an eminent English musician, who had visited Scotland in the train of the English ambassador. This person founded a school of music, which led to the scientific study of the art. He was afterwards knighted and constituted a member of the privy council,—distinctions which so enraged the nobility, that they caused him, with the other favourites of the monarch, to be ignominiously executed. The author of this work claims to be the representative of this ingenious but ill-fated musician.

The popular ballads of "The Gaberlunzie Man" and "The Jollie Beggar" were composed by James V. Queen Mary loved music, and wrote verses in French; and James VI. sought reputation as the writer of Latin poetry and of English psalms. Whatever were his defects as a sovereign, James VI. is entitled to approbation as a patron of the poets. The Earl of Stirling, Sir William Drummond of Hawthornden, and Sir Robert Aytoun, were severally honoured with his protection. They were the first Scotsmen who composed in English verse.

Among the various expedients to which James VI. had recourse for promoting the aggrandizement of his favourite, Sir William Alexander, afterwards Lord Stirling, was the privilege which he bestowed upon him of issuing base coins, denominated *turners*.

This description of money, though of inferior value to the coin issued from the Royal mint, was decreed to pass current; but the decree was extremely unpopular. In 1632, Lord Stirling built a house on the Castle Hill of Stirling, and having inscribed upon it his family shield, with the motto, " Per mare, per terras," some one satirically parodied it with the words " Per metre, per turners."

Sir William Drummond composed serious poetry, but he was essentially a humorist. His macaronic poem, " Polemo-Middinia, or the Battle of the Dunghill," is the most amusing composition of the sort in the language. It is a severe satire on some of the author's contemporaries. Happening to be in London, he proceeded to a tavern where several of his brother poets were in the habit of convening. Before presenting himself, he peeped into the apartment to discover who were present. He was observed, and the party called on him to enter. He found assembled Sir William Alexander, Sir Robert Kerr, Michael Drayton, and Ben Jonson. After an evening's enjoyment, the bards fell a-rhyming about the reckoning. They owned that all their verses were inferior to Drummond's, which ran thus:—

> "I, Bo-peep,
>   See you four sheep,
> And each of you his fleece.
>   The reckoning is five shilling;
>   If each of you be willing,
> It's fifteen pence apiece."

In 1645, when the plague was raging in Scotland, Drummond happened to arrive at the town of Forfar. Consequent on the regulations of the corporation, he was as a stranger refused admission into the place. He proceeded to the neighbouring town of Kirriemuir, where he was kindly entertained. The incivility which he had experienced at Forfar determined him to resent the affront. Learning that a feud existed between the towns respecting the right to a portion of common styled Muir Moss, he despatched a letter to the Provost of Forfar, which the messenger requested might at once be communicated to the corporation. The Estates of Parliament were sitting at St. Andrews, and the Provost, conceiving that the letter had proceeded from that quarter, ordered the Town Council to meet in the town-house. The parish minister was sent for, that his advice might be available. The communication was opened with much ceremony by the chief magistrate, and handed to the town-clerk, who was requested to read it aloud. The writing proceeded as follows:—

"The Kirriemarians and Forfarians met at Muir Moss,
The Kirriemarians beat the Forfarians back to the Cross.
Sutors* ye are, and sutors ye'll be ;
Fy upon Forfar, Kirriemuir bears the gree."

The insult was bitterly felt by every member of the corporation, who resolved to make individual exertion for the detection of the perpetrator.

* Shoemakers. The staple trade of Forfar was shoemaking.

Sir Robert Aytoun composed verses in several languages, but was not ambitious of fame as a poet. Many of his English poems remained in manuscript, and were supposed to be lost till about twenty-five years ago, when they were incidentally discovered by the author of the present work. Aytoun was the writer of "Old Long Syne," which, modernized by Burns, has become a universal favourite. Sir Robert Aytoun's satirical stanzas on a man dying for love are among his happiest efforts. The first stanza is charming:—

> "There is no worldly pleasure here below,
>   Which by experience doth not folly prove;
> But among all the follies that I know,
>   The sweetest folly in the world is love."

Sir Robert was a cadet of the same family which produced Professor William Edmonstoune Aytoun, whose poetical abilities as displayed in his "Scottish Cavaliers" and the "Bon Gualtier Ballads," together with his personal amenities, have caused a universal feeling of regret for his premature decease.

An anecdote of Professor Aytoun may not be unacceptable. Some years ago the writer met him at dinner at a fashionable watering-place. The guests were nearly all strangers to each other. Professor Aytoun was known only to a few. He took a leading part in the conversation, but chiefly directed his discourse to an elderly gentleman who had unadvisedly stated that he held the position of a county magistrate. The professor, conceiving that his new acquaintance valued himself on his magisterial status, seemed bent on obtaining a little harmless diversion at his expense. The robberies perpetrated by Italian brigands were then occupying public attention, and the county magistrate introduced the subject with the observation that the entire body of brigands should be exterminated. The professor took an opposite view, —considered that brigandage was not an unmitigated evil, and conceived that some of the brigand chiefs merited praise for their spirit of adventure. Besides, their system, he conceived, was a brave method of earning a livelihood. "Suppose," he proceeded, "you and I were to-morrow morning proceeding to the railway station with a brace of pistols in our vest pockets. What could be more easy than, by presenting these to the heads of well-to-do looking people in first-class carriages, to earn a number of purses easily, and without the possibility of detection?" "You may attempt this," responded the astonished magistrate, "but, for my part, I shall have nothing to do with it whatever." The subject changed. The administration of the Poor Law became a theme of discussion. The justice of the peace related that when he was on the bench he decided the cases referred to in a particular manner. "When I am on the bench," said the professor, "I decide quite in the opposite way." "Then I would not give much for your law," said the justice. The matter dropped, and the company soon proceeded to the drawing-room.

There, the writer having entered into conversation with Professor Aytoun, the county magistrate asked him aside, and inquired of him whether he knew the gentleman with whom he had been talking. He added, "I fear his principles are very lax." "Not at all, he is quite sound every way. He is the sheriff and vice-admiral of the Orkneys, a Doctor of the Civil Law, the Professor of Rhetoric in the University of Edinburgh, an Advocate at the Scottish Bar, and a leading contributor to *Blackwood's Magazine.*" "Oh, I see! Professor Aytoun, of course. What a facetious dog he is!" said the magistrate. "Pray introduce me to him."

When Professor Aytoun was making proposals of marriage to his first wife, a daughter of the celebrated Professor Wilson, the lady reminded him that it would be necessary to ask the approval of her sire. "Certainly," said Aytoun; "but as I am a little diffident in speaking to him on this subject, you must just go and tell him my proposals yourself." The lady proceeded to the library, and taking her father affectionately by the hand, mentioned that Professor Aytoun had asked her to become his wife. She added, "Shall I accept his offer, papa? He says he is too diffident to name the subject to you himself." "Then," said old Christopher, "I had better write my reply and pin it to your back." He did so, and the lady returned to the drawing-room. There the anxious suitor read the answer to his message, which was in these words,—"With the author's compliments!"

Professor Wilson was one of the most eccentric of the Scottish poets. He was uncommonly athletic, and was often tempted to afford indication of his physical powers. Shortly after his appointment to the Chair of Moral Philosophy at Edinburgh, he happened to be on a sporting excursion in the south of Scotland. He reached the border town of Hawick on a fair day. The people of this place were formerly celebrated for their pugnacity. As Wilson passed through the market-place two combatants were dealing blows at each other. He saw that one was a practised pugilist, and was disposed to deal unfairly with his opponent. His love of fair play led him to interfere. He called on the habitual pugilist to act fairly, which immediately drew upon him the ire of the bully, who threatened him with assault. With a single blow the Professor laid him prostrate, and then quietly walked on.

The Professor was in the course of a pedestrian tour in the Perthshire Highlands. A severe storm came on. Evening was drawing on, and there was no hotel or tavern near. The mansion of a surly old laird was not far off; but the cottagers reported that he lived in a state of seclusion, and was the most inhospitable of mankind. Wilson resolved to make an attempt at obtaining shelter under his roof. He proceeded to the mansion, and knocked loudly. The laird was alarmed, and presented himself in the hall,

"Who are you?" stuttered the irate gentleman, surveying the stranger's unshaven countenance and mud-bespattered costume. "I am Professor Wilson, of Edinburgh," said the stranger. "Being overtaken by this terrible storm, I have——" "You—you," interrupted the laird, "are nothing of the sort. An impostor, no doubt, looking after plunder. Get you gone." The Professor persevered, pouring forth eloquent sentences on the hospitality of Highland gentlemen. The laird, who was a reader of *Blackwood's Magazine*, was overpowered by the torrent of animated talk. "Come in, come in," he said; "for certainly you are either Professor Wilson or the d—l." The laird became delighted with his visitor.

The Professor, when in his holiday rambles, dressed very plainly. The late Principal Haldane, of St. Andrews, was travelling inside a stage-coach from Perth to Dunkeld. The only other inside passenger was a lady of prepossessing appearance and elegant manners. When the coach drew up at Dunkeld Hotel, the Principal was astonished to observe that a rough-looking personage, an outside passenger of the coach, handed the lady from the carriage, and familiarly proceeded with her into the hotel. He remembered stories of young ladies eloping with their fathers' grooms, and an apprehension of such an occurrence happening now passed across his mind. He called the landlord and inquired about the lady who had been his fellow-passenger. "Oh," said the landlord, "she is Mrs. Wilson; she has gone up-stairs with her husband, the Professor. May be ye ken him. He is sometimes called Christopher North." "Take my card to Mr. Wilson," said the Principal, quite relieved from his alarm. Principal Haldane was heartily welcomed by his fellow-travellers, and used to relate with much joviality his first impressions of the Edinburgh Professor of Ethics in his sporting jacket.

The late Lord Robertson, of Edinburgh, published two volumes of poems which did not sustain his reputation. Some time subsequent to the publication of his volumes, he met in company his old friend John Gibson Lockhart. "If you survive me, Lockhart," said the poetical judge, "you must write my epitaph." "I'll do it now," said the reviewer; "it will run thus:—

> ' Here lies a paper Lord,—
> The poet Peter;
> Who broke the laws of God,
> Of man, and metre.' "

Robertson was eminently facetious. His wit procured a happy retort on one occasion from Sir Walter Scott. Soon after the publication of "Peveril of the Peak," Sir Walter chanced to enter the Parliament House, the promenade room of the Edinburgh Law Courts, when Robertson, then an advocate, was amusing a number of his friends around the fireplace by the scintillations of his wit. As Scott came forward, Robertson exclaimed, "Hush, boys! here comes old Peveril—I see his peak!" There was a general laugh when Scott joined the circle. He asked his friend Lockhart to inform him as to the cause of the merriment. Lockhart related what had been said. Surveying Robertson's protuberant form, Scott said quietly, "Ay, ay, my man, as weel Peveril o' the Peak ony day as Peter o' the Paunch." The laugh was turned.

At a period considerably prior to his acknowledging the authorship of the Waverley Novels, Scott was spending an afternoon with the Ettrick Shepherd at Altrive Lake. The Shepherd was not one of the select few who were entrusted with the secret of the authorship; but he had never entertained a doubt as to the source whence these novels had proceeded. He had accordingly instructed his bookseller to enclose the Waverley series in a uniform style of binding, and to entitle each volume, "Scott's Novels." In examining the shelves of the Shepherd's library, Sir Walter's eye rested on the long line of handsomely bound volumes, one of which he took down. "I see," said he to his host, "your binder spells *Scots* with two *tt's*." "In this case," said the Shepherd, "I believe he has spelt correctly." Sir Walter smiled. The story was related to the writer by Mrs. Hogg, the Shepherd's widow.

When a youth of sixteen, Sir Walter Scott met Robert Burns. The great rustic bard had accompanied Professor Dugald Stewart to a conversazione at the residence of Professor Ferguson. There being several strangers present, Burns did not join in the general conversation, but proceeded to examine the pictures in the room. His attention was arrested by a print of Bunbury's, representing a soldier lying dead on the snow, his dog sitting by his side, and on the other his widow, with a child in her arms. Under the print were inscribed several lines of verse, descriptive of the scene; and Burns, who was melted to tears by the ideas suggested in the representation, inquired as to the authorship of the poetry. The philosophers were silent, or admitted their inability to make answer. Young Scott said, diffidently, "They're written by one Langhorne." On further inquiry, the pale-faced boy gave the name of the work from which the lines were quoted. He received in return a commendatory look from the bard of Coila, with these approving words,—" You'll be a man yet." This little speech, remarks a popular writer, constituted Scott's literary ordination.

Sir Walter retained a vivid recollection of his interview with the Ayrshire poet. He was particularly struck with his large dark eye. He writes, "It literally glowed. I never saw such another eye in a human head, though I have seen the most distinguished men in my time." The writer was informed by Mrs. Begg, the poet's sister, that the expression of her brother's eye, once seen, was never to be forgotten. She added, "His entire countenance beamed with genius. So striking was his look, that a stranger passing him on the highway would, though ignorant who he was, have turned round to look at him a second time."

Burns possessed the power of a crushing sarcasm, which he was not loth, on fitting occasion, to administer. He was standing on the quay at Greenock, when a prosperous merchant of the place happened to fall into the water. Being unable to swim, he had certainly perished had not a sailor at once plunged after him, and, at the risk of his own life, rescued him from his perilous situation. The merchant drew his purse, and gave the sailor a shilling. The bystanders protested as to the contemptible nature of the reward, when Burns, coming forward, entreated them to refrain. "Surely," said he, with a smile of scorn, "the gentleman is the best judge of the value of his own life."

An English commercial traveller, named Turner, met Burns in the King's Arms Hotel, Dumfries. Understanding that his new acquaintance was a poet, he professed attachment to his fraternity, and offered to treat him with a bottle of wine. But his conversation was chiefly about himself and his own merits. As Burns rose to take leave, the traveller asked him for a specimen of his versifying. Procuring a slip of paper, the poet wrote the following stanza, which he handed to his friend, and at once retired:—

"In seventeen hundred forty-nine,
  Satan took stuff to make a swine,
    And cast it in a corner:
But wilily he changed his plan,
  And shaped it something like a man,
    And ca'd it Andrew Turner."

Burns was dining with Mr. Miller, of Dalswinton. He was informed that one of the Lords of Justiciary had dined at Dalswinton the day before, and that, on entering the drawing-room, his lordship's vision being affected by his potations, he had pointed to one of his host's daughters, saying, " Wha's yon howlet-faced thing in the corner?" Burns tore off the blank leaf of a letter, and inscribed upon it these lines, which he presented to Miss Miller:—

> "How daur ye ca' me howlet-faced,
> Ye ugly, glowering spectre?
> My face was but the keekin' glass,
> And there ye saw your picture."

In a company where Burns was present some one had characterized the adherents of the Solemn League and Covenant as ridiculous and fanatical. He wrote and handed these lines to the sneerer:—

> "The Solemn League and Covenant
> Cost Scotland blood—cost Scotland tears;
> But it sealèd Freedom's sacred cause:—
> If thou'rt a slave, indulge thy sneers."

The following anecdote of the bard has not been recorded hitherto. It was obtained by the writer's father from a personal associate of the poet. Burns, at a public entertainment, was seated opposite a young foppish nobleman, who, to evince his contempt for one whom he regarded as a literary upstart, filliped some of his wine in the direction of the poet. We do it much better in our country," said the bard, as he raised his glass, and threw the entire contents in the face of the aggressor.

It is an error to suppose that Burns was not generally appreciated in his lifetime. He was eminently so. Before he had composed any of those exquisite songs which he contributed to Johnson's "Musical Museum," and Thomson's "Collection," he was hailed as a prodigy. He visited Edinburgh direct from the plough, and was received with honours and hospitalities by the leading persons of that lettered capital. His subsequent provincial tour was a continued ovation. When he was passing the second edition of his poems through Mr. Smellie's press at Edinburgh, the stool on which he usually sat while correcting his proof-sheets he found one day occupied. He looked annoyed, and the foreman, perceiving the cause, asked him to step a moment into the composing-room. Sir John Dalrymple, who was seated on the stool, was now asked to resign it for a chair, which was handed to him. "What!" said Sir John, "do you suppose I'll resign my seat to yon impudent, staring fellow?" "That is Robert Burns," said the foreman. "Robert Burns!" responded Sir John, at once dismounting from the stool; "that quite alters the case. Give him all the seats in the place."

Owing to his occasional excesses, Burns latterly forfeited the friendship of some who, at a former period, were proud to cherish his society. When keenly suffering from the loss of certain friendships, he began to apprehend, as Byron did afterwards, that his poetical fame was about to suffer an eclipse. On such occasions he would say to his wife, "Jean, they'll ken me better a hunder years after I'm gane than they do now." This anecdote is related by Colonel William Nicol Burns, the poet's surviving son.

Though abundantly conscious of his powers, Burns was free from the vanity so common to untravelled bards. His sister, Mrs. Begg, related to the writer that he was most attentive to the domestic duties, and entirely unobtrusive with his verses at the family circle. By his eldest son, Robert, who had a distinct remembrance of his father, the writer was informed that he encouraged his children to read poetry, but never presented to them his own. "My father died," said Robert, "when I was about ten years old; and though I had already read the compositions of the best English poets, I did not know that my father had written verses till considerably after the period of his death."

To the relics of Burns an extraordinary interest has attached. They have been dispersed over the habitable globe. Not a few of them have been made the subjects of special bequests. On this subject Mr. Bennoch, of London, relates, in the "Year-book," an interesting anecdote. Bacon, the host of the posting inn at Brownhill, twelve miles north of Dumfries, was an associate of the poet. From the bard he had received a snuff-box,—a horn neatly turned at the point, and mounted with silver. The landlord carried it to his dying day, out of respect for the ingenious donor. He died in 1825, when his effects were exposed to sale. The snuff-box was put up, and was being knocked down for a shilling, when the auctioneer, happening to look on the lid, discovered the inscription, which he read aloud,— "Robert Burns, officer of the excise." The words had just been pronounced, when rapid bidding followed, till the box was ultimately disposed of for five pounds. The writer was shown by his friend, Mr. Joseph Mayer, of Liverpool (whose collection of Burns's relics is unrivalled), a plain round "mull," inscribed with the poet's initials, for which an offer of five pounds had been declined.

A blacksmith at St. Ninians, Stirlingshire, is possessed of a sword-cane, which was gifted by the bard to a brother exciseman. For this relic the blacksmith has refused a tender of twenty pounds.

At the period of the Centenary celebration, the late Dr. Gillies, Roman Catholic Bishop of Edinburgh, presented to the Society of Scottish Antiquaries a pair of pistols which were said to have been used by the poet. A public notification of the event was followed by a statement in the *Illustrated London News* to the effect that the relics presented by the bishop were not genuine, the poet's pistols having been acquired by Allan Cunningham, and retained by his representatives. This announcement was acutely felt by Dr. Gillies, who determined to establish the genuineness of his gift. A thorough examination of the subject led to an unexpected result. It was proved that the pistols possessed by Allan Cunningham's representatives and those which the Catholic bishop had presented to the Antiquaries, had not belonged to the Scottish bard! But the genuine pistols turned up, and being acquired by Bishop Gillies, were by him deposited in the Antiquarian Museum.

A relic of the Ayrshire bard, of curious interest, may be mentioned. A son of the late Mr. James Gracie, banker, Dumfries, who was a kind benefactor of the bard, possesses a volume of Dr. Blair's Sermons, presented to Burns by the author. It contains numerous pencil-markings by the poet. Some years ago the writer examined this volume. A sermon on calumny was in many parts marked with approving sentences, as were passages in other discourses, referring to the ingratitude of the world, and the uncertainty of human friendship. The poet, it is easy to perceive, had been smarting under the sting of wounded pride and the desertions of friends.

Another interesting relic may be named. After composing his celebrated ode of "Bruce's Address to his Army at Bannockburn," he addressed a copy to his friend, Mr. Miller of Dalswinton. That copy, along with the poet's letter which accompanied it, was presented by a son of Mr. Miller to the late Mr. Wallace, of Kelly, as head of the Wallace family.

On the death of Mr. Wallace, the document

descended to his younger brother, the writer's late friend, Lieutenant-General Sir James Maxwell Wallace, who indicated his intention to bequeath it for preservation in the National Wallace Monument, so soon as that structure was completed.

In certain modern editions of his works, that eminently beautiful lyric, "The Land o' the Leal," has been ascribed to Burns. Several of his recent biographers allege that it was composed by him on his death-bed, and addressed to his wife. This is an error. The lyric was written by Carolina, Baroness Nairn, author of "The Lays of Strathearn." She wrote it for two married relatives of her own who had sustained bereavement in the death of a child. The original MS. has been in the hands of the writer. The correct version begins, " I'm wearin' awa', John," not " Jean."

Lady Nairn composed many other popular songs. In this respect she ranks next to Burns. From her pen proceeded such well-known compositions as "Will ye gang ower the lea-rig?" "Kind Robin loes me," "Oh weel's me on my ain Man," "Saw ye nae my Peggy?" "There's Cauld Kail in Aberdeen," "He's ower the hills that I loe weel," "The Lass o' Gowrie," "He's a terrible man, John Tod," "Bonnie Charlie's now awa'," "The Hundred Pipers," "Caller Herrin'," and "The Laird o' Cockpen." Several of these are attributed to Burns, and have been latterly included in his works. But Lady Nairn's MSS. prove her title.

The song "Caller Herrin'" was a favourite of John Wilson, the eminent vocalist. "The Laird o' Cockpen" was composed at the beginning of the century. The last two stanzas were added by Miss Ferrier.

When the late distinguished Marquis of Dalhousie, who owned Cockpen estate, was a rejected candidate for the representation of Edinburgh, he amused both his friends and opponents by quoting, in a hustings speech, a line of Lady Nairn's song. "I may only remark of Edinburgh," said his lordship, "that—

'She's daft to refuse the Laird o' Cockpen.'"

This song was founded on an older composition, beginning, "When she came ben she bobbit." That ditty was composed in the reign of Charles II. The Laird of Cockpen, hero of the piece, was an associate and military follower of the king. He was engaged on his side at the battle of Worcester, and afterwards accompanied the monarch to Holland, where he formed one of his little court. The laird excelled as a musician, and greatly delighted the king by his skilful playing. For the tune "Brose and Butter" Charles conceived a particular favour, and his companion gratified his royal wish in lulling him asleep at night, and awakening him in the morning, by playing that enchanting air.

At the Restoration, Cockpen found that his estate had been confiscated, and he had the mortification to discover that he had suffered on behalf of an ungrateful prince, who gave no response to his many entreaties for the restoration of his possessions. Visiting London, he was denied an audience, but he still entertained a hope that, by a personal conference with the king, he might gain his object. To accomplish this design he had recourse to artifice. He formed the acquaintance of the organist in the Chapel Royal, and obtained permission to officiate as his substitute when the king came to service. He did so with becoming propriety till the close of the service, when, instead of the solemn departing air, he struck up the king's old favourite "Brose and Butter." The scheme succeeded in the manner intended. The king, proceeding hastily to the organ gallery, discovered Cockpen, whom he saluted familiarly, declaring he had "almost made him dance." "I could dance too," said Cockpen, "if I had my lands again." The request to which every entreaty, on the score of humanity and justice, could not gain a response, was granted by the power of music. Cockpen was restored to his inheritance.

Lady Nairn was descended from the old Jacobite house of Oliphant, of Gask. Her father, Laurence Oliphant, of Gask, christened her Carolina in honour of Charles Edward; his father had attended the prince as aide-de-camp during his disastrous campaign of 1745-6, and his mother had indicated her deep sympathy in his cause by begging a lock of his hair on his accepting the family hospitalities. Lady

Nairn has celebrated this incident in her beautiful song of "The Auld House." She sings,—

> " The leddy, too, sae genty
> There sheltered Scotland's heir,
> An' clipt a lock wi' her ain hand
> Frae his lang yellow hair."

Lady Nairn's father would never permit the toast of the reigning family to be drunk in his presence. When he was old, and impaired eyesight compelled him to seek the assistance of his family in reading the newspapers, he would have angrily reproved the reader if "the German lairdie and his leddy" were designated otherwise than as "K. and Q."

Some one related to George the Third that there was a person in his dominions who would not drink to his Majesty's health, referring to the peculiarity of Mr. Oliphant, of Gask. "I respect that man," said the king.

Baroness Nairn was enthusiastic in her admiration of the genius of Burns, and began to compose verses to the older Scottish melodies on remarking the success of the Ayrshire bard in remodelling the elder ditties. She published all her compositions anonymously, or under the *nom de plume* of "Mrs. Bogan," and her identity was only made known after her decease.

The diffidence evinced by Lady Nairn on the subject of authorship was shared by two contemporary poetesses. Lady Anne Barnard, *née* Lindsay, eldest daughter of James, Earl of Balcarras, composed many precious lyrics, but she so dreaded publicity that she could never persuade herself to make them public. There was a single exception. The ballad of "Auld Robin Gray," composed in her twenty-first year, was printed by a member of her family, and speedily attained popularity. The hero of the ballad was the old herdman of Balcarras.

So great an interest was excited by the question as to the authorship of "Auld Robin Gray," which remained undetermined upwards of half a century, that the Society of Scottish Antiquaries made it a subject of investigation. The author was advertised for in the newspapers, a reward being offered for such information as might lead to his discovery. At length, in her seventy-third year, Lady Nairn revealed her secret to Sir Walter Scott, who printed an original copy of the ballad as his contribution to the Bannatyne Club.

Mrs. Agnes Lyon, like the preceding, is known only as the writer of a single composition. She composed the words of "Neil Gow's Farewell to Whisky." The MS. of the song, in Mrs. Lyon's handwriting, and attested as her composition, is now in the possession of a relative of the writer. Mrs. Lyon composed many poems and songs, which are still in MS. She has specified in her MS. book that the compositions are to be published only when the family funds are short.

It is well known that Burns was an enthusiastic

admirer of the poet Robert Fergusson, to whom he erected a tombstone in the Canongate Churchyard, Edinburgh. Fergusson is now almost forgotten, being eclipsed by the superior powers of the Ayrshire bard. As a true Scottish poet he is entitled to commemoration. He was singularly impulsive, and ultimately became a victim to mental disease. When a youth, he was residing with a maternal uncle, in the vicinity of Aberdeen. This gentleman was factor to a nobleman, and being a kind-hearted man, desired to introduce him to his noble constituent, who happened to be dining with him one day. Instead of appearing in a manner befitting the occasion, the juvenile poet entered the room in a state of *déshabille*, his clothes being torn from the effects of a ramble in the neighbouring plantation. Mortified by the youth's indifference, his uncle expressed himself indignantly. Fergusson proudly walked off. Hearing that he had left the premises, his uncle despatched after him a messenger on horseback. He was overtaken, but he doggedly refused to return. He walked to Edinburgh, a distance of two hundred miles, subsisting by the way as he best could.

He studied at the United College, St. Andrews. Here his poetical abilities recommended him to several of the professors, and preserved him from the effects of his occasional indiscretions. The father of the writer occupied the same rooms in the college which had been tenanted by Fergusson about fifteen years previously. He found the walls covered with rhymes, generally of a satirical order, both at the expense of the professors and certain of his less brilliant contemporaries. Two of the latter had been employed in agricultural operations before aspiring to academic honours. He inscribed one morning with red chalk, on the staircase conducting to their apartments, the couplet,—

> "Poet Cobb and William Moodie
> Left the plough and came to study."

He thus completed the verse in the evening:—

> "William Moodie and poet Cobb
> Never tried a worse job."

On one occasion the professors were made heavily to feel the bitter irony and reckless sarcasm of their poetical alumnus. The bursars, or students residing within the college, and entitled to be maintained by the institution, dined together daily in the common hall. The fare was mean, consisting generally of rabbits, from a warren in the neighbourhood. The bursars had often grumbled, but as a professor presided at table, none ventured openly to complain. Each bursar asked the blessing by turns. It was Fergusson's turn. He rose up reverently, and repeated the following:—

> "For rabbits young and for rabbits old,
> For rabbits hot and for rabbits cold,
> For rabbits tender and for rabbits tough,
> Our thanks we render, for we've had enough."

The presiding professor reported, as nearly as he could remember, the words of "the grace" to his colleagues, and a meeting of the Senatus Academicus was convened. It was ascertained that extensive dissatisfaction prevailed, and that Fergusson was the spokesman of many. His punishment might therefore have been attended with general insubordination. It was resolved to overlook the offence, and to provide a greater variety of food.

When Allan Ramsay commenced business in Edinburgh, he experienced the difficulties which usually attend the first step on the ladder of life. He was unable to meet his first half-year's rent. Some time after the rent had become due he chanced to meet his landlord, a country farmer, who was attending the Hallow Fair. The farmer hailed him to a neighbouring tavern. When they sat down, Allan referred to the subject of the rent, and expressed his distress of mind that he was unable to satisfy it. The farmer told him not to vex himself about the matter; he saw he was a lad of some genius, and would give him time. "Indeed," proceeded the farmer, "if you'll give me a rhyming answer to four questions in as many minutes, I'll quit you the rent altogether." Allan said he would try. The questions put were these:—"What does God love? What does the devil love? What does the world love? What do I love?" Within the specified time Ramsay produced the following verse:—

"God loves man when he refrains from sin ;
The devil loves man when he persists therein;
The world loves man when riches on him flow,
And you'd love me could I pay what I owe."

"The rent is paid," said the farmer, giving his young tenant a hearty slap across the shoulders, in token of high approval.

The distinguished author of "The Pleasures of Hope" was prone to some of the eccentricities which characterize men of genius. The late Professor Pillans, of Edinburgh, used to relate the following narrative concerning his early friend. When a student at Edinburgh University, Pillans happened to meet Thomas Campbell, who was then prosecuting his studies at the University at Glasgow. The youths became at once fast friends. Pillans invited his Glasgow friend to visit him in his father's house at Edinburgh, at the close of the session. The young poet accepted the invitation, but he proved a most unsocial visitor. Nothing could arouse him from a meditative mood; he seemed to have fallen into a condition of entire dejection—a sort of mental depression which could not be overcome. Mr. Pillans's father, an intelligent master printer, remonstrated with his son for bringing such "a woe-begone" person to the house. "I should not be surprised," he said, "though he would put an end to himself before morning." The future professor had likewise his misgivings as to his friend's sanity. But Campbell was then deep in the composition of "The Pleasures of Hope," which, on its appearance, at once established his claim to the highest poetical honours.

Campbell was singularly impulsive, and, as Dryden describes fortune, always in extremes. Attending the coronation of Queen Victoria in Westminster Abbey, he was moved to tears by the manner, so dignified and admirably self-possessed, in which her Majesty comported herself during the ceremonial. Returning home, he resolved to give expression to his sentiments by begging her Majesty's acceptance of a complete set of his works. He got his volumes bound in an appropriate style, and personally placed them in the hands of her Majesty's private secretary. He was informed by the secretary that the Queen was unwilling to receive gifts, since these placed her under obligations which she desired to avoid. The poet responded that there was nothing in her Majesty's dominions which he coveted, and that he simply claimed the privilege of rendering, as a subject, his devotion to his Sovereign. The secretary promised to place the volumes and his statement before the Queen. Next day a parcel from the palace was received at the poet's residence. He hesitated to open it. When he did he found his volumes returned, accompanied by a note. The Queen had graciously accepted the gift, but desired the author's autograph upon them. Campbell immediately complied with the royal wish, and in two days received another parcel from the palace, which contained an elegant engraving of her Majesty's portrait, inscribed with the royal autograph. The poet delighted to relate the anecdote and exhibit the engraving.

Campbell was walking down Regent Street, in company with the poet Southey. A poor woman with a child in her arms, and another half-clad little creature by her side, came up and solicited relief. Southey found he had no money, and Campbell, to whom such an appeal was at all times irresistible, had no smaller coin than a sovereign. He hastened into a mercer's shop, and presenting the sovereign, asked abruptly for change. The shopman was attending to a customer, but Campbell, unmindful of the fact in his desire to relieve the poor woman, insisted on his demand being complied with at once. His excited manner so alarmed the master of the shop, that after some words of an angry kind on both sides, he leaped over his counter and seized the poet by the collar. "You have come, both of you," said the irate mercer, "to make a disturbance for a dishonest purpose, and both of you shall go out at once." Campbell roared out, "Thrash the fellow! thrash him!" "You will not go out, then?" said the mercer. "Never till you apologize," said the poet. "Go, John, to Vine Street, and fetch the police," said the mercer to his assistant. Two policemen appeared forthwith, these at once placing themselves in ominous juxtaposition to the two poets. Campbell was unable to articulate from indignation. The Poet Laureate calmly explained the state of the case, adding, "This is Mr. Thomas Campbell, the distinguished poet, a man who would not hurt a fly, much less act with dishonesty." "Gudeness, man," said one of the policemen, starting back, "is this Maister Cammell, the Lord Rector o' Glasgow?" "Yes, he is; there is Mr. Campbell's card," said Southey. The mercer was appeased at once. "Had I known the gentleman," said he, "I would have changed fifty sovereigns for him." "My dear fellow," said Campbell, "I am not at all offended." And they shook hands, and parted excellent friends.

The poet's whimsical impulsiveness got him, on another occasion, into a kind of scrape. He was remarkable for his love of beautiful children. According to Mr. Jerdan, he was one day struck by the beauty of a child which he had seen in St. James's Park. To discover the abode of the young beauty, he put an advertisement in the newspapers. He had related what he had done to some persons, who could not resist the opportunity of indulging a joke at his expense. They answered the appeal, giving an address in Sloane Street. Next morning Campbell presented his card at the house, and was shown into the drawing-room. A middle-aged lady appeared, when the visitor proceeded to state that his errand was to see her lovely offspring. The lady made no reply, but rung the bell violently, and requested that the stranger might be conducted out. The poet had been sent to the house of a spinster!

At an argument, Campbell was apt to betray an

embarrassing keenness of speech. Dr. John Leyden, the eminent poet and Orientalist, was afflicted with similar impatience. The bards had quarrelled, but they remained, amidst their disputes, warm admirers of each other's genius. Sir Walter Scott relates how he repeated "Hohenlinden" to Leyden, who immediately said, in his own peculiar style, "Dash it, man, tell the fellow that I hate him; but dash him, he has written the finest verses that have been published these fifty years." Scott communicated this singular message, and received from the bard of Hope the reply, "Tell Leyden that I detest him, but I know the value of his critical approbation."

Repartee was not Campbell's forte; he occasionally succeeded. A poet, who had fancied his deserts overlooked, remarked to him one day, "I blush for the ignorance of the public; they have no taste—no perception of merit." "Ay," said the poet of Hope, "merit like yours, my friend, was born to blush unseen." He was fairly overcome at this species of banter by Turner, the celebrated painter. Meeting Turner at dinner one day, Campbell, with a view to his complimenting his brother artist, was asked to propose a toast. "I'll give you the painters and glaziers," said Campbell. There was the expected laugh; but Turner's turn came. He looked significantly at the bard of Hope, and proposed "The Paper-stainers."

Dr. Leyden was as impulsive as his poetical adversary. He could not be deterred from carrying out any resolution he had formed. His studies being at one period of a highly miscellaneous character, some one remonstrated with him on the circumstance. He replied, using his usual interjection, "Dash it, man, never mind; if you have the scaffolding ready, you can run up the masonry when you please." On board an Indian vessel he was boasting of his agility, when two gentlemen betted twenty gold mohrs that he could not go aloft. Leyden at once took to the shrouds and speedily reached the maintop. It was intended to inflict upon him the practical joke of tying him up till he should consent to pay a price for his liberty. Perceiving their intention, he seized a rope, and swung himself down—though at the cost of removing the skin from both his hands. He threw into the sea the order for the money which he had won.

On the eve of his departure for India, Leyden bid adieu to his friends at Edinburgh, with the intention of paying a farewell visit to his parents in Roxburghshire *en route* for London. A sudden impulse induced him to return to the Scottish capital, after he had proceeded some miles on his journey. He arrived in the city late of an evening, and proceeded at once to the residence of a friend, who chanced to be entertaining a party who had been toasting his health, and in kindly speeches regretting his departure. Sudden as an apparition, Leyden burst into the room with his familiar " Dash it, boys, I am here again."

James Hogg possessed the power of conjuring up ghosts, hobgoblins, and other frightful phantasmagoria, so as not only to exercise a spell over his auditors, but to haunt his own mind with viewless horrors. At the "Gordon Arms" inn, in the vicinity of his own residence of Altrive, he was one evening discoursing to willing listeners of phantoms and apparitions associated with a tale of terror. The riveted attention of the party induced him to call forth his utmost energies in depicting the frightful supernatural of his story, when a screeching female voice called into the room, "Maister Hougg, there's ane wantin' ye." "Preserve us, lassie! wha can want me at this time o' nicht?" exclaimed the bewildered poet, who started up, horror-stricken by the terrors of his own story.

During his visit to London a few years before his death, Hogg was fêted with hospitalities. At an entertainment given by Macleod of Macleod, he responded to an invitation to sing by chanting one of his Jacobite songs. When he had finished, some one remarked to him, jestingly, that he had surely forgotten that the Duke of Argyle was present. "Oh, your Grace!" exclaimed the shepherd, "never mind, I'll give you another." And he proceeded to sing "Donald Macgillivray," much to the amusement of the company.

Allan Cunningham, like the author of "The Pleasures of Hope," resided chiefly in the metropolis. His entrée to the literary world was somewhat after the manner of Chatterton. When a stonemason in Dumfriesshire, he had been introduced to Cromek, a London engraver, who was then collecting materials for his "Reliques of Robert Burns." Cunningham produced to Cromek some specimens of ballads apparently of an ancient origin, and so determined the enthusiastic engraver to publish another work, entitled "The Remains of Nithsdale and Galloway Song." The better portion of these Remains were composed by Allan himself. Cromek invited him to London, and entertained him at his residence. Trusting to his generosity, Cunningham at length revealed to his Mecænas his real connection with the *collected* poetry. Cromek, who was a man of narrow views, could not endure the idea of having been deceived. He indignantly threw off his protégé, who was obliged to resume his trade as a stonemason. But fortune attended him, and he soon obtained in Chantrey's studio a position worthy of his artistic skill and literary accomplishments.

Leyden and Hogg both practised on Sir Walter Scott the same species of imposture which Cromek suffered at the hands of Allan Cunningham. But Scott was gratified, rather than indignant, when, on the confession of the delinquents, he found that the spirit of the older ballad-writers had been transmitted to their descendants.

The Rev. James Grahame, author of "The Sabbath," occupied much of his time in verse-making, to the vexation of his excellent wife, who conceived that he was more likely to excel as a writer of prose and in other pursuits. From Mrs. Grahame he carefully concealed that he was composing a poem on the Sabbath. When the poem appeared in a handsome volume, he placed a copy on the drawing-room table, remarking to Mrs. Grahame that it was the latest poetical work which had been published. She proceeded to read a portion, and at length exclaimed, "Ah, James, if you could but produce a poem like this!" With feelings which may be imagined, Mr. Grahame proceeded to reveal the authorship.

The short-lived but most ingenious brothers, Alexander and John Bethune, the peasant poets, possessed, in the earlier portion of their career, a remarkable degree of diffidence. They were most careful in concealing from their neighbours their turn for verse-making. On the entrance of any stranger into their cottage, they hid their MSS., and removed all traces of literary occupation. This continued until the appearance of several of their volumes led to their being publicly recognized as men of letters.

A strong consciousness of power would seem to have been a characteristic of those Scottish bards whose genius early attained maturity. Robert Fergusson was painfully conscious of his poetical powers; the conviction was a burden to him, and ultimately upset his mind. On the approach of dissolution, Michael Bruce cherished the resignation of the Christian, but felt deeply that the extinction of "life's taper" would blunt his hope of the poetic wreath. Pollok was eminently pious, and gently resigned his harp. He died conscious of great powers; in his own words, he—

> " Heard from far the voice of fame,—
> Heard and was charmed."

Burns, we have seen, felt, amidst the unkindness of inconstant friendship, that his genius would, sun-like, rise above every obscuring cloud, and gain immortality. David Gray, the short-lived author of "The Luggie," wrote to his friend, Sydney Dobell, "I tell you that if I live, my name and fame shall be second to few of any age, and to none of my own. I speak thus because I *feel* power." When he had entered on the duties of his public office in Edinburgh, the late amiable Alexander Smith said to the writer, "If I live, I know that I shall make the name of Alexander Smith known from one end of the world to the other." He died at the age of thirty-seven, but fulfilled his prediction.

As a remarkable offset to these examples of a just self-consciousness of genius, it is sufficiently remarkable that several persons of transcendent literary and philosophic powers have entirely misapprehended where their strength lay. Hugh Miller published a volume of poems before he became known as a classic prose writer and an accomplished geologist. He was indifferent to reputation in the departments in which he excelled, but was covetous of fame as a poet, which his verses did not justify. Dr. Thomas Brown, the celebrated metaphysician, published a number of poetical volumes, all of which were still-born. The result was mortifying to him, for he would willingly have renounced his fame as a philosopher to have gained the credit of composing one popular poem. Lord Robertson has been named as the author of two volumes of poems. For a niche in the poetic temple, this highly accomplished person would have sacrificed his literary, judicial, and other honours; but his poetical efforts were universally condemned. Dr. William Tennant made many attempts to excel his first effort in "Anster Fair." He believed he had often succeeded, but the public decided otherwise. Apart from "Anster Fair," his numerous poetical volumes scarcely obtained a purchaser. The late Professor Aytoun informed the writer, before the appearance of his "Bothwell," that he would be content that his fame should rest upon it. It proved his only unsuccessful composition.

A venerated Scottish clergyman, some years deceased, who enjoyed a high reputation as a theological scholar and an eloquent preacher, was subject to periodical attacks of erysipelas, which affected his brain. During these attacks he abandoned his usual studies, and busily composed verses, which he took delight in reading to his family and visitors. So soon as he recovered from the attack, he committed his verses to the flames.

The remarkable success of Robert Burns in obtaining an early recognition of his genius led some of his poetical successors to expect that their own compositions would be similarly hailed. Robert Tannahill, in a fit of despondency on account of the supposed indifference to his songs, destroyed his manuscripts and committed suicide. Robert Allan, the author of "There's nae Covenant noo," and many other beautiful songs, left Scotland for America in his sixty-seventh year, disgusted with his native country for overlooking his merits as a poet. Elliot Aitchison, the Hawick bard, a person of remarkable poetical talent, was overcome by the neglect of his contemporaries. He ultimately dreaded that his name would be mentioned as a poet, and desired that after his decease he should be forgotten.

The humble circumstances of Scottish poets furnish some curious biographical particulars. Alexander Wilson, afterwards more distinguished as an ornithologist than a poet, composed his songs and ballads while carrying a wallet. James Macfarlan, whose extraordinary merits are not yet fully recognized, likewise commenced life as a pedlar. William Nicholson, author of "The Brownie of Blednoch," was a pedlar and gaberlunzie. Andrew Scott, who composed the popular ballad of "Symon and Janet," was a parish sexton. William Thom, author of "The Mitherless Bairn," was a poor handloom weaver. John Younger, a respectable poet, and author of the prize essay on the Sabbath, was an operative shoemaker. Nearly all the bards have been poor,—the children of misfortune. Some have brought discomfort upon themselves by that love of whisky which is so inherent in Scottish minstrels of the lowlier rank.

CHAPTER III.

LAWYERS AND THE LAW.

"Nemo me impune lacesset."
Scottish National Motto.

"I know you lawyers can with ease,
Twist words and meanings as you please."
GAY.

THE subtle character of the Scottish mind has rendered the legal profession one of the most prosperous. Scotsmen go to law about the veriest trifles, and debate the most paltry differences with singular energy. Compromise is seldom acceded to, and as there is a succession of tribunals before which nearly every description of process may be tried, lawyers enjoy a perpetual feast. Litigants seldom rest satisfied till they have either exhausted their finances, or at least the round of the courts. To the English mind it is quite inconceivable how important a Scotsman feels when he has a case in the Court of Session. Sir Walter Scott has delineated the Scottish litigant in the person of Peter Peebles; and his description of that personage presents no exaggerated picture of that class of persons whose names frequently figure in the reports of the law courts. Formerly a litigation in the Court of Session continued, on an average, seven years; and if either of the combatants died during the pending of the process, the war was prosecuted with unabated vigour by their representatives. When the parties were prosperous the process usually divided itself into several branches. The litigant who lost on one point was nearly certain to gain upon another. So he was encouraged to persevere. In cases involving actions for libel or damage to property, juries are empanneled. When the party receiving an adverse verdict is wealthy, his legal advisers recommend that the Court should be moved for a new trial. The grounds alleged on this motion are generally that the verdict of the jury has been contrary to the evidence, or that the presiding judge has misstated or omitted to state some point of law in summing up the evidence. It is remarkable how readily both judges and jurors admit their own errors. Judges have granted more than one new trial in the same cause on the alleged failure of the learned brother who had presided. In a recent celebrated cause the jury subscribed a memorial to the court, setting forth that had they heard the presiding judge properly, and so understood his meaning, they would have decided differently.

A most interesting volume might be written, tracing the rise and progress and issues of civil processes in the Scottish courts. Cases which have racked the minds of the combatants for the most precious years of their lives, and permanently impoverished their finances, have sprung from the most trivial causes. In every instance the kind offices of a few neighbours might have settled all differences without more expense than might be incurred at a social meeting. A few instances of the course of Scottish litigation may be quoted.

About the commencement of this century, two Stirlingshire lairds, whose estates adjoined, had, in arranging their boundaries, each laid claim to an aged hawthorn. The parties were mutually determined to possess it, and so entered on a litigation in the Sheriff Court. From the decision of the sheriff-substitute or resident county judge, the case was appealed to the sheriff. It was then entered in the Court of Session, passing under the review of the Lord Ordinary. Brought into the Inner House, the case was there debated and adjudicated. Several questions now arose out of the main process, and appeals on these as well as on the entire case were carried to the House of Lords. The various appeals having been heard by their lordships, a decree was pronounced, submitting the case with its many complications to arbitration. After a further period of exciting debate, the arbiter decided that both claimants had failed to establish a title to the hawthorn. He ruled that it should be enclosed by a walled fence, at the joint expense of the litigants, and that each party should settle his own legal costs.

What these costs were is not related, but they were of an amount sufficient to call for the sale of both estates.

An opulent landowner in the neighbourhood of Dunblane was passionately fond of litigation. He was wont to say that he had a pain in his stomach when he had no case in the Dunblane court. A young whale happened to strand in a quarry on his estate which opened into the Teith. The quarryman secured the animal, the value of which was inconsiderable. Hearing of the capture, the landowner proceeded with two attendants and claimed the whale as part of his estate. In accordance with the mode of taking possession of a newly-discovered island, he stuck his staff in the animal, and affixed his handkerchief to the staff as an apology for a flag. Proceedings were now entered in the Dunblane court, which ended in the Court of Session. The original discoverer was successful throughout; but the landlord gratified his peculiar tastes, and paid for them the value of many whales.

Another story about a whale may be related. About the year 1848, one of these ocean monsters was stranded in the bay of St. Andrews. The huge carcase was discovered close by the eastern shore. The tenant of the adjoining farm proceeded to claim the animal as his prize, his laird waiving his supposed prior title in his behalf. Meanwhile a lawyer discovered that the Earl of Crawford, as superior of the district lands, possessed certain rights in connection with the carcase. A third claimant came forward, the procurator fiscal of the county, as the representative of the Crown. This functionary took possession of the carcass, and in the Queen's name planted a guard upon it. The Earl of Crawford and the district laird and his tenant were content to avoid the certain loss of maintaining their respective claims by litigation. The Crown authorities called a public auction, and sold the blubber. About ten pounds were realized, and the loss to the Exchequer attendant on asserting the claim was inconsiderable.

Andrew Nicol, a native of Kinross, was thirty years a litigant in the courts about a *midden heap*, or small dunghill. Andrew was a sensible and judicious person save on the subject of his litigation, about which he was unreasonable and uncompromising. He was well known in the Parliament House, where he passed under the soubriquet of "Muck Andrew." He carried with him a plan of his dung-heap, and was ready to expatiate on the history of his case to any one who had the curiosity to address him, or listen to his details. Andrew closed his career in the debtors' prison at Cupar-Fife, in 1817.

Mr. Campbell, of Laguine, was an opulent and enterprising farmer in the north of Scotland. He introduced sheep-farming into the counties of Ross and Caithness. Possessed of many estimable qualities, generous, and even good-tempered, his single peculiarity was to spend a portion of his income in litigation. When he had sold his wool, he made a journey to

Edinburgh to consult with his lawyers, and he took care to pay for every meal double by the way, in the full expectation that his finances would be exhausted on the law before his return. Mr. Campbell consulted the most eminent counsel; he kept them long, but was most liberal in his fees. It is related of him that, in the absence of a distinguished lawyer on whom he called, he sought an interview with his wife, to whom in her drawing-room he explained the nature of his errand. The lady was patient, and listened for some hours to the statement of his pleas. Mr. Campbell was so gratified with her attention, that he left a sum of money as a fee, remarking that he had got quite as much satisfaction as if he had seen the lawyer himself. On one occasion, when his last case had been settled in court, he was asked by his solicitor what he would do now? meaning how he would feel for lack of his wonted excitement. "I suppose," said the litigant, " I must now dispute payment of your account."

A parish clergyman possessed a favourite dog. The animal was accused to its master by a neighbouring farmer of destroying two of his sheep. The clergyman was not satisfied that his cur was guilty, but consented to pay the cost of the sheep. The farmer wished that the dog should be killed. The clergyman refused to kill his dog, but was willing in the event of its being detected in the farmer's folds, to chain it up or send it into exile. The farmer led the clergyman into the provincial law courts. Subsequently the case was appealed to the Court of Session. Seven years did the parties pursue and defend in a series of law processes. The most eminent counsel were employed on both sides. The clergyman was victorious, but costs were not awarded him. He survived thirty years, and by living on the third of his stipend during that period was enabled to discharge his obligations.

The pertinacity with which Scotsmen pursue their real or supposed rights is in strict keeping with the national character. In the person of Sir William Wallace it thrust back English domination at Stirling Bridge, and established under Robert Bruce the national liberties at Bannockburn. But the indomitable spirit of the patriot has often degenerated into the sheer obstinacy of the partisan. The determination not to yield has been the fruitful source of disaster, insolvency, and ruin.

Captain Alexander Aytoun died in 1766, and under his father's testamentary deed was succeeded in his valuable estates of Kinaldie and Kippo by his maternal cousin, James Monypenny. The near relatives of the testator disputed the validity of the will. A litigation ensued which continued twelve years. The testamentary deed was found valid, but the decision was pecuniarily fatal to all the competitors. Mr. Monypenny, who was found legally possessed of the estates, was under the necessity of disposing of his acquisition to defray the costs of his defence.

The gentler sex have not been exempted from the national weakness of litigious pertinacity. A late female representative of the earldom of Crawford was constantly a plaintiff in one or other of the law courts. The case of succession to the estate of Roughwood, in Ayrshire, was, owing to the untiring energy of a gentlewoman, protracted in the law courts for upwards of half a century. Though suffering under the disheartening influences of successive defeats both in the courts of America and England, and though barristers had ceased to recommend a prolongation of hostilities, Miss Sheddon continued to prosecute her claims with determination and vigour. Her eloquence in addressing the courts on intricate points of law astonished learned senators, and excited on the part of many a feeling of regret that her powerful energies and remarkable powers of analysis had not been supported by more substantial claims.

Madame Lina Sassen, the reputed wife of Sir James Campbell, of Ardkinglass, became so enamoured of the law, consequent on prosecuting her alleged husband for a legal recognition of matrimonial rights, that for twenty years she was a constant attendant at the sittings of the Court of Session. That her suit against Sir James was unsuccessful did not diminish her legal ardour. She unceasingly renewed her claims, which she hoped would ultimately triumph. Her various pleas were only terminated by her death.

The following remarkable instance of pertinacity on the part of two married persons in humble life was related to the writer by the chief magistrate of a northern burgh, who vouched for the accuracy of the particulars. A married couple in the parish of Farnell had lived together happily for several years. One evening, when they were seated at their fireside, a mouse chanced to run across the floor. "There's a moosie," said the wife, "it cam frae below the bed." "Na," said the husband, "it cam oot below the kist."* The parties began to debate the point, a keen argument ensued, and angry words passed on both sides. The controversy was resumed in the morning, and continued with increasing violence from day to day, till the wife left the house and returned to her friends. The couple lived apart for twelve years, when, on the intercession of friends, they became reconciled. They resumed house-keeping together, and during five years the voice of discord was unheard. At length the wife ventured to refer to the cause of their long estrangement. "Wasn't it very absurd, dear John," said she, "that we should have separated about sic a trifle as a moosie comin' frae below the bed?" "I tell ye that it cam oot below the kist, woman," said the husband sharply. "It didna do that, John," retorted the wife, "I mind see'n 't, as if 'twere yesterday, comin' frae under the bed." The husband started to his feet, and vehemently maintained that his wife was speak-

* Chest.

ing falsely. The spirit of discord was again evoked. The parties separated, and were never reunited.

A story respecting the taming of a shrewish countess was communicated to the writer by an aged gentlewoman. A landowner near Forfar had an only daughter, who, having been much indulged, had become wilful and headstrong. Her prospects being considerable, a noble earl became a suitor for her hand. His lordship procured the lady's consent, and they were married. Before the marriage her ladyship was entreated by her sire to subdue her unyielding spirit, and duly warned that in the event of any difference with her husband, she would receive no countenance in the paternal home. The counsel did not avail, for a few weeks after the wedding she contrived to quarrel with her noble consort. Thereupon she ordered a carriage to convey her to her father's house. Her father, who had been daily expecting the arrival, was prepared, and so when the carriage drew up and the footman knocked, he personally demanded the visitor's name. "The Countess of ——," shouted the footman; while the lady, who was hastening to rush into the house, exclaimed how grievously wronged she had been by the earl. "Then," responded her sire, "since Lord —— has ill-treated my daughter, I'll take vengeance on his wife." And so saying, he displayed a large carriage whip, which he brandished about the lady's shoulders. It was enough. The countess fled to her carriage. Driving back to her husband's residence, she began to reflect on the necessity of imposing upon herself some measure of restraint.

The lady of John, twelfth Lord Gray, adopted a novel method of checking the obstinacy of her husband. When the Duke of Cumberland arrived at Dundee in 1745 to assume command of the royal troops, Lord Gray, as Lord Lieutenant of the county, waited on his Highness. The duke possessed an overbearing manner, and received his lordship haughtily. Lord Gray was excessively indignant. He hastily returned to his residence at Gray, and informing his wife of the rude reception which he had experienced, expressed his determination to be revenged. "I will let that Hanoverian know," said his lordship, "that I have as ancient blood in my veins as he can boast of, and that Scottish noblemen are not to be treated as if they were a pack of German land-lowpers. To-morrow I will join Prince Charles." Lady Gray knew that her lord could not by ordinary persuasion be induced to abandon any enterprise on which he had resolved. So she listened in silence. When bedtime came, his lordship expressed a desire to bathe his feet. Lady Gray instructed the attendant to bring to the apartment a pitcher of boiling water, and undertook personally to attend the process of the bath. When all was prepared her ladyship took up the pitcher, and discharged the entire contents on his lordship's legs and feet. One frantic roar fully testified that her object was attained. Lord Gray's limbs were so scalded that locomotion was impossible. Her ladyship screamed in affected horror at what she had done, and the family physician was sent for. When his lordship sufficiently recovered to resume the use of his limbs, his ire against Cumberland had abated, and it was too late, though the intention had remained, to offer service to the cause of the young adventurer.

These anecdotes may serve to illustrate that peculiar mood of the Scottish people which has so amply conduced to the business of the courts of law. It would, however, be most unjust to an honourable profession to ascribe to its more eminent members the encouragement of litigation. The most distinguished Scottish lawyers have uniformly discountenanced it.

Lord Chancellor Erskine, when at the bar, was consulted by his friend, Dr. Parr, in regard to a case which he thought of litigating. "Accommodate the difference amicably," said Erskine; "I can scarcely fancy a situation in which a lawsuit is not to be avoided." "A lawyer," said Lord Brougham, "is a learned gentleman, who rescues your estate from your enemies, and keeps it himself." "If any man," said Lord Cockburn, "was to claim my coat, and I believed that he was serious in his demand, I would rather part both with it and my vest than defend my title to it at the law." "Litigation," said Lord Jeffrey to the father of the writer, "is to be recommended to those only who possess a surplus of funds, and wish to get quit of it sensationally." To a client who insisted on having the last rights of the law, Sir James Gibson Craig remarked, "Well, let me tell you, the man who will have the last right and the last word at law is very like the man who will have the last drop in the tankard; he has the chance of getting the lid down on his nose."

Some of the most distinguished lawyers who have adorned the Scottish bench were persons of eccentric manners and strange peculiarities. The Hon. James Erskine, of Grange, a Lord of Session by the title of Lord Grange, was a person of singular character. He was younger brother of the Earl of Mar, who was attainted for exciting the insurrection of 1715, and bore in respect of unsettled principles no inconsiderable resemblance to that unfortunate nobleman. He was husband of that "Lady Grange" whose unwarrantable detention in the Western Isles forms one of the most remarkable episodes in modern history. The Hon. Mrs. Erskine, otherwise called Lady Grange, was daughter of Chiesley, of Dalry, who, on account of a decision of the Court of Session compelling him to maintain his wife and children, mortally wounded Sir George Lockhart, the Lord President, on returning from his place of worship. The disposition of Mrs. Erskine was too similar to that of her sire; she was a woman of ungovernable temper, revengeful, and unscrupulous in the accomplishment of her ends. She had, by concealing herself under a sofa in her husband's business chamber, become acquainted with certain circumstances which would certainly, on being publicly divulged, have cost him his office; for during the rising of 1715, some adherents of the House of Stuart frequently assembled in Lord Grange's mansion to concoct measures in support of the insurrection. Menaces of exposure, which were repeated by Mrs. Erskine on every occasion she happened to differ with her husband, rendered the domestic condition of Lord Grange singularly wretched. At length she was induced, in 1730, to accept a separate maintenance. She took lodgings at Edinburgh, but she now proceeded to vex her husband with angry missives containing her wonted threats. The daughter of one who in cold blood could deprive a high legal functionary of life for conscientiously discharging the duties of his office was not likely to make much scruple in sacrificing her husband to her resentment. Lord Grange consulted the members of his family—two adult sons and a daughter, married to the Earl of Kintore, and they unitedly concluded that it was necessary to place their unhappy relative under permanent restraint. Mrs. Erskine was accordingly seized in her lodgings on the evening of Saturday, the 22nd April, 1732, and conducted from place to place by night journeys till she reached the Hebrides. For two years she was kept on the lonely isle of Hisker, under the care of a peasant farmer. She was then removed to the remote and lonely St. Kilda, where she remained seven years. Having succeeded after nine years' captivity in conveying information to the authorities of her detention, her husband and children, who had become aware of her proceeding, caused her to be conveyed to the Isle of Skye. There she died in May, 1745, after a captivity of thirteen years. Her remains were interred in the churchyard of Trumpin, Waternish, Isle of Skye.

The demigration and confinement of Lady Grange have been justified on account of the unhappy condition of her mind, and the want of ordinary asylums at the period. Posterity would have been more willing to forgive the procedure had the conduct of her husband been otherwise commendable. But Lord Grange was, it is much to be feared, one of the most insincere and unscrupulous of his contemporaries. When at his country seat and among the clergy, he professed piety and exhibited the signs of a superior sanctity. In Edinburgh he was known as a debauchee. He was intensely ambitious. After being a Lord of Session for nearly thirty years, he resigned his post and entered the House of Commons, as member for Clackmannanshire. He expected the appointment of Secretary of State for Scotland, which would have enabled him to command its patronage. But his short-sighted policy put a check on his prospects. With a view to please the Scottish clergy, he warmly opposed the repeal of the statutes against witchcraft, and declared his belief in the necromantic arts. This procedure ruined his parliamentary influence. He retired from public affairs, and betook himself to inglorious seclusion.

His chief haunt was a coffee-house in the London Haymarket, the keeper of which was commonly believed to be his mistress.

Lord Monboddo, an eminent judge of the Supreme Court, laboured under the singular hallucination that the human race were originally possessed of tails. He had persuaded himself that these were removed by accoucheurs so soon as children were born. When a birth took place in his house, he kept watch at the door of the apartment, and demanded that the young stranger might immediately be presented to him. He was much disappointed that he could never discover any evidence of a caudal appendage having been wrenched off.

Lord Monboddo was impatient of contradiction, and insisted that the instructions which he conveyed to persons in his employment should be obeyed to the letter. He had entrusted a horse to a farrier, with directions that a certain medicine was to be given to the animal. The farrier administered the medicine in treacle. The horse having died next morning, his lordship narrowly inquired when and how the medicine had been given. Finding that treacle had been used, he prosecuted the farrier for the price of the horse. His lordship pleaded his own cause at the bar of the court, but failed to convince his colleagues that his claim was just.

Lord Monboddo regarded riding on horseback as the most gentlemanlike mode of. locomotion. His journeys to London were always performed on horseback. He to attempted to ride London in his eighty-fourth year, but was obliged to return when he had reached Dunbar. His lordship did not sit on the bench of the court, but at the clerk's table. Sundry odd reasons have been assigned for this practice, but it is believed the true cause was that he suffered from deafness, and was too conscientious to give judgment in any case without fully hearing the arguments of counsel on both sides.

Lord Monboddo was the patron of Professor John Hunter, of St. Andrews, the celebrated scholar. Mr. Hunter was born at Closeburn, Dumfriesshire; and having been educated at the famous academy of Wallace Hall, in his native parish, had been recommended to Monboddo for his scholarly attainments. The learned judge was surprised at the extent of Hunter's classical knowledge, and at once gave him employment as his amanuensis. When the Humanity Professorship in the University of St. Andrews became vacant, his lordship recommended Mr. Hunter to the patron, General Scott, who at once appointed him to the chair.

Lord Kames was a very eccentric judge. He had acquired the ridiculous habit of familiarly styling his friends by the term which designates a female dog. At an advanced age he retired from the bench. After taking farewell of his colleagues in a solemn address, and shaking hands with them all round, he was about to retire from the court-room, when the deep feelings of the moment re-awakened his peculiarity, and he cried, with a broken utterance "Fareweel — fare ye a' weel, ye bitches!" Dr. David Doig, Rector of the grammar school of Stirling, a person of remarkable learning, published anonymously two letters to Lord Kames respecting certain extravagant opinions advanced in his "Sketches of the History of Man." Having ascertained the authorship of the criticisms, his lordship called upon Dr. Doig, and finding him in his schoolroom, saluted him with, "Are you the bitch that wrote those letters?" "I am the Dog who did so, my lord," responded the rector.

Lord Kames was prodigiously fond of gossip. There was a lame porter, who bore the *sobriquet* of Linkum the Cadie, who was not more remarkable for his awkward gestures than for an extraordinary faculty for picking up news. Linkum hovered at his lordship's door every morning to convey to him his supplies of news in his progress to the Parliament House.

In the district of his estate of Blair-Drummond Lord Kames was noted as a zealous agriculturist. He was expatiating to a farmer in the Carse of Stirling on the alleged discovery of Baron von Haak, a German, who professed to fertilize an acre of land by a wonderfully small quantity of a kind of manure which he offered for sale. The farmer expressed a decided doubt as to the efficacy of the Baron's nostrum. "My friend," said Lord Kames, "there are such wonderful discoveries in science, that I should not be surprised if at some future time we might be able to carry the manure of an acre of land to the field in our coat pocket." "In that case, my lord," rejoined the farmer, "you would be able to bring back the crop in your waistcoat pocket."

Lord Braco was excessively fond of money. Walking in the avenue which conducted through his demesne, he saw a farthing at his feet, which he took up, cleaned, and deposited in his pocket. A mendicant who happened to come up, begged that his lordship would bestow upon him the small coin which he had picked up. "Fin' a farthing for yoursel', my man," said his lordship, as he slowly pursued his walk.

Lord Hermand was noted for his irritability of temper. When presiding at the Circuit Court at Inverness, a wag, aware of his weakness of temper, set a musical snuff-box a-playing on one of the benches. A pause in the business of the court immediately ensued. "Macer, what in the world is that?" exclaimed the irate judge. The officer looked about to discover the delinquent. "It's Jack's alive, my lord!" exclaimed the unsuspected offender. "Dead or alive, put him out this moment," said the judge. "We canna grup him, my lord," was the reply. "I say!" exclaimed the judge, "let every one assist to arraign him before me at once." The music having stopped, the Macer stated to his lordship that the offender had escaped. The trial was resumed, when in half an hour another tune sprung up. "He's there again!" cried his lordship. "Fence the doors of the court; let not a man escape." Search proved useless. "This is *deceptio auris*," said his lordship, somewhat subdued.

A large party was dining with Lord Hermand at his country residence. During dinner one of the attendants let fall a wine decanter, which was broken to pieces. The excited judge started to his feet, rushed after the unhappy waiter, who fled precipitately down-stairs. His lordship resumed his seat, as if nothing had occurred.

Lord Auchinleck was possessed of considerable powers of sarcasm. His son, James Boswell, was not exempted from its frequent application. Referring to his son's accompanying Johnson in his Scottish tour, and otherwise courting his society, the old judge remarked that he had often heard of bears being led about by men, but that Jamie was the first man he had ever heard of who was led about by a bear.

James Boswell was one day expatiating to his father on the learning and other good qualities of Dr. Johnson, in the hope of removing his prejudices against the lexicographer. "He is," concluded James, "the grand luminary of our hemisphere—quite a constellation, sir." "Ursa Major, I suppose?" drily responded his lordship.

In extracts from a journal, entitled "Boswelliana," by James Boswell, privately printed by Lord Houghton, occur the following notices of Lord Auchinleck:—

"My father," writes James Boswell, "had all along so firm, so dry a mind, that religious principles, however carefully inculcated by his father and mother, and however constantly they remained on the surface, never incorporated with his thoughts, never penetrated into the seat of his affections. They were a dead range, not a quickset hedge; the fence had a good appearance enough, and was sufficiently strong, but it never flourished in green luxuriance, never blossomed, never bore fruit. The ground within, however, produced plentiful crops of useful exertions as a judge, and improvements as a (laird) landed gentleman. And let it be considered that there may be a fine fence round barren, unprofitable land. 24th September, 1780."

"Lord Auchinleck," adds his son, "was one of the most firm and indefatigable judges that ever lived. Brown at Utrecht said, 'He was one of those great beams that are placed here and there to support the edifice of society.'"

"Brown at Utrecht," to whom James Boswell refers as thus eulogizing his father, was afterwards well known as the Principal of Marischal College, Aberdeen, and author of the prize essay "On the Existence of a Supreme Being." It may not detract from the character of Lord Auchinleck to assert that it is in the highest degree probable that Dr. Brown had passed his eulogy upon him more to gratify his vain and eccentric son than from any solid conviction of the truth of his assertion. Dr. Brown was known to the father of the writer, who used to speak of him as the most persevering satirist whom he ever met in society. His disposition was to assail rather than commend. Principal Hill, of St. Andrews, on being privately asked by Lord Melville his opinion of Dr. Brown before his appointment to Marischal College, stated that he was regarded as somewhat too impetuous in temper. By the mistake of a clerk, Dr. Hill's statement had been shown to Dr. Brown, who in consequence levied war on his brother Principal. He published a long poem, entitled "Philemon," in which, under the name of Vulpellus, he depicted Dr. Hill with fierce invective. The grandfather of Dr. Brown, as minister of Cortachy, distinguished himself by appearing armed in support of the reigning family in 1745. He was consequently promoted to the chair of Ecclesiastical History at St. Andrews. His lectures were composed in Latin. Six lectures of the course were entitled *Res gestæ ante mundum conditum.*

Another extract from his son's journal will conclude our notices of Lord Auchinleck :—

"Lord Auchinleck said, 'The great point for a judge is to conduct a cause with safety and expedition, like a skilful pilot. The agents always endeavour to keep a cause afloat; but I have my eye upon the haven, and the moment I have got him fairly in order, I give one hearty push, and then he is landed.'"

Lord Hailes was celebrated for his minute accuracy

in business affairs. He had an only daughter, whose succession to his estates depended on his having destined them to her by testamentary deed. But after his lordship's death no document of the nature of a will could be found. His daughter, Miss Dalrymple, was preparing, in consequence, to vacate the paternal home to make room for the heir male, when one of the domestics, in closing the window-shutters, discovered a document resting behind one of the panels, which she handed to her mistress. It proved to be his lordship's will, which was found to secure her in possession of his estates.

Sir George Mackenzie, the celebrated Lord Advocate, was an acute but unscrupulous lawyer. He possessed a valuable estate, which was likely to be inherited by his only daughter. The Earl of Bute was a suitor for the hand of the heiress, but he dreaded the opposition of her father in the event of his making proposals of marriage. Having obtained the young lady's consent, he adopted an amusing *ruse* to overcome the hostility of her sire. He called upon him in the capacity of a client, and submitted a case representing all the circumstances, the lady's name only being concealed. He then asked Sir George how he should proceed, and whether, in the event of their being married without the father's consent, they might be disappointed in enjoying his estates on his decease. Sir George, unconscious that he was concerned in the matter, gave counsel which led to his daughter becoming, by a clandestine marriage, the wife of his client.

Lord President Dundas had six clerks. He characterized them thus:—" Two cannot read, two cannot write, and the other two can neither read nor write." One of those who could not read was the eccentric Sir James Colquhoun. His lordship's remarks were of course hypercritical; but it is related of Lord Gardenstoun, as an historical fact, that he was unable to spell the most common words. His lordship was author of several respectable publications. James Boswell persisted in misspelling certain words. The word friend he uniformly wrote freind.

Lord Braxfield possessed eminent forensic talents, but was excessively coarse in his judicial procedure. During the trial of Muir, one of the political prisoners of 1793-4, he said to one of the jury, as he passed behind the bench to get into the jury-box, "Come awa', Maister Horner; come awa', and help us to hang ane o' thae daamned scoondrels."

The clerk of the Criminal Court, Mr. Joseph Norris, was an authority in forms and precedents. When any doubts were started regarding the validity of a criminal indictment, Braxfield used to say, "Hoot! just gie me Josie Norrie and a gude jury, an' I'll do for the fallow."

Lord Eskgrove is described by Lord Cockburn in his "Memorials of his Time" as a most eccentric personage. Cockburn heard him sentence a tailor for murdering a soldier in these words:—" And not only did you murder him, whereby he was berea-ved of his life, but you did thrust, or push, or pierce, or project, or propell the li-thall weapon through the belly-band of his regimental breeches, which were his Majesty's."

While summing up evidence in a case for the opinion of the jury, Eskgrove spoke thus:—"And so, gentlemen, having shown you that the pannel's argument is utterly *impossibill*, I shall now proceed for to show you that it is extremely *improbabill*."

A young lady of great personal attractions having come into court as a witness in a case, modestly drew down her veil. Lord Eskgrove called to her, "Madam, lift up your veil; throw off all modesty, and look me in the face."

Lord Eskgrove could not tolerate those counsel who evinced ingenuity or acuteness. He conceived a great aversion to young Brougham, then practising at the Edinburgh bar. He designated Brougham *the Harangue*. "Well, gentlemen," he said to a jury, "what did the Harangue say next? Why, it is this [his lordship misstated it]; but here, gentlemen, the Harangue was most plainly *wrangg*, and not *intelligibill*."

Lord Cockburn was the last Scottish judge who habitually used the vernacular. His easy manners and intimate familiarity with provincial phrases rendered him expert in examining witnesses from the country. He was, as a counsel, associated with

Francis Jeffrey in a cause in which their client sought to prove that the heir of a landed property was incapable of administering his affairs. A country farmer, who was understood to be favourable to the views of the pursuer, was examined by Mr. Jeffrey, who failed to procure satisfactory answers to his questions. Cockburn came to the assistance of his learned colleague. "Ye ken Davie, I suppose?" said he to the witness. "Ou aye," responded the farmer, "I've kent him since he wasna muckle bigger than ma loof." "Ay, an' what d'ye think o' the cratur?" "Think o' him?" said the farmer. "The cratur has naething in him ava." "Wad ye trust him in the market to sell a coo?" proceeded the counsel. "Deed no," answered the witness; "I maist think he disna ken a coo frae a calf." "That will do, John," said Mr. Cockburn," who resumed his seat.

A prosecution in the Justiciary Court was likely to break down, consequent on the counsel for the Crown being unable to elicit from a witness the particular position of the prisoner at the time when the crime was committed. The witness had deponed that the prisoner was neither standing, nor sitting, nor lying, nor crouching. "Was she on her cutty hunkers?"* inquired Mr. Cockburn, coming to the rescue of the Crown counsel. "That's it," responded the witness.

* A peculiar bending of and resting upon the lower limbs, common among the peasantry.

During a jury trial at Jedburgh, Messrs. Jeffrey, Cockburn, and Moncreiff, all subsequently judges, were engaged as counsel. When Mr. Moncreiff was addressing the jury, Mr. Jeffrey playfully handed the following case to his learned brother, Mr. Cockburn, for his opinion:—" A legacy was lately left by an elderly gentlewoman in the north to the *Peer* of Aberdeen. As the will was written by the lady herself, and was generally deficient in spelling and accuracy of expression, a dispute has arisen as to the intent of the testator, and the following claimants have appeared for the legacy. *First*, the Earl of Aberdeen; *second*, the commissioners for erecting the pier at Aberdeen; and *third*, the manager of the Charity Workhouse, who grounds his right on the fact that the old lady was in the habit *more majorum* of pronouncing poor *peer*. To which of the parties does the money belong?" Mr. Cockburn appended his opinion in these words:— " The legacy belongs to none of the three claimants, but to the Horticultural Society of Scotland, for the purpose of promoting the culture of a kind of fruit, called, or to be called, the *Pear of Aberdeen*."

Lord Jeffrey, it is stated, refused to be appointed a Lord of Justiciary, lest, in passing the last sentence of the law, he might be compared with that friend of capital punishment, the infamous Judge Jeffreys of England. A similar sensitiveness led to his retaining his own name as a Lord of Session, instead of assuming the designation of his estate of

Craigcrook. "A Lord Craig-crook,"* said his lordship, "would alarm everybody."

The youngest son of Henry David, fifth Earl of Buchan, became the celebrated Lord Chancellor Erskine. He was a famous humourist.

A barrister, named Lamb, was of an extremely nervous and sensitive nature, and he usually prefaced his pleadings by offering an apology for these constitutional defects. On one occasion when he was opposed to Erskine, he remarked in court that he found himself growing more and more timid as he grew older. "No wonder," rejoined Erskine; "every one knows the older a Lamb grows the more sheepish he becomes."

Polito, keeper of the menagerie in Exeter Change, brought an action against the proprietors of a stagecoach for negligence, his portmanteau having been stolen from the boot of the coach behind while he had been sitting on the box. Erskine was retained as counsel for the coach proprietors. He said to the jury, "Why should not the plaintiff take a lesson from his own sagacious elephant, and travel with his *trunk* before him?" The joke gained the case for the defendants.

Lord Erskine, when at the bar, was consulted by the Duke of Queensberry as to whether a tradesman might be sued for a breach of contract about painting his house. Mr. Erskine returned the papers to his

* Those unfamiliar with Scottish forms of expression may be informed that to crook a craig is to hang some one.

Grace with this opinion expressed on an enclosed slip, —" This action will not lie unless the witnesses do."

The future Chancellor was taken ill one evening at Lady Payne's. On her ladyship expressing a hope that his indisposition might not prove serious, he replied in the following impromptu :—

> " 'Tis true I am ill, but I need not complain,
> For he never knew pleasure who never knew *Payne*."

With the celebrated Dr. Parr Lord Erskine maintained terms of close friendship. "If I survive you," said the doctor to him one day, "I'll write your epitaph." "It is a temptation to commit suicide," responded the wit.

In his latter years the Chancellor became eccentric and credulous. He became a believer in apparitions and the second sight, and used to relate to his friends that John Burnet, his father's valet, who had been long dead, had reappeared to him.

Alexander Wedderburn, Earl of Rosslyn, Lord Chancellor from 1793 to 1801, was originally a member of the Scottish bar. His removal to London was consequent on a dispute with Mr. Lockhart, Dean of the Faculty of Advocates. The Dean possessed a fiery temper, and was extremely overbearing towards his juniors. He had on one occasion termed Wedderburn "a presumptuous boy,"—a rude speech, which the young counsel resolved, on the first suitable occasion, to resent. Being opposed to the Dean in a case before the court, Wedderburn took occasion to allege respecting his learned opponent that "he had been disgraced in his person and dishonoured in his bed," referring to his having been menaced with a horsewhipping, and to a rumour of his wife's infidelity. This monstrous outrage on the Dean called from the Lord President a severe rebuke on the offender, who immediately disrobed and left the court. He started for London the same day, and joining the English bar, attained, after thirty-six years' successful practice, the Lord Chancellorship and an earldom.

The Hon. Henry Erskine, an advocate at the Scottish bar, was, like his younger brother, Lord Chancellor Erskine, a noted wit. His name was vulgarly pronounced Askin. When he was Dean of Faculty, a foppish advocate, wishing to avoid a question put to him by the Dean, said testily, "I never meet you but I find you *Askin*." "And I," rejoined the Dean, "never meet you but I find an *anser*" (a goose).

Erskine was dining with Mr. Creech, the bookseller, who was rather penurious, and who on one occasion entertained his guests with a single bottle of Cape wine, though he spoke of some fine Madeira which he had in his cellar. Having failed in his efforts to induce the host to produce his vaunted Madeira, Erskine summed up, "Well, since we can't get to Madeira, we must just double the Cape."

On being introduced by James Boswell to Dr. Samuel Johnson, in the Edinburgh Parliament

House, Erskine took out a shilling and, slipping it into Boswell's hand, whispered to him, "It's for a sight of your bear."

When informed that Knox, the doorkeeper of the Parliament House, had been killed by a small cannon fired in honour of the king's birthday, he remarked that it was strange a man should live by the *civil*, and die by the *canon* law.

A friend ventured to remonstrate with Mr. Erskine on his habit of punning, observing that it was, in his opinion, the lowest species of wit. "Precisely so," rejoined the humourist, "and hence it is the foundation of the whole."

John Clerk, afterwards Lord Eldin, was sent to London to plead before Lord Chancellor Eldon in an important property cause. He was inveterate in his use of the Scottish accent. In the course of his speech he pronounced the word *enow* for enough. The Chancellor drily remarked, "Mr. Clerk, in England we sound the ough as *uff*—enuff, not enow." "Vera weel, ma Lord," said Clerk, "of this we have said *enuff*; and I come, ma Lord, to the subdivision of the land in dispute. It was apportioned, ma Lord, into what in England would be called *pluff* land, a pluff land being as much land as a *pluffman* can pluff in one day." The Chancellor was convulsed by the happy repartee, and said, "Proceed, Mr. Clerk, "I know *enow* of Scotch to understand your argument."

When the learned citizens of Edinburgh indulged

deeply in their potations, it is related that on a dark, misty night Clerk was wending his way homewards along Queen Street, towards Picardy Place, but became bewildered. Accosting a passenger, he blandly asked if he could direct him to John Clerk's house. The person thus accosted, looking the inquirer in the face, exclaimed, "Dear me, you are John Clerk yoursel." "I know that well," was the answer, "but it is not John Clerk I want, but John Clerk's house."

A son of Mr. Grahame, the author of "The Sabbath," was very tall and exceedingly lean. One day walking on the floor of the Parliament House, he attracted the notice of Mr. Clerk. "Who is that?" asked the wit. He was answered, "The son of the *Sabbath*." "Is he indeed?" said Clerk; "he looks much more like the son of the *Fast-day*."

When Clerk was on the bench, an advocate who had been pleading before him apologetically concluded a speech of six hours by remarking that he was afraid he had gone beyond his time. "Oh no," answered the witty judge, "these last three hours you have been speaking to eternity."

John Hagart of Bantaskine was a celebrated counsel. When he undertook a cause, he devoted his entire energies to the benefit of his client. In one instance he clearly exceeded the duty of an advocate. He was defending, in the Justiciary Court, a person who had been indicted for murder. The crime was alleged to have been committed on a moonlight night, and two witnesses were, on the part of the Crown, prepared to depone that they had seen the prisoner red-hand in the act. Mr. Hagart perceived that it was in vain, by ordinary means, to invalidate the testimony of the witnesses. He had recourse to a stratagem. He caused a new leaf to be inserted in his copy of the "Edinburgh Almanac" at that portion of the calendar which included the date of the alleged crime. The substituted leaf indicated that there was no moonlight on the night when the witnesses testified that the murder had taken place. When the almanac was produced by Mr. Hagart in the course of his speech, the deputy advocate, conducting the prosecution, was quite taken aback, and at once consented to abandon his charge against the prisoner. Such a dangerous experiment could not be repeated.

Hugo Arnot, the historian of Edinburgh, held the status of an advocate, though he seldom practised before the courts. He was remarkable for his eccentric humour and singular impulsiveness. He was one day waited upon by a lady, who requested him to advise how she might best get rid of an admirer, whose importunities caused her annoyance. The lady was the reverse of fascinating, and Arnot, being indisposed to flatter her vanity, replied, "Oh, you had better marry the fellow." "Marry him!" replied the astounded lady, "I would see him hanged first." "Marry him then," persisted the humourist, "and I'll bet on it he'll soon hang himself."

Arnot had got into the habit of ringing his bell violently. A maiden lady, who lived on the upper floor, complained to him that his bell made her start, and begged him to be more gentle in ringing it. Wearied with her messages, Arnot at length said he would cease to use the bell altogether. He did so, but in its place discharged a pistol when he desired the attendance of his servant. The lady was horror-struck, and sent a message entreating him to resume the use of his bell.

One of the most distinguished of the Edinburgh advocates happened to possess a somewhat forbidding aspect, of which, however, he was happily unconscious. An accidental circumstance served to inform him of the fact. Taking a ride into the country, he found, on reaching a toll-bar, that he had forgotten his purse. Mentioning the circumstance to the toll-keeper, he said he would pay him when he next passed. The official seemed rather doubtful. "Look in my face," said the advocate to him indignantly, "and say whether you think I am likely to cheat you." "I'll thank you for the twopence," responded the toll-keeper.

Mr. William Ross, another lawyer of the capital, was more successful in an effort to attain his purpose. He occupied a country house at Stockbridge, then an isolated suburb of the city. Having been annoyed with thieves breaking into his garden and grounds, he issued a handbill bearing this inscription,—

"'THOU SHALT NOT STEAL.'

"All persons whom it may concern are desired to take notice that steel traps, of the largest size, for catching breakers of the eighth commandment, are every night placed in the garden of St. Bernard's, between Stockbridge and the Water of Leith, on the north side of the water; that spring guns are set to rake the walls with shot upon the touch of a wire; and that a tent, having in it an armed watchman, is pitched in the middle, with orders to fire without mercy. If, therefore, any evil-disposed person or persons shall attempt to break into the grounds of St. Bernard's, their blood will be upon their own heads!"

The alarming nature of this menace at first created a suspicion that the whole was a fiction, and some inroads began to be attempted on the premises. Mr. Ross now had recourse to a new method of alarm. He procured the limb of a body from the dissecting-room, and dressing it with a stocking and shoe, sent it through the streets with the public crier, proclaiming that it had been found last night in St. Bernard's garden, and would be restored to the owner on application. The *coup de main* succeeded.

One of the most difficult duties of Scottish advocates is to conduct the examination of witnesses. An acute member of the faculty was overcome by the smartness of a celebrated physician. Professor

Gregory was in the witness-box, in a case of alleged insanity. His testimony went to prove the insanity. In cross-examination it was elicited from him that the party in question was a skilful whist-player. "And do you seriously consider, Dr. Gregory," proceeded the learned counsel, "that a person having a capacity for a game so difficult, and which requires memory, judgment, and combination, can be at the same time deranged?" "I am no card-player," replied the Professor, "but I have read in history that cards were invented for the amusement of an insane king."

A country farmer was examined before the Presbytery of Brechin, in the case of the Rev. John Gillanders, minister of Fearn, who was charged with intemperate habits. The lawyer who conducted the prosecution asked the farmer whether he had heard Mr. Gillanders acknowledge that he had been in the habit of drinking to excess. "I never heard him say that," responded the farmer, adding with emphasis, "but I have often heard him say that he was not."

The writer was present at a meeting of the Presbytery of Meigle, when a case in which a parochial schoolmaster was charged with drunkenness was tried before the court. A provincial lawyer of considerable eminence conducted the prosecution. A lad was placed in the witness-box who had some years before attended the school of the accused. The examination proceeded thus:—

Lawyer. When you attended Mr. C.'s school, did you remark that he had a habit of frequently proceeding to a small closet which opened from the schoolroom?

Witness. I did.

L. Did he very frequently enter this closet?

W. I should say very frequently.

L. Have you ever been in the closet?

W. I have.

L. And did you remark what it contained?

W. I believe I can remember what I saw in it.

L. Now will you tell the court what you saw in the closet?

W. There were a good many bottles in it arranged on shelves.

L. Very good. And when Mr. C. repeatedly entered the closet, had you the curiosity to remark what he did when he was there?

W. I often joined the other boys in looking into the closet after the master.

L. You did. And tell us now what you saw Mr. C. doing on these occasions.

W. He was handling bottles.

L. Handling bottles; ay. And do you know what the bottles contained?

W. Yes.

"What then did they contain?" proceeded the prosecutor, as he resumed his seat with an air of relief and composure.

"They were ink-bottles," said the witness.

The sudden overturn of the prosecutor's hopes may be conceived.

A shrewd shopkeeper in a central burgh, who desired to stand well with his customers, was examined as a witness in an action for libel. He had privately assured the prosecution that he had heard the defendant use malicious language concerning the plaintiff. When placed in the witness-box he was asked, "Did you ever hear the defendant speak in a vituperative manner of the plaintiff?" "I have," was the reply, "He did so in his *own jocular way!*"

Though as a nation the Scottish people are to be remarked for their integrity, there are occasional exemplifications in the courts of justice of aberrations from the strict path of truthfulness. The writer happened to be present in a Scottish court when a witness was examined in an important case, in which he was directly implicated. He was probably stating the truth; but it was an awkward circumstance respecting the aspects of his testimony, that he was guided in his answers by signs which were communicated to him by his country solicitor, who sat before him in the court.

In 1817 the Edinburgh Jury Court was occupied with a case between the burgh of Kirkcaldy and the trustees of the Kinghorn ferry. A witness gave evidence on behalf of the trustees of a very decided character. The counsel for the plaintiffs, having been informed that an agent of the trustees had presented the witness with a coat, sought to elicit the fact in a cross-examination. The examination proceeded thus:—

Counsel. Pray, where did you get that coat?

The witness, looking obliquely down on the sleeve of his coat, and from thence to the counsel, exclaimed,—"Coat! coat, sir! Whar got I that coat?"

C. I wish to know where you got that coat.

Witness. Maybe ye ken whar I got it.

C. We wish to know from whom you got it?

W. Did ye gie me that coat?

C. Tell the jury where you got that coat.

W. What's your business wi' that?

C. It is material that you tell the court where you got the coat.

W. I'm no obliged to tell aboot ma coat.

C. Do you not recollect whether you bought that coat, or whether it was given to you?

W. I canna recollect everything aboot ma coats; whan I got them, or whar I got them.

C. You said you remembered perfectly well about the boats forty-two years ago, and the people that lived in Kirkcaldy then, and John Marr's boat; and can you not recollect where you got that coat you have on at present?

W. I'm no gaun to say onything aboot coats.

C. Did Mr. Douglas, clerk to the trustees, give you that coat?

W. I didna get the coat to do onything wrang

for't; I didna engage to say onything that wasna true.

As the witness was leaving the box, the Lord Chief Commissioner called him back and observed, "The court wish to know from you something further about this coat. It is not believed or suspected that you got it improperly or dishonestly, or that there is any reason for your concealing it. You may have been disinclined to speak about it, thinking there was something of insult or reproach in the question put from the bar. You must be sensible that the bench can have no such intention; and it is for your credit, and the sake of your testimony, to disclose fairly where you got it. There may be discredit in concealing, but none in telling where you got it. I ask then, where did you get the coat?"

W. I'm no obliged to tell aboot ma coat.

Chief Commissioner. True; you are not obliged to tell where you got it, but it is for your own credit to tell.

W. I didna come here to tell aboot coats; but to tell aboot boats and pinnaces.

C. C. If you do not tell I must throw aside your evidence altogether.

W. I'm no gaun to say onything aboot ma coat; I'm no obliged to say onything aboot it.

The witness retired, but was afterwards recalled by Lord Gillies, and his examination was resumed.

Lord Gillies. How long have you had that coat?

W. I dinna ken hoo lang I hae had ma coat. I

hae plenty o' coats. I dinna mind aboot this coat or that coat.

L. G. Do you remember anything near the time? have you had it a year, a month, a week? Have you had it a week?

W. Hoot aye; I daresay I may.

L. G. Have you had it a month?

W. I dinna ken; I cam here to speak aboot boats and no aboot coats.

L. G. Did you buy the coat?

W. I dinna mind what coat I bought or what coat I got.

The witness puzzled the court, but his evidence was rejected.

"I've gained my cause," said a litigant exultingly, on retiring from the court-room. "Indeed," said his friend, "I did not expect that it would have been decided so soon." "Oh, it's not just decided," rejoined the litigant, "but it's put upon my oath." The jubilation was suspicious.

A country farmer applied to a country solicitor for advice. Having related the circumstances of the case, the practitioner remarked that he hoped he had been careful in his statement of the facts, as they actually occurred. "Ou aye," said the farmer, "I thocht it better to tell you the plain truth; you can put the lees till't yoursel."

The delay which occurs in Scottish law courts in the conduct of civil causes is most inimical to the ends of justice where oral testimony is concerned.

The principal parties in a cause may preserve a distinct recollection of particulars in which they are individually interested; but persons who are incidental spectators or auditors cannot be expected to retain a minute and lively recollection of events in which they may only possess a remote or passing interest. In an action in the supreme court, connected with events which had taken place about two years previously, the writer was distressed to remark that of two clergymen examined as witnesses, one emphatically contradicted the other in respect of certain occurrences enacted when both were present and both were actors.

An ingenious Scotsman, author of some standard novels, was, many years after their publication, and at a somewhat advanced age, a witness in one of the law courts. A learned counsel in the cause remarked to the witness that he believed he had composed some works of fiction. The witness responded in the negative, adding that he had only written sketches of real life, in which all the characters were introduced by their names. In one of his prefaces the accomplished author had disclaimed the idea that he had in real life found any one resembling certain of his characters, and asserted that one of them in particular was purely imaginary.

Criminals are generally frank in confessing the truth to those who have undertaken their defence. The writer was present at a criminal trial, when the impressive eloquence of his counsel drew from the prisoner an unwitting acknowledgment of his crime. The prisoner, a lad of eighteen, was accused of plundering the contents of a gentleman's pocket. By the evidence of the witnesses for the prosecution the prisoner was entirely unmoved. He was equally unconcerned by the address of the prosecutor, which demonstrated his guilt. When his own counsel, however stood up, he leaned forward in the dock, and listened most eagerly. "If this young man had taken the money," proceeded the learned counsel, "where, I ask, would he have placed it? Not in his pockets, for they were likely first to be examined. Not in his shoes, for these, too, were sure to be inspected. I say, gentlemen of the jury, where was this lad likely to place the money?" The counsel made a short pause, when the prisoner, fearing that his defender was actually at a loss, exclaimed, "I put it in here, sir," pointing to his bosom.

In the times of feudal jurisdiction, the principal landowners were "Lords of Regality," and so exercised the power of inflicting capital sentences on those who resided on their estates. Any one who was sentenced by the *laird* to suffer death was, however precious his life might be to his family, readily resigned to the executioner. A young Highlander, condemned by the Laird of Grant for sheep-stealing, was reluctant to mount the fatal drop. The executioner having failed to induce him to ascend, that functionary called on the wife of the condemned to render her assistance. The woman went up to her husband, tapped him gently on the shoulder, and said coaxingly, "Noo, Donald, gang awa up, and be hangit like a shentleman,* and no anger the laird."

Mr. William Roger, great-grandfather of the writer, was a county magistrate of Perthshire. He had on some occasion displayed leniency towards John Gunn, the noted freebooter. Not long after, at a market held at Coupar-Angus, a female cottar of Mr. Roger sold her cow, the price of which, about four pounds, she rolled in her handkerchief, which she deposited in her pocket. Gunn's men were on the alert, and very soon after the handkerchief was gone. In great distress, the poor woman informed Mr. Roger of her mishap, who immediately ascertained that Gunn was present in the market. Accompanied by the woman, he sought out the freebooter, to whom he related the story of her loss. The leader of banditti blew a small whistle, which immediately secured the presence of his gang. He parleyed with one or two of the number, and then produced the handkerchief with the money. "Any other little favour I can do you, Mr. Roger, shall be done," said the bandit. Gunn was afterwards hanged.

The municipal system permits many persons to attain magisterial rank who are scarcely qualified to sustain the dignity. Provost Anderson of Stirling was so elated with his honours, as chief magistrate of his native town, that he became the hero of the most whimsical extravagances. He was most ambi-

* Gentleman.

tious of dying in office, that he might obtain a public funeral—and actually got up a programme of the ceremonial to be observed on the occasion. "It is," said the provost, "most excellently planned, and so gratifying to think that I will be the principal person on the occasion."

Municipal dignitaries have occasionally got hard hits. An elderly woman in Dundee, who made her living by selling fruit, received a visit from the provost, who stated that he had received complaints as to orange peel being thrown on the pavement near her shop. The woman expressed her regret that her customers should be so careless of the public safety; but quaintly added, "Deed, provost, I've often remarked that the streets were never sae weel keepit, as when your grandfaither sweepit them." The grandsire of the chief magistrate was a scavenger.

Civic functionaries are disposed to resist any interference with their dignity. A public entertainment was given by the citizens of Aberdeen to the celebrated Lord Melville shortly after the honourable termination of his state trial. Deacon Webster, who was present, desirous of testifying his personal respect for his lordship, said aloud to him across the table, "I was unco gled to hear ye war acquitted." The intended compliment having failed to elicit any observation from the noble guest, the deacon was repeating the remark in a louder tone. Mr. Crombie, of Phaesdo, advocate, who sat near the loquacious deacon, mildly remonstrated with him on the injudiciousness of his speech. "An' do you, sir," said the deacon, "presume to teach me what is proper? Many a time your father has shaved me for a farthing." The elder Crombie was a hairdresser and barber. When a number of persons came into his shop to be shaved, it was his practice to arrange them in a row, placing a towel round each and soaping them, so that they were obliged to remain till the shaving process was completed.

A bailie having imposed a fine of ten shillings on a familiar friend for a drunken brawl, the offender remonstrated, saying, "You are surely not in earnest, bailie." On this pleading the bailie so far relented as to reduce the fine to five shillings. Still the persistent culprit pled for leniency. It was reduced to half a crown. Another effort was made, and at last the fine was made one shilling, with the remark, which shut up the pleading, "As sure as death, John, though you were my very born brither, I could not make it less."

There is extant a bond by the magistrates of Perth to the Earl of Perth, agreeing, on getting the loan of his lordship's hangman from Crieff, that he would under a heavy penalty be safely sent back, so "as to serve his lordship's friends."

A magistrate of a western burgh who was fond of using learned words, was at a dinner in the mansion of a nobleman. By the peer he was asked his opinion of the wines which were served. The answer startled the company when the bailie replied,

"My lord, I'm no *accoucheur.*" He probably meant *connoisseur.*

Rutherglen, under the old system of burgh election, was united with Glasgow, Dumbarton, and Renfrew, to return one member of parliament. In case of equality the burghs in rotation had a casting vote as returning burgh. On the occasion of a contested election Rutherglen was the returning burgh, and therefore the votes of the deacons, who as such were town councillors, were of great value. The friends of the two candidates from Glasgow kept up for weeks a system of continual feasting. The election being over, the deacon of the weavers returned to his humble diet of porridge and milk. Recollecting the slang of his late retainers he irefully ordered his wife to remove the milk, declaring *the same to be corked.*

CHAPTER IV.

ABOUT ROYAL PERSONAGES.

"A monarch's crown,
Golden in show, is but a crown of thorns;
Brings dangers, troubles, cares, and sleepless nights,
To him who wears the regal diadem."
MILTON.

"Then happy low, lie down,
Uneasy lies the head that wears a crown."
SHAKSPEARE.

QUEEN MARGARET ATHELING, wife of Malcolm Canmore and niece of Edward the Confessor, was one of the most pious of royal princesses. She retained the services of a private chaplain, who conducted divine worship daily in her royal household. An illuminated missal lay on the table of her boudoir, and its pages bore marks of her frequent use. To her little private oratory she frequently retired for the purposes of devotion. She built many hospitals for the infirm and aged. Among a number of orphans she dispensed provisions every morning; and every evening she personally ministered to the sick. She introduced the manufacturing arts, and personally illustrated the benefits of a life of industry. Queen

Margaret died at the age of forty-seven. Her remains were at the Reformation borne from their resting-place at Dunfermline, and deposited in a chapel built for their reception, by Philip II. of Spain, in the palace of the Escurial.

In the beginning of the fifteenth century two extraordinary events were enacted at the Scottish and English courts. The rightful monarch of each country was detained a captive at the court of the other. The detention of James I. at the court of Henry IV. is matter of well-known history, but Mr. Tytler * was the first to establish that Richard II. was similarly detained in Scotland. It is commonly believed that Richard perished in Pontefract Castle. This, Mr. Tytler has shown, did not occur. He contrived to escape from his imprisonment at Pontefract, and found his way to the Western Isles, where he was recognized in the disguise of a harper, and brought to the court of Robert III. By Robert, and afterwards by his brother the Regent Albany, he was kept at Stirling, and entertained in a style becoming his rank. He died at Stirling Castle, in 1419, and was interred in the Dominican monastery of the place. The Latin inscription which adorned his tomb is included in the "Extracts from the Scottish Chronicles," printed for the Maitland Club. Referring to these remarkable captivities, Mr. Tytler observes that Henry IV. and the Duke of Albany "played off their two royal prisoners against each

* Tytler's "History of Scotland," vol. iv., p. 12. Edinburgh, 1831.

other." After the death of Albany, James I. regained his liberty. His first act of government was to procure the condemnation and execution of the son and other near relatives of the usurper of his throne. They were beloved by the people, who wept aloud when they were decapitated. A series of hillocks, at Stirling, from which the populace witnessed the executions, still bear the name of the *Gowling* or weeping hills.

The first reigning members of the House of Stuart were weak princes. James I. profited exceedingly by his long detention at the English court. He became a master of accomplishments, an intelligent ruler, and a firm though somewhat severe dispenser of justice. He was the inventor of Scottish music. He promoted the amenities of life. He found his subjects plundered by a set of lawless persons, who subsisted by spoliation. In order to suppress their practices he caused purses of gold to be suspended on trees by the highways, and watchers to be set in the vicinity. Just as a purse was cut down by a vagabond thief, he himself was forthwith suspended in its place.

Another method adopted by James I. to discover the condition of his subjects was that of moving about among them in disguise. He commonly assumed the costume of "a gudeman" or inferior yeoman. Proceeding on foot in this attire between Edinburgh and Linlithgow, he was assailed near Cramond Bridge by a band of gipsies. He defended himself with his accustomed valour, but was at length overpowered. Just as he had been smitten down, a farmer, familiarly called Jock Howison, and his son, who were thrashing in a barn not far off, hearing the noise, proceeded to the scene of action. Finding one man ruthlessly assailed by so many, they dealt about their flails among the gipsies so vigorously as to put them to flight. Howison raised the wounded stranger, and conducting him to his cottage, handed him a basin and towel that he might wash, and furnished him with other means of refreshment. When the stranger removed his cloak, the farmer perceived that he was a person of the better sort, and offered him a seat at the head of the board. This was at first declined; but Howison persisted, saying, "Do as I tell ye, for I'm maister here." Before leaving, the stranger heartily thanked his benefactor, and, informing him that he lived in Edinburgh Castle, said he would be glad to see him there. Howison replied that he would be particularly pleased to see the castle, and promised soon to avail himself of the stranger's invitation. "Wha shall I speir * for when I come?" said the farmer. "Ye'll ask for ane James Stuart," said the stranger, "and they'll bring ye to me at once."

After a few weeks Howison presented himself at Edinburgh Castle. He was ushered into an assembly of the nobles, among whom was his former guest, who saluted him cordially. Howison asked whether the king was present. "He is here now," answered his

* Enquire.

friend. "Where?" said Howison; "how will I ken him?" "Why," said the supposed "gudeman," he is the only one present who keeps his hat on." "Then," said Howison, looking round on the company, "he maun be either you or me!" The king smiled, and said that he was James Stuart, who wore the crown, and assured him that the good service rendered him should not be forgotten. His Majesty next requested Howison to name any boon he might desire. "The lairdship o' my farm o' Braehead," said the farmer, with alacrity. "The lands are yours," said the king; "and I couple the gift with this proviso, that you and your representatives shall bring a basin of water and a towel to wash the king's hands every time he passes Cramond Brig. The monarch invited the honest farmer to dinner, and called on him to sit beside him. As Howison hesitated to accept the honoured seat, the king gave him a sharp slap on the shoulder, adding, "Do as I tell ye, for I'm maister here."

Mr. William Howison Crawfurd, of Braehead and Crawfurdland, did service to George IV., in 1822, in fulfilment of the stipulation under which his ancestor received his lands. At the grand civic banquet in the Parliament House, after the different courses had been served, the heir of Jock Howison, attended by the son and nephew of Sir Walter Scott, as pages, dressed in crimson and white satin, approached the king with a basin and ewer of silver, for his Majesty to wash his hands. In offering the basin

Mr. Howison Crawfurd knelt down, and the king acknowledged the service with his accustomed graciousness. The rose-water used on the occasion has been hermetically sealed up, and the towel which dried his Majesty's hands has never been used for any other purpose.

James II. was oppressed by the haughty assumptions and rebellious practices of his nobles. Their combined opposition was so formidable that on one occasion he lost heart. He called for James Kennedy, the shrewd Bishop of St. Andrews, and asked him to suggest some method of securing his prerogative. The bishop produced a bunch of arrows. Handing an arrow to the king, he asked him whether he could break it. "Easily," said the king, who, suiting the action to the word, snapped it on his knee. The bishop next presented a bundle of arrows to his Majesty, and inquired whether he could snap these. "I certainly cannot," said the monarch. "When your enemies remain banded together," rejoined the prelate, "your Majesty cannot subdue them; let them be detached, and each one will be broken as readily as the arrow." James returned to his palace, and contrived to follow the counsel of the ingenious prelate.

The union of the crowns of England and Scotland sprung from the marriage of James IV. with Margaret Tudor, daughter of Henry VII. The event was preceded by an occurrence connected with the personal history of the royal bridegroom, which is very imperfectly set forth by the ordinary historian.

Three plain blue marble slabs in Dunblane cathedral, one paving the choir, and the two others resting at its entrance, were placed in this ancient church to protect the remains of the three daughters of John, first Lord Drummond—Margaret, Euphemia, and Sybella,—who were there interred. These ladies, of whom the second, Euphemia, was married to Lord Fleming, died in their father's house of Drummond Castle, in 1502, from the effects of poison. The object of the poisoners was to accomplish the death of Margaret, the eldest daughter, consequent on her being betrothed to the young king, James IV. When Duke of Rothesay, and believed by his royal father to be strictly confined within the precincts of Stirling Castle, he was making love pastimes with fair Margaret Drummond in her father's bowers of Stobhall. He had met the young lady when she attended court as one of the maids of honour of his mother; and a fine melody, entitled "Tay's Banks," is said to have been composed by him in honour of her charms. A few lines of the song have been presented by Miss Strickland. We modernize the spelling:—

> "The river through the rocks rushed out
>   Through roses raised on high;
> The shenè birds full sweet 'gan shout
>   Forth that seemly shaw.
> Joy was within, and joy without,
>   When Tay ran down with streames stout
>   Right under Stobbeshaw."

On the demise of his father, and his accession to the throne, James betrothed himself to the object of his early love. As the parties were related within the degrees prohibited by the Church, the solemnization of the marriage was deferred till the requisite dispensation should be obtained from the Pope. But the members of the Privy Council were opposed to the connection, and entreated their sovereign to contract a union which might promote a permanent alliance with England. He pretended to yield to their remonstrances, and actually formed a matrimonial contract with the Princess Margaret, while he was privately negotiating with Rome regarding his proposed marriage with fair Margaret Drummond. Tidings of the monarch's secret determination to wed the lady whom he heartily loved having been propagated, it was resolved by the ruthless nobility that she should perish. She was cut off, with her sisters, by poison being mixed in her morning meal. The king was long inconsolable. He pensioned two priests to celebrate mass for the soul of his intended spouse. After waiting a year, he married the English princess. Their great-grandson ascended the British throne.

James V. acquired his popular title of "King o' the Commons" by the frequency with which, in disguise, he associated with the humbler classes. Sometimes he appeared as a "Gaberlunzie," or beggar, carrying a wallet. In reference to this disguise, he is believed to have composed the "Jollie Beggar" and the "Gaberlunzie Man," two popular songs. "The Wife of Auchtermuchty," an amusing ballad, has also been ascribed to him. James commonly took the disguise of *a gudeman*, a character which he was well qualified to sustain. When resident at Stirling, he left the castle in disguise by a small postern at the Ballengeich Pass; from this arose the designation which he assumed of "Gudeman of Ballengeich."

In one of his rambles from Stirling, James was benighted at the base of the Ochil hills, near Alloa. He sought shelter in the cottage of John Donaldson, a small farmer. Though ignorant that his visitor was a person of quality, Donaldson gave him a kindly reception, and desired the gudewife to fetch for the stranger's supper the hen that roosted nearest to the cock, which, he said, was always the plumpest. The king, who was highly pleased with his entertainment, wished Donaldson to visit him in Stirling Castle, saying that he was known there as the "Gudeman o' Ballengeich." Like Jock Howison, the gudeman of the Ochil farm found his way to the royal presence, and was amazed to discover that he had entertained the king. His Majesty called him "king o' the muirs," and gave him a grant of his farm in reward for his evening's hospitality. The farm was retained by the family till a recent period. On the death of John Donaldson, the last "king o' the muirs," about forty years ago, the chair in which the king sat was purchased for the Crown, and deposited in Stirling Castle. When Queen Victoria visited the Castle, in 1842, Sir Archibald Christie, the governor, exhibited the chair to her Majesty, briefly detailing these particulars of its history.

From Falkland Palace James often sauntered about the adjoining district in his favourite disguise. One evening he experienced hospitality from the miller of Ballomill, a place on the north bank of the Eden, near Crawford Priory. On parting with his entertainer he said he would be glad to see him at Falkland. "Jist gang to the palace yett,* and ask for the gudeman o' Ballengeich, an' I'se come t'ye." The miller found his way to the royal residence, and was duly welcomed. The king revealed himself at once, and insisted that the miller, who was very athletic, should engage with himself and his nobles in various muscular feats, such as "tossing the caber" and "putting the stone." The miller remained some days at the palace. At first he beat all the courtiers in the athletic exercises, but he afterwards lost strength, and was occasionally overcome. The king perceived that the dainty food of the royal table did not suit the miller's constitution, and so asked him on what he usually lived. He replied that his fare was "broken water and slain meal." "Then," said the king, "that you may always have plenty of both, you shall have a portion of the land of Ballomill. Whether," proceeded the king, "will you take

* Gate.

the aught part or the twa part of the land?" The miller was less of an arithmetician than an athlete, so, according to the story, he chose the eighth part of the land, which in his view seemed the better part of the alternative.

The king was, as *gudeman*, on a visit to the hamlet of Markinch. To obtain some refreshment he stepped into the village inn. The landlady informed him that the *ben-house*, or stranger's apartment, was engaged by the parish priest and the village schoolmaster, but she supposed they would allow him to join them. He was received readily, and caroused with his new acquaintances for several hours. When the reckoning came to be paid, the schoolmaster proposed that the priest should join him in paying the stranger's share. The priest objected, remarking that "the birkie should pay higglety-pigglety with themselves." So the disguised monarch paid his share. As they separated the stranger thanked the schoolmaster for his intended generosity, and added, "I shall make your living higglety-pigglety with the priest's; I am the king."

Some time after, the king, who had conceived a strong aversion to the priest, called him to his presence. "I understand," said the monarch, "you are proud of your learning. I am to propose to you four questions, and if you cannot answer them within four days you shall no longer retain the living of Markinch."

Returning home the priest found that the questions were of a most puzzling character. Utterly perplexed, he proceeded to seek counsel from the miller of the Middle Mill, on the Leven, a person greatly reputed for his sagacity.

The miller offered to personate the priest at the palace, and to bring him out of his difficulty. The impersonation was rendered easy from a natural resemblance which subsisted between the miller and the ecclesiastic. At the appointed time the miller, in clerical attire, presented himself before the king, and undertook to answer the royal queries. "Where is the middle of the earth?" said the monarch. "Just here," responded the miller, beating the ground with his staff; "if your Majesty will measure all round, you will find that it is just at this spot." "Ay," said the king, "that may do. How long will I take to go round the world?" "Twenty-four hours," said the miller, "if you rise with the sun, and travel with him all the day." "Not so bad," said the king. "Now can you tell me how much I am worth?" "Twenty-nine pieces of silver," said the miller; "our Saviour was valued at thirty, and you cannot be worth more." "Very ingenious," exclaimed the king. "Now for the last question. What am I thinking?" "You are thinking," replied the miller, "that I am priest of Markinch, but I am only miller of the Middle Mill." "Well," said the king, "you're a clever fellow, and should be the priest. But your answers have saved your friend."

Many highway robberies had been committed in

the neighbourhood of Falkland, the perpetrators always contriving to escape detection. Suspicion rested on the four sons of a person named Seaton, who lived in the castle of Clatto, about four miles east of the palace. The king was riding in that neighbourhood in his disguise as a *gudeman*, when a stout young man seized his horse by the bridle, and demanded his purse. With a small sword the rider chopped off the hand of the assailant, who instantly betook himself to flight. Next day the king, attended by his nobles, visited Seaton in his castle. He asked for all his sons, and was informed that one was ill and in bed. Expressing a desire to see the invalid, he was conducted to the sick chamber. The king offered to shake hands with the ailing man. Young Seaton held out his left hand, and proceeded to explain that he had by an accident been deprived of the other. "I have a hand in my pocket," said the monarch; "perhaps it may suit you." The king blew his bugle-horn, and his attendants took possession of the castle and its inmates. A gibbet was erected, and Seaton and his sons were executed.

James was on one occasion overpowered in a scuffle with three gipsies, who took him prisoner, and compelled him to lead their ass, and otherwise minister to their wants. As they were drinking in a public-house in Milnathort, James contrived to despatch a messenger to Falkland Palace, to inform his nobles of his detention. In the course of a few hours an armed body, led on by some of the courtiers, surrounded the gipsy encampment, and liberated the monarch. Two of the gipsies were hanged.

James VI. was the only coward in his illustrious house. His intense apprehension of personal danger has been ascribed to the alarm sustained by his mother on the murder of Rizzio, some time previous to his birth. The affair of the Gowrie conspiracy no doubt increased his weakness. Desirous of inspecting a coal mine, he accepted an invitation from Sir George Bruce, of Culross Abbey, to visit the extensive mines on his estate. The coal on the Culross property was then wrought under the sea, and was brought out for shipment at a moat within sea mark. To this moat James being suddenly conducted from the chambers of the mine, the idea of treachery took sudden possession of his mind, and he lustily bawled out, "Treason!" Sir George succeeded in allaying the royal fears by pointing to an elegant pinnace, which he had provided to convey his august visitor to the shore.

In 1617, James VI. visited Scotland for the second time since his accession to the English throne. He invited the Edinburgh professors to meet him in the Chapel Royal of Stirling Castle, in presence of many of the English and Scottish nobility. Several subjects were debated before him, after the manner of the times. After supper the king sent for the disputants, whose names were John Adamson, James Fairlie, Patrick Sands, Andrew Young, James Reid, and William King. He then proceeded to compliment them in these words:—

"Adam was the father of all, and Adam's son had the first part of this act. The defender is justly called Fairlie; his theme had some fairlies * in it, and he sustained them very fairly, and with many fair lies given to the oppugners. And why should not Mr. Sands be the first to enter the sands? But now I clearly see that all sands are not barren, for certainly he hath shown a fertile wit. Mr. Young is very old in Aristotle. Mr. Reid need not be red with blushing for his acting this day. Mr. King disputed very kingly, and of a kingly purpose concerning the royal supremacy of reason above anger and all passions." The monarch added that the College of Edinburgh, to which they belonged, should henceforth be called *The College of King James*.

The interesting traditions which lingered among the people respecting the homely ways of the old sovereigns conduced towards the insurrectionary movements of 1715 and 1745. The first insurrection was considerably checked by the appearance of the Chevalier de St. George, which did not justify the sanguine hopes of his adherents. But Prince Charles Edward, when he appeared, in 1745, caused the uninviting aspects of his sire to be forgotten. His fine manly form was the admiration even of those who denied his claims. Highland dames and damsels strove to kiss his hand. Many gentlewomen carried

* Wonders.

miniatures of the young adventurer in their bosoms. Lady Anadowal and Miss Flora Macdonald caused sheets in which he had slept to be constantly carried with them in their journeyings, that they might not lose the opportunity of being buried in their folds.

When George IV. visited Scotland, in 1822, all classes were equally enthusiastic in yielding him a proper reception. The Highlanders regarded him as their lawful king, since the Stuart line had failed. Some of the English nobility entertained apprehensions respecting the loyalty of the Gael—and a gallant colonel, on their behalf, suggested to Sir Walter Scott that it might be prudent that the Highland guard at Holyrood should remove the flints from their pistols. Sir Walter invited the Colonel to meet a number of the Highland chiefs at his house at dinner, which he suggested might be a favourable opportunity for introducing the subject of the *flints*. The evening was spent amidst the most enthusiastic manifestations of loyalty. When the proceedings had considerably advanced, Sir Walter said to the colonel, "Will you now speak about the flints?" "It would be utter madness," replied the colonel; "the men are loyal to the backbone."

The loyalty was exuberant. It was whispered that the king, like some of his royal predecessors, occasionally moved about *incognito*—a rumour much to the inconvenience of those stout burly gentlemen who appeared in the thoroughfares, these being constantly cheered and jostled as disguised sovereigns. One portly yeoman, who considerably resembled the monarch, was pounced upon as veritable Majesty, and the more he attempted to protest that he was not, the huzzas became the louder. At length, when fairly driven into a corner by the populace, he shouted at the pitch of his voice, " Upon my honour I'm no king—not even a baronet or a knight, but a plain man just as any of yourselves."

Sir Walter Scott, who was received into the royal presence before the king had left his ship, was so overwhelmed by the honour of having his health drunk by the monarch, that he begged the wineglass from his Majesty, that it might be preserved in his family. When the glass was accidentally broken, the great minstrel regarded the occurrence as a personal affliction.

In congratulating his Majesty on his arrival, the chief magistrate of Leith eloquently conveyed the sentiments of assembled thousands as he said, " I feel an elevation of mind which is inexpressible, in bidding welcome to Scotland the descendant of more than a hundred of her kings."

An Edinburgh advocate had some time before been presented to the king at St. James's Palace. In the confusion of the hour he forgot the usual act of fealty, and took hold of the royal hand, which he shook with Scottish cordiality. When the state levée was held at Holyrood, the advocate, who had undergone some ridicule on account of his former awkwardness, knelt down and saluted the royal hand in the customary manner. He was passing on, when the king recognizing him said, "Stop, friend. I always part with my old acquaintances as I meet with them." The king then seized the gentleman by the hand and gave him a hearty shake.

The king took occasion to express the extreme gratification he had experienced by his reception in the Scottish capital. "I had been accustomed," he said, "to regard the Scots as a loyal race—an independent people, but now I perceive that they are a nation of gentlemen."

Our present gracious Sovereign has been so long accustomed to reside during a portion of the year in the Highlands, that the enthusiasm which attended her Majesty's first visit in 1842 has subsided into quiet and respectful greetings. To the occupants of the Balmoral estate the Queen has endeared herself by many acts of condescension and kindness. She has manifested a personal concern in their welfare, has sat familiarly by their firesides, and paid visits to them in their afflictions. Some years ago, Mr. Mackenzie, farmer, Ardoch, had been severely indisposed for a period of six months. The Queen sent word that she proposed to visit him in his sick chamber next day, and expressed a hope that he would not be annoyed by the intention. The visit was paid, and on the following day her Majesty despatched a messenger to Mr. Mackenzie's dwelling to inquire how he was, lest her visit had in any manner disturbed him.

L

The Queen was seated at the fireside of a cottar wife. The broth-pot was simmering on the fire. Her Majesty was informed by the honest housewife that she was preparing her broth. "And what is broth made of?" asked the Queen. "There's beef intilt,"* answered the gudewife, "and there's neeps intilt, and there's carrots intilt, and there's barley intilt." "But what's *intilt?*" said her Majesty. "Just as I'm telling your Majesty,—there's carrots intilt, and neeps intilt, and——" "Yes, I know all that very well," again interjected the Queen; "but what's *intilt?* I don't know what that is." "Just precisely as I'm telling your Majesty. There's beef intilt, and there's barley intilt, and there's neeps intilt, and there's carrots intilt, and there's greens intilt." Her Majesty only ascertained the meaning of intilt on her return to the castle.

There are some remarkable instances of regal personages having sprung from Scottish families. The great-grandfather of her Majesty the Empress of the French was a landless baronet in Dumfriesshire. Miss Charlotte Paterson of New York, granddaughter of Robert Paterson, the Dumfriesshire stonemason, prototype of "Old Mortality," was the first wife of Jerome Bonaparte, ex-King of Westphalia, younger brother of the Emperor Napoleon.

The daughter of a plain family named Nelson, residing in St. Ninians, Stirlingshire, was the late Sultana of the Crimea. Miss Gloag, daughter of the

* Into it.

blacksmith of Mill o' Steps, a small hamlet near Muthill, had an adventurous history, terminating in royal honours. Her father, after being many years a widower, contracted a second marriage. His daughter, who had attained her sixteenth year, was unkindly treated by her stepmother. At that period, about a century ago, many Scottish maidens emigrated to America. Miss Gloag joined several others, and embarked in an emigrant ship bound for some port on the American coast; but evil fortune seemed to pursue her. The vessel was seized by African pirates, and the passengers and crew were carried to Morocco and there sold as slaves. Miss Gloag was purchased by the Emperor, who admitted her into his harem. At length she became Empress. She corresponded regularly with her humble relatives in Scotland. About the beginning of the century, two sons of the late Emperor of Morocco applied to the British Government for protection against the pretensions of an ambitious relative, who aspired to their father's throne. They pled a claim for assistance on account of their mother being a British subject. The claim was admitted, and a fleet was being fitted out at Gibraltar for their defence, when intelligence arrived that they had been secretly assassinated.

CHAPTER V.

ECCENTRIC CHARACTERS.

> "Learned men oft greedily pursue
> Things that are rather wonderful than true,
> And in their nicest speculations choose
> To make their own discoveries strange news."
>
> BUTLER.

WHEN it does not proceed from an affectation of singularity or superiority, eccentricity may be traced to the preponderance of one faculty, or to habits of concentration respecting particular subjects of thought to the exclusion of all others. An eccentric person is the comet of the social circle; he moves in an orbit of his own, but, unlike the comet of the heavens, he occasionally impinges on the toes or the feelings of his neighbours.

Henry David, fifth Earl of Buchan, was a most eccentric person. When Prince Charles Edward held court at Holyrood, in 1745, he formed a strong desire to obtain a private interview with the young adventurer without committing himself to his cause. In order that this might be carried out without compromise to his interests as an adherent of the reigning family, he asked his friend Lord Elcho, who had joined the insurrection, to effect his seizure at the cross, with a view to his being apparently dragged into the presence of the Prince. The capture was negotiated, but the design failed, for Charles Edward declined to give audience to any one who would not pledge himself to his cause.

Lord Buchan was succeeded, in 1767, by his eldest son, David Stuart, a person of even greater eccentricity than his father. He was extremely vain. "I belong to a talented family, madam," his lordship remarked to the witty Duchess of Gordon. "Yes," responded the Duchess, "and I suppose the talent has come from the mother, since it has been settled on the younger branches." The Duchess referred to the Hon. Henry Erskine, Dean of Faculty, and the Hon. Thomas, afterwards Lord Chancellor Erskine, who were the younger brothers of this pedantic nobleman.

A most ridiculous story of the Earl is related by J. G. Lockhart. In 1819 Sir Walter Scott was very ill, confined to his bed in his house in Castle Street, Edinburgh. Though aware that all visitors were strictly prohibited, the Earl determined on seeing him. Finding the knocker on the front door tied up, he descended to the area door, and, despite the remonstrances of the coachman, mounted up-stairs on his way to the invalid's bedchamber. Miss Scott met him and expostulated. It was useless. The Earl would proceed—must see Sir Walter. Meanwhile the coachman, who had again come upon the scene, gave his lordship a shove, and, with menacing gestures, indicated that any further intrusion would be resisted. The Earl reluctantly made his retreat. Sir Walter was informed of the adventure, and forthwith despatched James Ballantyne, who happened to be with him, to explain matters, and so relieve his lordship's disappointment. Ballantyne found the Earl in his library in a state of great excitement. He had gone, he said, to embrace Sir Walter before he died, to remind him that they should rest together in the same burial-place, and to show him a plan of the funeral procession which he had prepared. In the programme it was specified that his lordship should pronounce an elòge over the remains of the departed minstrel when they had been lowered into their last resting-place.

While nominally a patron of the arts and their cultivators, Lord Buchan was careful to avoid any draft on his finances. He was extremely penurious. A young portrait painter in the capital had been recommended to his notice, and was forthwith honoured with a commission to delineate his lordship on canvas. On the completion of the work, which was deemed quite satisfactory, the needy painter eagerly expected a handsome recompense. As none was forthcoming, he contrived, through a friend, to convey to the Earl a hint that he required the money. His lordship invited him to breakfast. The youth accepted the invitation with delight. The meal being concluded, his lordship sauntered forth into Princes Street, and, taking the artist by the arm, proceeded to walk him up and down this public thoroughfare. At noon he remembered another engagement, and parted with his protégé, remarking to him as he moved off, "Your fortune is now as good as made, since you have been seen in Princes Street walking familiarly with the Earl of Buchan."

James Boswell, the biographer of Johnson, was extremely eccentric. He entertained the most overweening idea of his own importance. The following are excerpts from his note-book:—

"Boswell was presented to the Duke of Argyle at Whitton in the year 1760. The Duke talked some time with him and was pleased, and seemed surprised that Boswell wanted to have a commission in the Guards. His Grace took Boswell's father aside and said, 'My lord, I like your son; that boy must not be shot at for three and sixpence a day.'"

"Boswell compared himself to the ancient Corinthian brass. 'I am,' said he, 'a composition of an infinite variety of ingredients. I have been formed by a vast number of scenes of the most different natures, and I question if any uniform education could have produced a character so agreeable.'"

"My freinds* are to me like the cinnamon tree, which produces nutmeg, mace, and cinnamon. Not only do I get wisdom and worth out of them, but amusement. I use them as the Chinese do their

* So Boswell spelt the word.

animals. Nothing is lost there. A very good dish is made of the poorest parts; so I make the follies of my freinds serve for a dessert after their valuable qualities."

"When Wilkes and I sat together, each glass of wine produced a flash of wit, like gunpowder thrown into the fire—puff! puff!"

"Mons. D'Ankerville paid me the compliment that I was the man of genius who had the best heart he had ever known."

Boswell was not unconscious of his foibles and weaknesses. His note-book contains the following :—

"Boswell, who had a good deal of whim, used not only to form wild projects in his imagination, but would sometimes reduce them to practice. In his calm hours he said with great good humour, 'There have been many people who built castles in the air, but I suppose I am the first that ever attempted to live in them.'"

"Boswell complained that he had too good a memory in trifles, which prevented his remembering things of consequence. 'My head,' said he, 'is like a tavern in which a club of low punch-drinkers have taken up the room that might have been filled with lords that drink Burgundy; but it is not in the landlord's power to dispossess them.'"

Captain Erskine complained that Boswell's handwriting was so large that his letters contained very little. "My lines," said Boswell, "are like my ideas, very irregular, and at a great distance from each other."

Unlike the majority of egotists, Boswell could heartily enjoy a jest at his own expense. The most severe home-thrust never disturbed his complacency. His note-book proceeds:—

"Boswell was talking away one morning in St. James's Park with much vanity. Said his friend Temple, 'We have heard of many kinds of hobby-horses, but, Boswell, you ride upon yourself.'"

"Boswell was one day complaining that he was sometimes dull. 'Yes, yes,' cried Lord Kames, 'Homer sometimes nods.' Boswell being too much elevated with this, my lord added, 'Indeed, sir, it is the only chance you have of resembling Homer.'"

"Rather than borrow one half-guinea of Lord ———, I would borrow ten shillings of ten chairmen, and the odd sixpence of a shoe-black."

On one occasion Boswell admits he lost his temper under the tongue of censure. His wife was the reprover. These are his words:—

"When I was warm, talking of my own consequence and generosity, my wife made some cool, humbling remark upon me. I flew into a violent passion; I said, 'If you throw cold water upon a plate of iron much heated, it will crack into shivers.'"

The good-natured egotist thus expresses his sentiments respecting social meetings:—

"I have not an ardent love for parties of pleasure,

yet, am I once engaged in them, no man is more joyous. The difference between me and one who is the promoter of them is like that between a water-dog and an ordinary dog. I have no instinct prompting me. I never go into the water of my own accord; but throw me in, and you will find that I swim excellently."

Sir John Dinely, an English baronet, but associated with Scotland from a lengthened residence in the country, holds a first rank among members of the eccentric school. He was the last heir-male of an old family in the county of Worcester, descended on the female side from the royal House of Plantagenet. The family had gradually experienced reverses, and the means which accrued to Sir John on his succession in 1761 were very circumscribed. These were soon entirely exhausted by his prodigality, so that in his state of indigence he willingly accepted the situation and emoluments of one of the Poor Knights of Windsor. He had originally studied medicine, and had attempted to practise as a physician, but he seems to have abandoned the trammels of a professional existence to betake himself to a career of Platonic gallantry. His days were spent in assiduous devotion to the fair sex, with a view to his being enabled to select a wife who should be the paragon of beauty, elegance, and worth. In order to achieve this grand aim, he pursued a course of eccentricity exceeded only by that of the fictitious knight of La Mancha. Not content with advertising from time to time in the English journals as to his admiration of the fair, and in terms of glowing enthusiasm soliciting the notice of ladies of every rank and age as candidates for his hand and affections, he resided for a lengthened period of his life in different parts of the country, in quest of a fair object who might be found permanently worthy of his love. From various entries in the burgh records, it appears that after residing some time both in Edinburgh and Glasgow, he had come to Stirling in 1768, and purchased a house in the principal street. He had the house altered to suit his peculiar tastes; the roof was made flat, and a garden was laid out on its summit. A fish-pond in the centre was surrounded with a bordering of gooseberry bushes and some rare plants; and from a walk encompassing the whole the eccentric baronet could amuse himself by looking on the gold-fish sporting in the basin, or on the fair passing down Broad Street. But the roof gave way from the superincumbent pressure, and Sir John, unable to repair it, had to dispose of the property about two years after he had acquired it. He left Stirling for a period, and his name first reappears in the records as having been subjected to pecuniary difficulties by the prosecution of a female to whom he had not fulfilled an alleged promise of marriage. In 1778 he returned to Stirling, and as a burgess and guild brother, which he had been appointed in March, 1768, he preferred a claim to be pensioned from the funds of Cowan's Hospital. The claim, owing to his poverty, was admitted, and the indigent baronet had paid to him half a crown weekly till the old term of Martinmas, 1792, when he surrendered his rights and left the place. In his transactions with the guildry he laid aside the use of his title, and assumed the name of John Baronet, by which designation he is generally entered in the registers, the qualifying expression, "or such person now so styled," being added to his assumed name in the property conveyance. By several persons in Stirling Sir John is well remembered. Arrayed in a costume consisting of a velvet vest, satin breeches, and silk stockings, with a scarlet cloak thrown over to conceal their faded and tattered aspects, his feet generally protected by a pair of high timber sandals, and his hat and wig secured to his head by a large cotton handkerchief tied under his chin, he sauntered about daily, paying his courteous *dévoir* to every female who would good-humouredly address him. As none of the sex were too young for his admiration, a train of very young Misses were not unfrequently attending him, listening to his sighs and smiling at his foibles. He knew each beauty of the district by name, and kept a catalogue of them in which their names were entered according to his estimate of their charms. On leaving Stirling he returned to Windsor, where he indulged in his peculiar eccentricities till his death, at an advanced age, in May, 1808. Mr. Burke, in the "Anecdotes of the Aristocracy," allots a chapter to the eccentric baronet, and has recorded some of his oddities and advertisements. He lived entirely alone, dispensing with the assistance of a servant; his chief haunts in London being the auction-rooms and pastry-shops, at the latter of which he made, in his advertisements, his assignations with the fair sex. He valued himself much on his family connections and hereditary distinction, and estimated his fortune at £300,000, should he be able to recover it. Several of his advertisements for a wife are inserted in a work by Captain Grose, entitled, "A Guide to Health, Beauty, Riches, and Honour."

Francis Macnab, of Macnab, valued himself on being the chief of an ancient Highland clan. He therefore rejected the usual prefix of "Mr.," and desired to be known and addressed as "Macnab." A gentleman called on him one day at his residence in Edinburgh according to invitation, but inadvertently on asking if he was within used the objectionable prefix. The servant stated he would make inquiry, but soon returned to say that *Mr.* Macnab was not in the house. The visitor retired, though he was confident he had heard his friend's voice from an inner apartment. Bethinking himself, he went back and asked "if Macnab was at home?" The answer was in the affirmative, and the laird received him cordially.

Macnab's education had been neglected. Some one ventured to remark on his inaccurate spelling in a document he was writing. He promptly replied, "Who could spell wi' sic a pen?"

At the Leith races one year Macnab had the misfortune to lose his horse, which fell down dead. At the races of the year following, a young fellow, who had witnessed the catastrophe, said to the laird with flippant air, "Macnab, is that the same horse you had last year?" "No," said Macnab, "but this is the same whip," which he brandished as if about to apply it to the querist's shoulders.

An amicable contest once existed for the chieftainship of the clan Macnab. One of the claimants was officially located in Canada. The other, being on a visit to the colony, was waited on by his rival, who left a large card, inscribed "The Macnab." Next day the visit was returned, and a card twice the size of the former left, inscribed, "The other Macnab."

Maxton, the laird of Cultoquhey, in Strathearn, was one of the most eccentric of Scottish landowners. He was surrounded by four potent families, each of whom he conceived was anxious to appropriate his patrimonial acres. He prayed daily that he might be delivered—

> "From the greed of the Campbells,
> From the ire of the Drummonds,
> From the pride of the Grahams,
> And from the wind of the Murrays."

The Duke of Atholl, who was the chief of the Murrays, having invited Cultoquhey to dinner, asked him to repeat his addition to the litany, believing that he would decline to do so in his presence. He was, however, mistaken, and the Duke demanded that he would promise to omit his name, otherwise he would crop his ears. "That's wind," said the undaunted laird; an imperturbable reply, which restored the Duke to his equanimity.

Francis Semple, the ingenious author of "Maggie Lauder," and other popular songs, was possessed of considerable eccentricity and humour. From his residence at Beltrees, Renfrewshire, he proceeded to Glasgow, some time in 1651, there to visit, along with his wife, an aged maiden aunt, his father's sister. On his arrival his aunt informed him that she must immediately apprise the captain of Cromwell's soldiers, then occupying the city, of his arrival, otherwise the soldiers would distrain her property. Semple undertook to prepare a missive supplying the needful information. Receiving a sheet of paper, he wrote these lines, which he folded in the form of a letter, and addressed "To the Commander of the Guard:"—

> "Lo doon near by the city temple,
> There is ane lodg'd wi' Auntie Semple,
> Francis Semple, of Beltrees,
> His consort also, if you please;
> There's twa o's horse, and ane o's men,
> That's quartered down wi' Allan Glen.
> Thir lines I send to you, for fear
> O' poindin' of auld auntie's gear,
> Whilk never ane before durst stear,
> It stinks for staleness I dare swear."

The writer subscribed his name and address, and by

special messenger transmitted his communication to the military official.

Having read the document, the English commandant conceived that the writer had intended a deliberate insult, and ordered a party of soldiers to arrest him. Semple was apprehended and arraigned before the Lord Provost. When the libel was read, the civic chief could not restrain his laughter, in which the commandant heartily joined, when the epistle was explained to him in English. From that moment Semple and the commandant became friends; the latter introduced the poet to his officers, who enjoyed his society and his songs. On their return to England the officers made Semple's songs known in the south, where they were long popular.

James Sibbald, editor of the "Chronicles of Scottish Poetry," was very eccentric, but withal possessed considerable humour. He resided several years in London, without informing his friends in Scotland of his proceedings, or even where he lived. At length his brother, a Leith merchant, got a letter conveyed to him, in which he entreated him to relieve the anxieties of his relations by stating, just in two lines, where he lived, and what he was doing. Sibbald made the following laconic answer:—

"I live in Soho,
And my business is so-so."

Dr. Walter Anderson, minister of Chirnside, was possessed of very ordinary talents, but was ambitious of fame as an author. Meeting Mr. Hume, the historian, in company, he said to him, "Mr. David, I dare say other people might write books too, but you clever folks have taken up all the good subjects." Mr. Hume replied, "Oh, there is room for a history of Crœsus, king of Lydia." This remark, made by the historian in jest, the worthy clergyman accepted in perfect earnest, and positively prepared and published a huge quarto on the history of Crœsus, with an elaborate dissertation "On the ancient notion of Destiny or Dreams." On the outbreak of the French Revolution Dr. Anderson published a pamphlet on the subject, which, like his other publications, proved unsaleable. With a view of inviting attention to the work, he prepared an appendix, much exceeding the size of the original publication. Having called on Principal Robertson, and informed him of his plan, the Principal remonstrated with him on the absurdity of his proposal. "When your pamphlet is already found to be heavy," said he, "do not think to lessen it by making it ten times heavier." Anderson's reply was sufficiently smart :—"Why, Dr. Robertson, you may have seen a kite raised by boys? If you have, you must have remarked that when they try to raise the kite by itself, they do not succeed, but when they add a long string of papers to its tail, up it goes like a laverock." *

Professor William Wilkie, of St. Andrews, author of "The Epigoniad," suffered from a perpetual chill.

* Lark.

In order to secure himself sufficient warmth in bed, he slept under the load of twenty-four pairs of blankets.

Lord Gardenstone indulged a fondness for the race of pigs. One of these animals he had trained to follow him like a dog. When it was little, his lordship allowed it to share his bed. This became inconvenient, but he continued to permit the creature to occupy the same room. He appropriated his clothes as its couch, which, he used to say, it kept comfortably warm.

The celebrated Dr. Adam Smith, author of "The Wealth of Nations," was singularly eccentric in his habits. When he was engaged in composition, he got into a sort of reverie, which rendered him nearly unconscious of events in the external world. One Sunday morning he happened to walk into his garden at Kirkcaldy, his mind occupied with a train of ideas. He unconsciously travelled out of his garden into the turnpike road, along which he proceeded in a state of profound meditation, till he reached Dunfermline, a town nearly fifteen miles distant. The people were proceeding to church, and the sound of the bells awakened the philosopher to reflection. He was arrayed in an old dressing-gown, and presented a figure of no inconsiderable oddity.

Dr. Robert Hamilton, Professor of Mathematics in Marischal College, Aberdeen, was remarkable for his absence of mind. He had repeatedly proceeded to his class-room wanting in several essential articles of apparel. It afterwards was arranged that he should not leave his dwelling without undergoing inspection by some member of his household.

The following anecdote of Professor Hamilton was related to the writer by the late Professor Pyper of St. Andrews. When the Professor was in the act of drawing mathematical figures on the black-board, many of his students were in the practice of throwing peas at him, from the effects of which he sheltered himself by placing his hand protectively on the back of his head. On one occasion an assailant, having waxed bold from the impunity which had attended his frequent perversity, cast at the board a *toy cracker*, containing a few particles of fulminating powder, which exploded near the Professor's head. With one bound the learned preceptor darted from the class-room. A deputation of the better conducted members of the class were immediately despatched after him to plead an apology and entreat his return. Pyper acted as spokesman, but was met by the Professor with these words,—"Gentlemen, I have no objection to the peas, for I can easily protect myself with my hand; but I entreat you to spare my life. The ball hit the board within an inch of my ear." On a proper explanation of the nature of the missile, with a promise that such projectiles should not again be used, the Professor resumed his duties.

Dr. Thomas Blacklock, the blind poet, was occasionally subject to extraordinary conditions of reverie. On the day of his ordination to the ministry at Kirkcudbright, he fell into a state of stupor or profound slumber immediately after dinner. He had retired to a private room, but being aroused some hours after, he rejoined his friends at table. He sung several songs and conversed on different topics, though some of his friends observed him to be absent in manner. After supper he began to speak to himself in a very low and unintelligible tone. At last he awoke with a sudden start, and declared himself unconscious of all that had happened since the hour of dinner. His settlement had been strongly opposed by the parishioners, a circumstance which preyed deeply on his sensitive mind.

The first wife of the Hon. Henry Erskine was uncommonly eccentric. Among her peculiarities was the custom of gadding about half the night, examining the family wardrobe, and ascertaining whether everything was in its proper place. One night she was unsuccessful in a search, and about three in the morning she awoke Mr. Erskine from his sleep, and put to him the question, "Harry, lovie, where's your white waistcoat?"

John Barclay, author of "Argenis," and his wife were both eccentric persons. Barclay spent the afternoons in his garden. He conceived a passion for the cultivation of the tulip, and became so much attached to that flower that he occupied an ill-aired and uncomfortable dwelling in order to feast his eyes constantly upon it. When he had occasion to be absent, he placed two mastiffs as sentinels upon the garden to guard his beloved plant. After his death, Mrs. Barclay caused a handsome monument to be raised to his memory; but learning that an erection of a similar character had been reared in the same place by a Roman ecclesiastic to the memory of his tutor, she caused her husband's cenotaph to be destroyed. "My husband," said the irate gentlewoman, "was a man of family, and famous in the literary world; I will not suffer him to remain on a level with an obscure pedagogue."

Thomas Coutts, the celebrated London banker, was a native of Edinburgh. He was a man of very eccentric tastes. Being miserly in his habits, he caused his garments to be repaired so long as they could possibly be made to hold together. The process of mending, which he caused to be executed by his female servants, became extremely irksome, and several of them in consequence left his employment. At length a young woman, named Susan Starkie, entered his service, who, perceiving her master's peculiarity, contrived to introduce into his wardrobe, out of her savings, new stockings instead of those which had become useless. The careful banker was gratified to find his garments assume a renovated aspect under the care of his new handmaid, and conceiving that he could not procure a more economical wife, he married her.

Alexander Cruden, author of the "Concordance of the Bible," was subject to mental derangement, and was, at three different periods, confined in a lunatic asylum. When he had regained his freedom after the third occasion, he endeavoured to induce several relatives, who had been instrumental in confining him, to submit to imprisonment in Newgate as a compensation for the maltreatment he conceived he had experienced at their hands. To his sister he proposed the alternative of Newgate, Reading, and Aylesbury jails, or the prison at Windsor Castle!

Several Scottish clergymen have evinced eccentricity by constantly dwelling, in their pulpit prelections and writings, on the illustration of a single doctrine or particular duty. A clergyman of the seventeenth century is described as accommodating every text towards enforcing the duty of supporting the "Solemn League and Covenant." Another Scottish divine preached so frequently on the subject of faith that his ministrations became irksome. A friend suggested to him a text, in the hope that on one occasion, at least, the wonted topic might be avoided. He named these words (Exod. xxxix. 26),—" A bell." Next Sunday the clergyman, having read this short text, proceeded thus: " Brethren, a bell is the symbol of faith—for faith cometh by hearing, and how can we hear better than by a bell ? " In a history of the Bible,* the Rev. George R. Gleig

* " The History of the Bible," by the Rev. G. R. Gleig, M.A., M.R.S.L., &c., &c., vol. ii., p. 370.

contrives to indicate his aversion to Scottish Theology by describing the apostle Paul as "no Calvinist."

Hugh Miller, the distinguished geologist, was for many years engaged as a quarrier and stonemason. He was singularly indifferent as to his personal attire. When he used to visit the printing-office of the *Inverness Courier* on the Saturday afternoons, he uniformly presented himself with his mason's apron folded up about his person. He was then an operative, but when he proceeded to Edinburgh to undertake the editorship of the *Witness* newspaper, he could scarcely be persuaded to lay aside the badge of his original employment.

The name of Mr. Durham of Largo is familiar to every reader of Scottish anecdote, from his love of setting forth stories of the marvellous. A servant who had long been in Mr. Durham's employment informed him that he could no longer remain in his service. "Why should you leave, John?" said Mr. Durham; "have I not always treated you well?" "Oh," responded John, "I have nothing to complain of on that score. But there is a reason." Mr. Durham said that he would endeavour to make him comfortable, and asked him to state his reason at once. "Weel then, sir," said John, " gin ye maun hae it, I must just tell you that the folks on the street often point to me and say, 'That's the man that has the leein' maister,' an' I dinna like this." "But, John, did you ever observe that I told an untruth?" said Mr. Durham.

"Weel, sir," responded John, "ye maun excuse me if I say you sometimes gang a little owre far." "I am not sensible of it, John," said Mr. Durham; "but, John, when you are standing behind me at table, and think I am going at all wrong, just give me quietly a wee dunch* on the back." Shortly after there was a dinner-party in Largo House, and Mr. Durham was entertaining his friends with his reminiscences of travel. In America he said he had seen monkeys of prodigious size, with tails twenty feet long. There were expressions of surprise. John gave his master a nudge. "Well, gentlemen," said the laird, "if the tails were not quite twenty feet long, I am sure they were fifteen." There were still expressions of surprise. John administered another nudge. "Certainly I did not measure the tails, but they could not be less than ten feet long." There was another nudge. This was too much for the laird's endurance. He turned round and exclaimed, "What do you mean, John; would you have the monkeys without tails at all?"

The following anecdote respecting Mr. Durham's unfortunate habit has often been incorrectly told. Mr. Durham was present among a party of gentlemen, when a bet was taken as to whether he or another gentleman of the company, also noted for bouncing, would tell the greatest lie. Informed of the wager, Mr. Durham observed that, "it was singular he had the reputation of being a liar, since he was quite sure

* Slight blow.

he had never told a lie in his life." "The bet is gained," exclaimed the gentleman who had been inclined to support the claims of the other bouncer. "A greater lie than this could not be told."

Mr. Finlayson, town-clerk of Stirling, in the latter half of the seventeenth century, was notorious for coining marvellous stories. He had been on a visit to the Earl of Menteith at Talla, in Lake Menteith. On his being about to leave, the Earl asked him whether he had seen the sailing cherry-tree. He said he had not, and begged that his lordship would give him an account of it. The Earl stated that the tree had grown out of a goose's mouth from a stone which the bird had swallowed, and which she carried about with her round the lake. "The tree is now," added his lordship, "in full fruit, of the most exquisite flavour." Finlayson admitted that the story was very interesting, but could inform his lordship of one still more remarkable. "Did your lordship ever hear of the ball fired from one of Cromwell's cannon, when he was encamped at Airth?" The Earl said he had not. "Then," said Finlayson, "it so happened that the ball fired from Airth reached Stirling Castle, four miles off, and lodged in a trumpet which was being sounded by one of the soldiers." "And the trumpeter was killed of course?" said the Earl. "Not at all," responded Finlayson; "and this is the most marvellous part of the story,— the soldier blew the ball back again, and it killed the artilleryman who had fired it." The Earl admitted that Finlayson's fiction fairly eclipsed his own.

The Hon. William Ramsay Maule,* afterwards Baron Panmure, was, in the earlier part of his career, celebrated for his strange escapades. Several stories of his eccentric doings have been preserved. Mr. Maule had been making merry at an hotel in Montrose. At a late hour he sallied out in quest of adventure. A street lamp happened to attract his attention. With a stroke of his ponderous walking-stick he fractured it to atoms. "You have broken a lamp, Mr. Maule," said one of the watchmen. "The price is seven shillings." "Just so," responded Mr. Maule; "can you change a guinea note?" The watchman responded in the negative. "Never mind," said the young squire, "I'll just take pennyworths." So he proceeded to destroy other two of the lamps, and then handed the note to the watchman.

There is a better known story of Mr. Maule connected with a similar escapade at Perth. At a late hour one evening he had proceeded from street to street of that city, extinguishing the lamps and smashing them to pieces. The city corporation met next morning to deliberate on obtaining a restoration of their property, and punishing the offender. Just as they had taken their seats in the council-chamber Mr. Maule presented himself, and respectfully addressing the Lord Provost, requested permission to make a statement. "My lord and honourable gentlemen,"

* This benevolent nobleman died on the 3rd of April, 1852.

proceeded Mr. Maule, "on walking last evening through your beautiful city, I was struck with the inferior appearance of your street lamps, which were quite unworthy of so fine a city. I therefore took the liberty of destroying them, that I might enjoy the satisfaction of presenting a set of lamps of a handsome and appropriate character. This I now beg leave to do." The Lord Provost conveyed to Mr. Maule the acknowledgments of the corporation, and he retired from the council-chamber amidst the plaudits of the assembly.

The mother of the late Joseph Hume, M.P., was early left a widow, and contrived to support herself and her young family by keeping a store of earthenware at the market-place of Montrose. At the weekly fair she spread out her wares on the street to attract customers. On a fair day Mr. Maule and a companion entered Montrose on horseback, and discovering Mrs. Hume's goods in the street, proceeded to gallop through them, to the entire consternation of the bystanders. Mrs. Hume remarked that "the weel faured * honourable wad hae his diversion." She had been paid by Mr. Maule for her goods in double their specified value.

Walking one day through a plantation on his estate, Mr. Maule heard a sound like the hewing of wood. Proceeding in the direction of the sound, he saw a young man deliberately levelling one of his trees. "What are ye aboot, man?" said he, in as

* Well-favoured, good-looking.

provincial a tone as he could command. "Do you no see what I'm aboot?" answered the fellow, with an air of indifference. "I see," said the stranger; "but what if Maule were to come upon you?" "Hout, man!" replied the youth, "he wadna say a word. There's no a better gentleman in a' the country. Wad ye lend me a hand?" The stranger assented, and when the tree had been placed on the cart, which was waiting at some distance, the peasant proposed to reward his assistant with a dram at the alehouse. To this request the stranger would not accede, but said to the youth that if he would call next day at the castle, he should have a glass out of his own private bottle. The countryman promised to call, and kept his word. He was immediately ushered into the presence of Mr. Maule and a company of gentlemen. "You will get your dram in the hall," said Mr. Maule to the bewildered and trembling rustic; "but when you next go to cut wood, I would advise you first to ask Maule's permission."

The old highland chairmen of Edinburgh were notorious for their love of money. The discontent of these persons happened to be talked of in an Edinburgh club where Mr. Maule was present. He undertook the defence of his northern countrymen, and took a bet of five guineas with one of the company that he would readily satisfy their demands. The bet was accepted. Mr. Maule threw himself into a sedan, requesting that he might be carried a short distance down the Canongate. On alighting he handed a guinea note to his conductors. "Thank yer honour," said the recipient, "but surely ye'll gie me anither sixpence to get a gill." "An' any odd bawbees* for sneeshin,"† said the other. "Your greed has cost me five guineas already, besides what you have got," said Mr. Maule, as he walked off, resolving never again to espouse the cause of highland chairmen.

In the manner of his times Mr. Maule occasionally disguised himself as a mendicant. One cold wet evening he entered the house of an old woman, and in his character of gaberlunzie sought shelter and refreshment. He received a welcome, but had no sooner seated himself than he began to complain of the insufficiency of the fire for so severe a night. The poor cottager said she had no more fuel in the house. "Oh, I'll soon find fuel," said the supposed vagrant. And so saying, he seized hold of the spinning-wheel, which he broke to pieces, and heaped upon the fire. The poor woman was utterly appalled, and upbraided the audacious wanderer for destroying her only means of earning a living. After submitting to the full torrent of her wrath, he suddenly cast aside his tattered vestments, and drawing forth a well-filled purse, placed ten guineas in her hand. "Buy plenty of fuel for the winter, and a good new wheel," said the gentle beggar, as he hastened his departure amidst showers of benediction.

The last Duke of Gordon was, as Marquis of

* Halfpence.   † Snuff.

Huntly, celebrated for playing the gaberlunzie. This exploit being mentioned in company, a gentleman present took a bet with him that under no possible disguise could his lordship deceive him. In the course of a few days he appeared at the house of his friend, in his guise as a mendicant. The owner of the mansion was walking in his avenue, when the pseudo-beggar saluted him with becoming reverence and asked an *awmous*.* The gentleman told him to step into the hall, and there to see what could be found for a keen appetite. The gaberlunzie humbly thanked his honour, and proceeding into the hall, had placed before him an abundant supply of cold meat, bread, and beer. Having partaken of the cheer, he again crossed the path of the gentleman, who asked him how he had fared. "Very poorly, very poorly," replied the mendicant; "I had nothing but cold beef, sour bread, and stale beer." "You must be a saucy scoundrel," said the gentleman, who called to some of his people to hasten his departure. The beggar threw aside his rags, and appeared before his astonished friend as the Marquis of Huntly!

The most remarkable adept at mystification who has appeared in Scottish society is Miss Stirling Graham, a distant relative of the writer. A publication of this estimable gentlewoman, descriptive of the mystifications which she practised in her youth, should be procured by all those who wish to enjoy an insight into the manners of Scottish life fifty years

* Alms.

ago. Two of Miss Graham's mystifications are suitable to the present work.

One Saturday evening Mr. Francis Jeffrey met Miss Graham in society, and expressed to her a wish that he might be introduced to the old lady she was in the habit of personating. She consented, and promised that he should see the old lady very soon. On the afternoon of the following Monday a carriage drove up to Mr. Jeffery's door, and "the Lady Pitlyal," ascertaining that the learned gentleman was within, stepped out and was duly ushered into his business room. She was accompanied by her daughter, "the heiress of Pitlyal." Her ladyship was received with the ceremony befitting her rank. She proceeded to detail with much minuteness the particulars of a law process, in which she was desirous of retaining Mr. Jeffrey as her counsel. Jeffrey undertook to examine her papers on the case being presented to him by her agent. She then handed him a fee, adding a pinch of snuff from her massive gold box. Taking a folded paper from her silver-clasped pocket-book, she stated that it contained an extract from a muckle book, called the "Prophecies of Pitlyal," and that she was anxious to have his explanation of it. Jeffrey promptly excused himself, remarking that her ladyship would find him more skilled in the law than the prophets. Nothing daunted, Lady Pitlyal handed to him the paper, and begged him to read it aloud. He read, among other lines, these :—

"O'er the Light of the North,
 When the glamour breaks forth,
 And its wild-fire so red
 With the daylight is spread,
When woman shrinks not from the ordeal of tryal,
There is triumph and fame to the house of Pitlyal."

Jeffrey could not comprehend such symbolical phraseology, and her ladyship hinted her belief that it might be realized in her obtaining a good marriage for her daughter.

A pause in the conversation having occurred, her ladyship asked Mr. Jeffrey to inform her where she could procure a set of *fause teeth*. He politely informed her of the names of two celebrated dentists, and at her request wrote their addresses on a slip of paper. She now informed him that she read his *buke*, meaning the *Edinburgh Review*. She retired, leaning on her daughter's arm and her gold-headed cane, and complaining loudly of "a *corny* tae." Jeffrey was late for dinner, in consequence of the interview, and explained to his family that he had been detained by one of the oddest and most tiresome old women he had ever met with. Next day he learned that he, too, had been "taken in" by Miss Stirling Graham's old lady.

Miss Graham was on a visit to her friends, Mr. and Mrs. Guthrie, of Craigie. The Misses Guthrie proposed she should "take in" their father and mother. A letter accordingly was handed up to Mr. Graham from his friend Mr. Dempster, of Dunnichen, announcing the visit of an old acquaintance of his—Mrs. Macallister, from Elgin, who was on her way to Edinburgh, as a witness in Lord Fife's cause. She was represented as amusing, a great traveller, and somewhat of an oddity. "Where's the lady?" said Mr. Guthrie, on glancing at the letter. "In her carriage at the door," said the servant. The laird hastened to receive her, and found Mrs. Macallister in the hall. "Bless me, Mrs. Macallister, are you standing there?" said the laird, as he offered his arm, and conducted the supposed stranger into the drawing-room. He introduced her in due form to Mrs. Guthrie and to every one of the party. A smile, which increased into a decided laugh, arose among the Misses Guthrie, and Mrs. Macallister was obliged to plead a spasmodic pain in her side to account for her whole frame being moved by a fit of laughter, which she struggled to suppress. An elderly gentleman of the party reproved the young ladies in another part of the room for laughing at an old person, even allowing that she was a little outré in her attire.

The laird ordered that Mrs. Macallister's horses should be attended to, and was particularly attentive to her during that afternoon and evening. "I have met a gentleman of your name in London," said Mrs. Macallister; "he is connected with a mercantile house." "My son Charles," said the laird. "I met another Mr. Guthrie at Gow's ball in Edinburgh— a very facetious young gentleman. He introduced me to some of his acquaintances, and called aloud to the music to play—'Such a pair was never seen.'"

"That is my son Sandy," said the laird, laughing heartily.

At supper, Mrs. Macallister took a fancy for the laird's snuff-box, and presenting her own valuable gold one, offered to exchange with him. Mr. Guthrie politely excused himself, stating that his box was a keepsake from his valued friend, the late Mr. Graham, of Duntrune. But Mrs. Macallister persisted, and at length deliberately placed Mr. Guthrie's snuff-box in her pocket. He looked extremely annoyed, but was too polite to complain.

Mrs. Macallister proceeded, in reply to a question by Mr. Guthrie, to give an account of her family of "four sons," and as she hesitated to speak of the youngest—her equanimity having momentarily wavered—an elderly gentleman present, conceiving that painful associations had been excited, covered his face with his handkerchief, and wept.

At eleven o'clock, Miss Guthrie offered to escort Mrs. Macallister to her room, but she said that Mr. Dempster had always conducted her to the door of her apartment himself, and kissed her when he bade her good night, and that he had assured her his friend Craigie would not be behind him in gallantry. The laird accordingly led the ancient dame up-stairs, but when at the door of her chamber, she took off her bonnet to conclude the scene, and the features of Miss Graham met his eyes, he stood for some seconds as if overwhelmed with surprise. Then laughing heartily, he exclaimed, "Now, Clemy, give me back my snuff-box."

Sir Hugh Lyon Playfair of St. Andrews, another relative of the writer, was singularly eccentric in his habits. He was many years chief magistrate of St. Andrews, a city which he converted from a state of dirt and dilapidation into a condition of elegance and beauty. In the course of his operations he had to encounter the usual prejudices against reforms common in the smaller Scottish burghs. Desirous of removing certain porches which, projecting from the older houses, interfered with the symmetry of the streets, he obtained the signatures of the owners and occupants to a memorial in which those excrescences were condemned. One morning every porch was found in ruins. The owners were astounded—many of them menacing law proceedings. The provost presented the memorial to the town council, who voted thanks to the subscribers for their enterprise and public spirit. The compliment overcame every hostile feeling.

There was a convenient promenade in a suburb of the city which the professors of St. Mary's College were desirous of closing up, since it was likely to lead to a permanent thoroughfare through a portion of their estate. The professors caused a wall to be erected across the footpath. During the following night the wall disappeared. Again it was reared, and once more the interruption was cleared off. The professors of St. Mary's proceeded a third time to assert their rights, when a formidable barrier was constructed. In the course of a few weeks this also was levelled, and on its site was erected a board containing the following couplet :—

> "This fence, three times built by St. Mary's,
> Was thrice demolished by the fairies!"

At an early period of his labours as a civic reformer, Sir Hugh had made application to Government to obtain funds for completing the unfinished structure of the United College. Some of the professors felt aggrieved that they had not been consulted in regard to the application, and a letter of remonstrance on the subject was addressed to Sir Hugh by the Faculty. The gallant knight did not relax his efforts, and at length procured a grant of £12,000 for the college buildings. He now received from the university the degree of LL.D. in recognition of his services; but the eccentric magistrate suspended the letter of remonstrance in his business room, with the title in large letters,—"Vote of Thanks from the Professors of the United College for procuring the completion of their College buildings."

Sir Hugh was actuated by a strong sense of duty, which he combined with an entire disregard of popular applause. Some years before his death he reared a monument to himself in the public cemetery of the burgh. The writer suggested to him that he might have saved the expenditure, since the citizens would certainly not fail to raise a memorial stone to one who had done so much for the improvement of their city. "Don't you think," said the knight, "that if they intended to honour my memory, they would do something for me when living? Would they not encourage my literary efforts? I lately published a catechism; it is well got up, it contains matter of universal interest, it has been favourably received by the press, the price is sufficiently moderate—being only one penny; and how many copies have my fellow-townsmen purchased of my little work, which was published a year ago? I believe not more than three, and one of these is still unpaid!"

The Rev. Dr. U——, an accomplished clergyman of the Scottish Church, is said to have been indebted for his living to an occurrence which scarcely promised such a satisfactory result. He had, early in the century, been sent by his father, the clergyman of a Highland parish, to prosecute his classical studies at the High School of Edinburgh. The bully of the school was a young laird, who made it a point to try the mettle of every new comer. The hero of our tale was a lank lad of fourteen, whose retiring manners almost precluded the possibility of his giving offence; but Bully contrived to fasten a quarrel on him, and it was arranged that their mutual honour and prowess should be determined before sufficient witnesses in a retired part of the King's Park. Contrary to all expectation, the Highlander parried the blows of his antagonist, and ingeniously striking where least expected, fairly overthrew the Goliath of the school ring. The juvenile spectators were delighted, and cheered lustily. Not less so the discomfited hero of a hundred school fights. He pronounced his adversary the only boy of the school whom he could not lick,* and in consideration of his prowess, he promised that as he intended for the ministry, he would present him to a living, of which he expected in due time to be patron.

The boys separated—the ministerial aspirant leaving his native country and obtaining educational employment, first on the Continent and afterwards in America. Thirty years elapsed till the living promised at the school-fight became vacant. Bully did not forget his promise. He made inquiry concerning the locality of his old friend, which was at length discovered. The long-promised living was conferred on him in a kindly communication reminding him of the struggle in the King's Park.

Sheriff Barclay supplies the following. On a curling pond, a landowner, who was patron of several livings, was on a rink with a young probationer. The last stone to be played was in the hands of the aspirant to a pulpit. The reckoning was much against his side. The patron exclaimed to his curling *confrère*, "If you take this shot, I promise you the first living in my gift." Fortunately, the stone won the game. Ten years after, a church in the landowner's gift became vacant. He did not forget his promise at the bonspeil.† The probationer received a presentation from his curling acquaintance. "He still lives," writes Dr. Barclay, "proving by the efficient discharge of his sacred duties that he did *not lead his patron on the ice.*"

* Beat, subdue. † Curling match.

The present chapter shall be closed with some anecdotes of the famous violinist, Neil Gow, and his son Nathaniel, the accomplished musician.

Neil Gow was a native of Inver, near Dunkeld, where he continued to reside, under the patronage of the Duke of Atholl, his hereditary chief. Though present at the most refined gatherings of his day, Gow retained his native simplicity of manners. At Dunkeld House he was regarded as a privileged person, and his rough drolleries were not only tolerated, but heartily enjoyed. There was a brilliant assemblage at the mansion. Dancing had been continued throughout the evening. Supper was at length announced, but some of the ladies lingered in the drawing-room, reluctant to leave the dance. Gow was somewhat fidgety, for he had not then bid "farewell to whisky," and he longed for refreshment and rest. At length, losing patience, he surprised the fair lingerers by exclaiming, "Gang doun to yer suppers, ye daft limmers, and dinna had me reelin' here as if hunger and dearth were unkent in the land. Gang doun wi' ye."

One day Gow was summoned to Dunkeld House to note the musical performances on the piano of Lady Charlotte Drummond, one of the Duke's daughters, who had lately "finished" her education. Hearing her play, Neil said to the Duchess, "That lassie o' yours, my leddy, has a gude ear." A gentleman remarked, "Neil, do you call her Grace's daughter a lassie?" "What would I ca' her," answered the minstrel; "sure she's no a laddie."

The celebrated Duchess of Gordon paid Neil a visit in his cottage. Her Grace complained to him of suffering from giddiness and swimming in her head. "I ken the complaint weel," said Neil. "When I've been a wee fou the nicht afore, I've thocht as if a bike * o' bees were bizzin'† i' my head the next mornin'."

The Duke of Atholl made himself familiar with Gow. Walking with the Duchess one day on Stanley hill, near Dunkeld, Neil chanced to come up. The Duke seized hold of him, and sportively engaged him in a wrestling match. Neil had the worst of it, and rolled down the incline. The Duchess ran towards him and expressed a hope that he was not hurt. "Naething to speak o'," replied Neil, "I was the mair idiot to wrestle wi' sic a fule."

Several gentlemen met Gow walking in the neighbourhood of his cottage. "Are you Neil Gow, may I ask?" said one of them. "Deed am I," was his answer. "Oh, we are so glad, for we have walked all the way from Aberdeen on purpose to see you." "The mair fules," replied the musician, "I wadna gane half so far to see you."

Neil's son, Nathaniel Gow, was also distinguished for his powers as a violinist. When George IV. made his state visit to Scotland in 1822, he was specially retained to discourse the national airs at a great assembly, which his Majesty consented to attend. One tune especially attracted the royal

* Nest.   † Buzzing.

notice. "What do you call that tune, Gow?" said the King. "'Wha'll be King but Charlie?' please your Majesty," replied the musician. All were embarrassed by the answer, save the king and Gow —the latter entirely unconscious of his uncourtly speech. But "the first gentleman in Europe" asked the musician to repeat the tune, and desired that it might be often played to him during his visit to the northern capital.

CHAPTER VI.

THE WISE AND THE WEAK.

"Eye Nature's walks, shoot folly as it flies,
And catch the manners living as they rise."
Pope.

THERE are two distinct classes of Scotsmen—one shrewd and sagacious, the other extremely foolish. The observation, commonplace as it may seem, is strictly descriptive of the Scottish character. Intensity is peculiar to the mental condition of northern races. Lacking the vivacious sprightliness of the Irish Celt, and equally removed from the listless content of the unlettered Saxon, the Scotsman is impassioned and fervid. With his mind he deals as with the soil of his country; he endeavours to make the most of it. He supplements original deficiencies by observation, and steadily acquires knowledge in the school of experience. Hence weak persons are a distinct class among the Scots. Their dulness of apprehension and poverty of thought have rendered them conspicuous. Such were, no doubt, the Scottish associates of Mr. Sydney Smith, of whom he humorously said that a surgical operation was required to get a joke into their understandings.

Mr. John Welch, son-in-law of John Knox, the reformer, was one of the most fervid and ingenious of the older Presbyterian clergy. On a false charge of sedition he was deprived of his living and banished to France. When he was residing at St. Jean d'Angely, a fortified town in Lower Charente, that town was besieged by Louis XIII., who was then at war with his Protestant subjects. Mr. Welch warmly counselled the burgesses to make resistance, and personally assisted in serving the guns. When the place capitulated, the monarch requested the Duke d'Epernon to arrest him and bring him to court. The Duke proceeded on his mission with a party of soldiers. He found Mr. Welch preaching in his place of worship. Observing the Duke enter, Mr. Welch requested him to be seated and listen to his discourse. The Duke obeyed. He declared to the preacher at the close of the service that he felt edified. Mr. Welch accompanied him to the king's presence. The monarch asked him how he dared to preach since the exposition of Protestant doctrines was forbidden in those places where the court resided. Mr. Welch replied, "Sir, if your Majesty knew what I preached you would come to hear what is spoken, and command your people likewise to hear it. I preach that you must be saved by the merits of Jesus Christ, and not your own; and I further preach that, as you are king of France, there is no man above you in this kingdom. But these men, whom you permit to preach, teach that there is one above you in authority, the Pope of Rome. To this I could not assent." The speech so pleased the monarch that he received Mr. Welch into favour, constituted him "his minister," and assured him of his constant protection. He kept his promise.

When Scotland was overrun by an English army during the Protectorate, the Estates of Parliament caused the Regalia, consisting of the crown, sceptre, and sword, to be deposited in the stronghold of Dunnottar Castle. This became known, and the castle was besieged by a portion of Cromwell's army. After a prolonged resistance, the garrison resolved to capitulate. Such a course would have implied the surrender of the national trophies. Ogilvie, who commanded the garrison, was a landowner at Kinneff, and Mr. James Granger, minister of that parish, and his wife were deeply concerned that one of their parishioners should be placed in the condition of surrendering the ancient insignia of the national honour. Mrs. Granger, accompanied by her maid, proceeded to the castle. She claimed permission from General Morgan, who commanded the besiegers, to enter the castle to visit her friend Mrs. Ogilvie. The request was courteously granted. After a short interval Mrs. Granger and her maid returned. The maid bore a bag of hards of lint Mrs. Granger carried a small bundle. General

THE WISE AND THE WEAK. 205

Morgan handed the lady to her horse. The castle surrendered soon after, and Mr. Ogilvie was severely menaced unless he would deliver up the regalia. He protested that it was impossible to comply, since these insignia had been removed. He spoke truly. Mrs. Granger and her maid had borne them off in presence of the besieging army. Her little bundle contained the crown, and the bag of hards borne by her maid concealed the sceptre and sword of state. The precious relics were carefully deposited under the pulpit of Kinneff church.

After the Restoration two parties were rewarded for their supposed share in this transaction. Mr. Ogilvie was created a baronet, and John Keith, son of the Countess Marischal, received the earldom of Kintore. The latter was represented by the Countess as having carried the regalia to France, but in reality he had no share whatever in their preservation. The patriotic minister of Kinneff, and his adventurous helpmate, went unrewarded.

When William Wallace, a youth of fifteen, slew young Selby, son of the English constable, at Dundee, he was saved from the consequences of his rashness by the ingenuity of a woman. Flying from his pursuers Wallace took refuge in a peasant's hut at Innergowrie. Relating his story, the *gudewife* arrayed him in female attire, and placed him at her spinning-wheel. He had just begun to spin, when the pursuers entered, and demanded whether a young murderer had been there. " There's nae ane here," said the gudewife, "but the carlin* at the wheel and mysel." The soldiers searched the premises and passed on.

The late Sir Alexander Boswell, Bart., of Auchinleck, son of the celebrated James Boswell, was a person of great ingenuity and public spirit. He formed the scheme of rearing a monument to the poet Burns at his birthplace, on the banks of the Doon. Having procured many promises of support, he convened a meeting on the subject, to be held in the county rooms at Ayr. When the hour of meeting arrived, two persons only were found in the room, these being the convener, and his factor or land-agent. This result had been discouraging to most persons; but Sir Alexander did not lose heart. He took the chair, on the motion of his factor, and in return he nominated the factor clerk to the meeting. He read a series of resolutions, which the factor seconded. These, as unanimously agreed to at a public meeting held at Ayr, and duly subscribed by the chairman and clerk, were printed and circulated. A committee which had been nominated met and acted. In the course of twelve months the sum of £2,000 was at the credit of the committee. A monumental design was procured, and the work of its construction was begun. Sir Alexander Boswell now publicly related the story of the Ayr meeting, and his enthusiasm and ingenuity were duly applauded.

James Boswell has been already referred to. Though in many respects a weak man, he occasionally said

* A familiar term for a female.

good things. His note-book * contains the following:—"A dull fool was nothing, that never showed himself; the great thing is to have your fool well furnished with animal spirits and conceit, and he will display to you a rich fund of risibility."

A stupid fellow was declaiming against that kind of raillery called roasting, and was saying, " I am sure I have a great deal of good nature, I never roast any." "Why, sir," said Boswell, "you are an exceeding good-natured man, to be sure; but I can give you a better reason for your never roasting any. Sir, you never roast any because you have got no fire."

"Asparagus is like gentility; it cannot be brought to table till several generations from the dunghill."

"The minds of some men are like a dark cellar, where their knowledge lies concealed; while the minds of others are all sunshine and mirror, and reflect all that they read or hear in a lively manner."

"I said in a dispute with Sir Alexander Dick, on the different estimation to be put on sons and daughters, that 'Sons are truly part of a family, daughters go into other families. Sons are the furniture of your house; daughters are furniture in the house for sale. No man would wish to have his daughters fixtures; such of them as are well-looked are like certain marked pictures at the exhibition.'"

"I said of a rich man who entertained us luxuriously, that although he was exceedingly ridiculous,

* " Boswelliana," privately printed by Lord Houghton.

we restrained ourselves from talking of him as we might do, lest we should lose his feasts. Said I, 'He makes our teeth sentinels on our tongues.'"

During Dr. Johnson's visit to Scotland, one Campbell, a St. Andrews student, published an amusing pamphlet in ridicule of the Doctor's style. The pamphlet, which has long ceased to be in print, represents a supposed conversation between the lexicographer and some persons seeking etymological information. "What is the simplest definition of a window, Dr. Johnson?" said one of the inquirers. "A window, sir," responded the sage, "is an orifice cut out of an edifice for the introduction of illumination." The candle had required snuffing. "Pray, sir," said the lexicographer to one of the party, "will you deprive that luminary of its superfluous eminence?"

For the following anecdote, related by old Lord Elcho, we are indebted to a work lately published by Mr. Jerdan:—

"I once presided," said his lordship, "over a jolly company, when it was more customary than it now is, —and the more's the pity—to call upon every guest in turn for a song or a tale, under the penalty, in case of refusal or non-compliance, of a strong tumbler of salt and water. I at last came to a contumacious chap, who protested he could neither sing a song nor tell a tale. This would not pass with me, and especially as I had had my eye on this Billy for some time, and did not at all like his jeering leers and scoffing manners. So I said to him peremptorily, "Well, sir, if you can do neither the one nor the other, you must oblige me by tossing off the tumbler I will now order to be brought to you." " Stop !" he cried, hastily, "let me try first." Silence ensued, and he proceeded: "There was once a thief who chanced to find a church door open, of which carelessness he took advantage and stepped in, not to worship but to carry off whatever of the portable he could find. He put the cushions under his arms, hid as much as he could, and impudently wrapped the pulpit cloth about him like a plaid; but lo and behold! whilst he was thus employed the sexton happened to pass by, and seeing the church door open, got the key and locked it; so that when our irreligious friend thought he had nothing to do but slip out as he had slipped in, he discovered he was a close prisoner, and all egress stopped. What to do he knew not; but at last it struck him that he might succeed in letting himself down to the ground by the bell-rope. Accordingly, with it in hand he swung gently off, and you may be certified set up a ringing that alarmed the neighbourhood. In short, he was captured with his booty upon him as soon as he reached mother earth; upon which, looking up to the bell, as I now look up to your lordship, he remonstrated, 'Had it not been for your long tongue and empty head, I might have escaped.'"

Robert Pollok, author of "The Course of Time," was delivering in the Theological Hall of the Secession Church a trial discourse, of which the subject was Sin. The diction was considerably inflated, and as the preacher proceeded, the students gave audible expression to the amusement which they experienced. At last the Professor smiled too. This was not unobserved by Pollok, who was just on the point of a climax respecting the evils which sin had caused. He closed it with these words, emphatically spoken, "And but for sin, the smile of folly had never been upon the brow of wisdom."

Mr. Cochrane, a Jacobite landowner in Stirlingshire, was requested to allow a stone to be quarried on his estate for a monument to Sir Robert Munro, Bart., of Foulis, an officer in the royal army, who fell at Falkirk. "I'll gie ye headstanes for them a'," was Cochrane's reply, meaning all the adherents of the House of Hanover.

Dr. Cullen entertained strong views respecting the loquacity of the fair sex. The Rev. John Aitken, minister of St. Vigeans, had consulted him on account of incipient deafness. Cullen wrote a prescription, on which Mr. Aitken tendered a fee. "I thank you," said the physician, "but I have long made it a rule not to accept a fee from a country clergyman; he cannot afford it, sir." "There may be some who cannot," said Mr. Aitken, "but I can; for my living is good and I have no family." "What, are you a bachelor?" said the doctor. "I am," replied Mr. Aitken. "Then," said the physician, "go home, destroy my prescription, and get married, and I'll hazard my reputation that, a month after, you shall hear on the deafest side of your head."

Lady Wallace, who was reputed for her sallies of wit, was overcome with her own weapons by David Hume. "I am often asked," she said to the philosopher, "what age I am; what answer should I make?" "When you are asked that question again," replied Hume, "just say that you are not come to the years of discretion."

Dr. Davidson, Professor of Natural Science at Aberdeen, gave occasional lectures in natural history. In order to puzzle him, some of his students contrived to put together portions of various insects, so as to present the appearance of a single original. The medley being placed before the Professor, one of the rogues remarked, "We think it is a sort of bug." The Professor, inspecting it through his glass, promptly replied, "Yes, gentlemen, a humbug."

Andrew Gemmels, the Teviotdale gaberlunzie, prototype of *Edie Ochiltree*, was a person of no inconsiderable humour. When Sergeant Dodds was haranguing a group of rustics at St. Boswell's Fair on the glory of a soldier's life, Gemmels, who was close behind him, reared aloft his meal-bags on the end of his pike-staff, and exclaimed, "And behold the end o't!" The sergeant retired amidst the laughter of the bystanders.

Gemmels was standing before an expensive and fantastic mansion, built by a laird, one of his patrons, whose circumstances were none of the best. The laird came out and said, "Well, Andrew, you're admiring our handiworks?" "Atweel am I, sir?" was the reply; "I have just been thinking that ye hae thrown awa' twa bonny estates and built a gowk's* nest."

The celebrated Henry, first Viscount Melville, was on a visit to Edinburgh shortly after the passing of some unpopular public measure to which he had given his support. On the morning after his arrival he sent for a barber to shave him at his hotel. This functionary, a considerable humourist, resolved to indicate his sentiments respecting his lordship's recent procedure as a legislator. Having decorated his lordship with an apron, he proceeded to lather his face. Then, flourishing his razor, he said, "We are *obliged* to you, my lord, for the part you lately took in the passing of that odious bill." "Oh, you're a politician!" said his lordship; "I sent for a barber." "I'll shave you directly," added the barber, who, after shaving one-half of the beard, next came to the throat, across which he drew rapidly the back of his instrument, saying, "Take that, you traitor." He then hastily withdrew. Lord Melville, who conceived that his throat had been cut from ear to ear, placed the apron about his neck, and with a gurgling noise shouted "Murder!" The waiter immediately appeared, and, at his lordship's entreaty, rushed out to procure a surgeon. Three members of the medical faculty were speedily in attendance; but his lordship could scarcely be persuaded by their joint solicitation to expose his throat, around which

* Fool's.

he firmly held the barber's apron. At length he consented to an examination; but he could only be convinced by looking into a mirror that his throat had been untouched. His lordship was mortified by the merriment which the occurrence excited, and speedily returned to London.

Mrs. Glen Gordon, who acted as deputy keeper of Linlithgow Palace, remonstrated with General Hawley on the danger likely to result from the large fires kindled by his men in the immediate vicinity of the palace. The General rudely answered that he did not care though the palace was burnt to the ground. "An that be the case I can rin awa' frae fire as fast as you," responded the indignant lady, alluding to the General's recent rout at Falkirk.

Miss Maxwell, afterwards Lady Wallace, was a celebrated beauty. She resided in Edinburgh, and the style of dress which she adopted regulated the fashions of the capital. The family were about to attend the races at Leith, and the carriage was waiting, when a milliner, who had been making a bonnet for Miss Maxwell, rushed into the house, protesting that in her haste to deliver the head-dress in time, she had unfortunately brought it in contact with the buckle of a street-porter, by which it was rent. "Ne'er mind," said the lady, who, placing the torn bonnet on her head, drove off. In the course of next day the milliner was besieged with orders for bonnets of the new and becoming style worn by Miss Maxwell!

A young farmer at Cumnock, Ayrshire, considered that the daughter of a neighbour at Auchinleck would suit him as a wife. Having made up his mind, he made proposals to the fair one without the usual preliminaries. The young lady's reply was, "Deed, Jamie, I'll tak' ye, but ye maun gie me my dues o' courtin' for a' that."

Alexander Wood, the eminent Edinburgh surgeon, was fortunate, at an early period of his career, in winning the affections of a lady whose social position was at the time superior to his own. He waited on the lady's father, who was known in the city as "honest George Chalmers," and made known to him that he proposed to marry his daughter, Veronica. "On what do you mean to support her?" said Mr. Chalmers. Taking out his lancet, Mr. Wood replied, "I have nothing but this, and a determination to use it." "It is enough," said Mr. Chalmers, "Veronica is yours."

Mr. William Roger, of Ryehill, Perthshire, great-grandfather of the writer, was frequently employed to arbitrate in agricultural concerns. Though a person of substance and known probity, he had been, in an affair of arbitration, offered a bribe by both parties. The monies supposed to be the price of his conscience were sent him shortly before the period when he was to make his award. He placed the two budgets of guineas one in each pocket of his upper coat, and proceeded to meet the parties. Having taken his seat he said, striking his hands on his sides, "There is a rogue on this side, and a rogue on that, but an honest man in the middle." He then made his award, and drew forth the *rogues* from his pockets, which he returned to the owners.

Dr. Guthrie relates the following :—A small croftsman came to Mr. Linton, of the Grammar School of Brechin, with his son, a stripling, who had taken it into his head to obtain a little learning. The father said, "Oh, Mr. Linton, you see my laddie's fond o' lear.* I'm thinkin' o' making a scholar o' him." "Oh," said Mr. Linton, "what are you to make of him?" "You see, Mr. Linton," was the father's reply, "if he gets grace we'll mak' a minister o' him." "But if he does not get grace," persisted Mr. Linton, "what will you make of him then?" "Weel, in that case," replied the croftsman, resolving to repay Mr. Linton in his own coin, "I suppose we'll just hae to mak' him a schulemaster."

An honourable baronet was canvassing the stewartry of Kirkcudbright in the Conservative interest. Calling on a farmer to solicit his vote, he found that the object of his visit was not at home; but he obtained an interview with the farmer's daughter, and endeavoured to enlist her influence on his behalf. "I might try to induce my father to vote for you," said the damsel, "if you would get me the situation of maid of honour to the Queen." "I fear you would scarcely be fit for such an appointment," said the baronet. "That is," rejoined the damsel, "just

* Learning.

what my father was thinking respecting your being member for the stewartry."

The Rev. Mr. Aitken, of St. Vigeans, was examining a fisherman regarding his scriptural knowledge. Finding him very deficient, Mr. Aitken expressed his regret that a person of his age should be so ignorant respecting such important truths. "Weel, sir," said the fisherman, "just allow me to speir* a question at you. How many hooks will it tak' to bait a fifteen score haddock line?" "Really, John," said the minister, "I cannot answer you; that is quite out of my way." "Weel, sir, ye should na be sae hard upo' poor folk—you to your trade, an' me to mine."

A story is related in a recent publication of an incident which occurred in a London clubhouse, when several gentlemen thought to discover the peculiar idiosyncrasy of the inhabitants of the three kingdoms by putting the same question to one individual of each. Three street porters were called in, these being natives of England, Ireland, and Scotland. "What would you take," said the president to the Englishman, "to run three times round Russell Square, stripped to the shirt?" "I'll take a pot o' porter, sir," was the reply. The question being put to the Hibernian, he shrugged his shoulders, and with the *naïveté* of Irish humour exclaimed, "Sure I'd take a mighty great cowld." Sandy was next asked. He scratched his head, and archly replied by the cautious interrogatory, "What will ye gie me?"

* Ask.

An elderly gentlewoman had employed the village mason to execute some work of repair. During his operations John repeatedly remarked that "it was a very stourie* job, and that he would not be the worse of something to synd † it down." The bottle was at length produced, with a small thistle glass, which was filled a little way from the brim and handed to the mason. "Ye'll no' be the waur o' that, John," said the lady, congratulating herself on her liberality. "Atweel, no, mem," responded the mason, holding up the dwarfish glass; "I wadna be the waur o' that though it had been vitriol."

A country laird, riding in an unfrequented part of Kircudbrightshire, came to the edge of a morass, which he considered not quite safe to pass. Observing a peasant lad in the vicinity, he hailed him, and inquired whether the bog was hard at the bottom. "Ou ay, quite hard," responded the youth. The laird passed on, but his horse began to sink with alarming rapidity. "You rascal," shouted the laird to his misinformant, "did you not say that it was hard at the bottom?" "So it is," rejoined the rogue, "but ye're no halfway till't yet."

"An old lady," says Dr. Guthrie, "was walking in Hanover Street, Edinburgh, with a large umbrella in her hand. A little urchin came up who had no cap on his head, but plenty of brains within; no shoes on his feet, but a great deal of understanding for all that. Well, I saw him fix upon that venerable old lady.

* Dusty. † Wash.

He appealed to her for charity; she gave him a grunt. He went up again; she gave him a poke. He saw there was no chance of getting at her through her philanthropy, and he thought to get at her through her selfishness; so he pulled up his sleeve to his elbow—his yellow, skinny elbow,—and running up, he cried out, displaying the limb, and exhibiting his rags and woeful face, 'Jist oot o' the infirmary wi' the typhus fever, mem.' The old lady put her hand to the very bottom of her pocket, and taking out a shilling, thrust it into his hand and ran away."

Blind Alick, of Stirling, was blind from his birth, and his intellect, with the exception of one faculty, was an entire blank. But his memory was retentive to an extraordinary degree. A person who had once addressed him he remembered ever after. He had heard the Scriptures read in the different schools of the place which he was in the habit of visiting, and he could repeat almost the entire sacred volume, beginning at any chapter or verse. A gentleman, to puzzle him, read, with a slight verbal alteration, a verse of the Bible. Alick hesitated for a little, then told him where it was to be found, but said that it had not been quoted correctly; he then gave the proper reading. The gentleman next asked him for the ninetieth verse of the seventh chapter of Numbers. Alick replied, "You are fooling me; the chapter has just eighty-nine verses."

Daft Jamie was a natural, well known on the east coast of Forfarshire. A farm servant was one day teasing him in a very provoking manner. "Ye ill-looking scoundrel," said the maniac, in a fit of wrath, "if I werena sure the Almighty made all mankind, I wad say ye were a coonterfeit."

Some anecdotes on the score of simplicity will close the chapter.

A Countess of Strathmore lost the friendship of a neighbour by her ignorance of Scottish modes of speech. Mr. Skene, of Carriston, was dining with the Earl and Countess at Glammis Castle. In the course of conversation the Countess remarked to her guest, "I have heard a great many persons say, Mr. Skene, that you are not to ride the water on. Pray what may they mean?" "Oh, I suppose they mean," said Mr. Skene, "that my legs are so short, that if they were to cross a river on my back, they would get themselves wetted." Mr. Skene perceived that he had been represented to Lady Strathmore as one not to be trusted, and whether her ladyship had arrived at this explanation of the metaphorical language or not, he felt that it was better to decline in future the hospitalities of the castle.

Dr. Glen, who resided in Edinburgh about the close of the last century, was extremely parsimonious, but was withal fond of popular applause. He was regular in attending church, and used to deposit his weekly charity in the collection plate in a column of copper pieces, which he laid down carefully, so that it might attract the attention of passers by. He presented the Orphan Hospital with a bell, so that his fame might be sounded abroad. When in company, if the bell happened to ring, he took occasion to remark its fine tone, and so introduce the subject of his generosity.

"What three things would you desire most to have?" said a gentleman to a highlander. "For the first," he replied, "a Loch Lomond o' whisky." "And for the second what would you have?" persisted the gentleman. "A Ben Lomond of sneeshin,"* responded Donald. "And what for the third?" "Atweel," said Donald, after a little reflection, "I think I wad hae just anither Loch Lomond o' whisky."

The almanack has only of late years been introduced in some of the isolated districts. The Ettrick Shepherd has recorded that even in Selkirkshire, within a short distance of the capital, the natives, chiefly sheep farmers and shepherds, were wont to preserve the memory of occurrences in their personal and family history by enumerating them in connection with "the year of the great storm," "the summer of uncommon drought," and so on. The following was transcribed from the family Bible of a farmer in Watten parish, Caithness:—" Our Bessy was born on the day that John Cathel lost his grey mare in the moss. Jamie was born on the day they began mending the roof o' the kirk. Sandy was born the night my mother broke her leg, and the day before Kitty gaed awa' wi' the sodgers. The twins, Willie and Margaret, were born the day Sandy Bremner biggit †

* Snuff. † Built.

his new barn, and the vera day after the battle of Waterloo. Kirsty was born the night o' the great fecht on the Reedsmas, in Barlan, atween Peter Donaldson and a south country drover; forbye* the factor raised the rent that same year. Annie was born the night the kiln gaed on fire, six years syne. David was born the night o' the great speat,† and three days afore Jamie Miller had a lift frae the fairies."

A clergyman was prosecuting his pastoral visitations. He came to the door of a house where his knock for admission could not be heard amidst the noise of contention within. After a little he stepped in, saying authoritatively, "I should like to know who is the head of this house?" "Weel, sir," said the husband and father, "that is just the point we've been trying to settle."

There was a mixture of shrewdness and simplicity in the following. Shortly after the establishment of the Ministers' Widows' Fund, the minister of Cranshaws asked in marriage the daughter of a small farmer in the neighbourhood. The damsel asked her father whether she should accept the clergyman's offer. "Oh," said the sire, "tak him, Jenny; he's as gude deid as leevin'." The farmer meant that his daughter would, owing to the new fund, be equally well off a widow as a wife.

That simplicity which develops in a blind and morbid obstinacy is illustrated by the following anecdote:—A man and his wife were walking together

* Besides.   † Flood.

near a farmyard at Troqueer, when they were attracted by the appearance of a well-dressed stack of hay. The man remarked that it was neatly pulled, while the wife insisted that it was "clippit." The controversial spirit was excited on both sides. The husband was wedded to his opinion, and the woman would not yield. "Clippit, I say; I'll say it's clippit yet; any one but a fule wad ken that it's clippit," are specimens of the rhetoric with which she regaled the ears of her offended lord. They were passing the farm mill-pond. The gentleman gave his obstinate helpmate a push, and she fell into the water. Believing that she was about to perish, she held up two fingers, imitating the action of scissors, to intimate that even in death she would not surrender her opinion. She was dragged out of the pond, and having shaken herself, she exclaimed, "I'll say clippit yet."

In Shakspeare Square, Edinburgh, some forty years ago, lived Lucky Johnston, mother of Harry Johnston, the famous theatrical humourist. One night during his engagement at the theatre, Lucky had invited a number of her cronies to supper, in honour of his visit. Harry told his drollest stories, which excited great merriment at the supper-table. A dame seated at the upper end of the table rose up, after a great explosion of laughter, and holding a handkerchief to her face, said, addressing the humourist, "Maister Harry, ye maun excuse me for no laughin', for I hae got a sair mouth."

Dr. Guthrie relates the following:—A woman went to her minister for advice. She said, "My husband and me don't agree. We quarrel very often. He comes in sometimes tired and ill-tempered, and I fire up. Then we go to it with tooth and nail." "Well," said the minister, "I can cure that." "Oh, can you, sir? I am so delighted, for I do love my husband, when a's come and gone," said she. "It's a certain cure," said the minister, "and will work a charm." "Oh, I am so happy to hear it," says she. "Well," continued the minister, "when your husband comes home from his work, fractious and quarrelsome, and says a sharp thing to you, what do you do?" "Oh, I answer back, of course." "Very well," says the minister, "the singular charm is this: whenever your husband comes in and commences to speak sharply, the first thing you do is to run out to the pump, fill your mouth with water, and keep it in for ten minutes." The woman came back to the minister three or four weeks after, and said, "The Lord bless you, sir, for that's the most wonderful charm I ever heard o'! Deed is't."

Parish schoolmasters are, on their appointment, examined as to their literary qualifications. One of the fraternity being called by his examiner to translate Horace's ode beginning,—

"Exegi monumentum œre perennius,"

commenced, "Exegi monumentum—I have eaten a mountain." "Ah," said one of the examiners, "ye needna proceed any further; for after eatin sic a dinner, this parish wad be a puir mouthfu' t' ye. You maun try some wider sphere."

A Government official was examining a military school. Desiring to ascertain the progress of the pupils in Scripture knowledge, he proceeded, "How long did Noah warn the inhabitants of the old world to repent?" The pupils hesitated. "One hundred years," said the official. "Now, children, can you tell me the names of the twin sons of Isaac?" "Jacob and——" said a little girl. "Yes, my child; Jacob and——? Don't you remember? why, Ishmael, my dear." The examiner remarked to the teachers that the children were most imperfectly instructed in Bible knowledge, and that he must withhold the usual holiday!

A desire to surprise by some new discovery is a failing of weak persons. A Scottish author, who has written a "Family History of England," has introduced an air as having been played by the band at Fotheringay Castle while Mary was proceeding to her execution, and which the writer remarks "a fortunate accident threw in my way." The air is no other than "Joan's Placket" arranged as a march! It is scarcely requisite to say that no air was performed at the execution of the unhappy queen. A similar *discovery* was made by one Findlay, a printer at Arbroath, who, in reprinting Dr. Buchan's work on "The Cure and Prevention of Diseases," substituted the word "Preservation" for "Prevention," which he alleged was the word evidently intended by the physician!

A clerical friend relates the following. When a student at St. Andrews, he and his companions frequented the workshop of a loquacious cobbler, who was a considerable humourist, and, according to his own account, no inconsiderable hero. The cobbler cured his own bacon, of which he had an ample supply arranged in the chimney of his one-roomed dwelling. Some of the students proposed to have a *gaudeamus*, or supper-party, before returning to the country, and it was resolved to seize one of the cobbler's hams for the occasion. Three delegates engaged in the affair of capturing the ham, and for this purpose, one of the number, chosen by lot, descended the cobbler's chimney. He got safely to the floor, and having fastened a ham to his shoulders he proceeded to ascend. Losing his hold, he fell heavily. The noise awakened the sleeping shoemaker, who got out of bed and struck a light. Retreat was impossible; so the chimney descender blackened his face and looked as formidable as he could. "What are ye?—where d'ye come frae?—what d'ye want here?" were questions which the cobbler put in rapid succession to the sooty-faced intruder. "I come from Pandemonium. Satan, my master, has sent me to you with the present of a ham," was the reply. "I defy the devil an' a' his works," said the cobbler. "I' the name o' a' gude begone." "Well," said sooty-face, "shall I blow the roof off your house, or will you

P

light me to the door?" The cobbler walked backwards towards the door, which he opened, allowing the intruder to depart without further questioning. Next morning he missed one of his hams, but received a sum of money in its stead which more than compensated him for the loss; but the cobbler ceased to obtain credit as one of the heroic.

The following is a verbatim copy of a letter lately addressed by a poor woman to a Sheriff Substitute in one of the central counties. It illustrates the mistaken reading of Scripture frequently to be found among the humbler ranks:—

"HONORED SIR,—When I saw you in the Watergit last Thursday, it was renning, and you were rinning, and I didna like to stepp you to spake about my boy. Sir, you promised to do for him, and you have not done for him, and i am not abel myself to keep him; for his father does nothing for him, but gist goes about a vagaybond on the face of the airth. When i married him he was a respectible laeberer, and then turned spinner; but now, like Solomon's lillie, he neither toils nor spins, and i bees not able for to keep the boy. Sir, he is 5 yers of ag, and i will bring him to your honor next week. Sir, I remans till death

"Your humbil Servant."

These anecdotes may be summed up by a brief narrative of a recent movement. For some years Scotland had lacked her fair share of public grants and other national privileges. Discontent was general. A public meeting was held at Edinburgh. Resolutions were passed, and the "National Association for the Vindication of Scottish Rights" was constituted. Under proper management something might have been accomplished, for the country had been suffering from Imperial neglect, or the indifference of her Parliamentary representatives. Unfortunately, the wise were content to initiate, and the weak were permitted to administer. An attorney discovered that there was a defect in the national shield—the Scottish Lion was in its wrong place! The alleged grievance was put forward prominently—too prominently for the cause of the "Rights." Ridicule assailed the movement from all quarters. Original promoters withdrew. Adherents fell off. The attorney was left to bemoan in solitude the decay of Heraldic science, and the degeneracy of Scottish patriotism.

CHAPTER VII.

INSCRIPTIONS, RHYMES, AND POPULAR SAYINGS.

> " A thousand fantasies
> Begin to throng into my memory,
> Of calling shapes, and beckoning shadows dire
> And airy tongues that syllable men's names."
>
> MILTON.
>
> "'Tis education forms the common mind,
> Just as the twig is bent, the tree's inclined."
>
> POPE.

THE manners of a people are better indicated by the character of their floating traditions and their scattered rhymes than in the pages of their historians. Traditions denote the nature of the channel through which they have flowed. The rhymes of the people, whether inscribed or orally transmitted, may be held as the spontaneous utterances of their convictions. Such simple lines had been forgotten unless they had contained the germ of truth. The quaint old inscription had suffered obliteration unless successive generations had found the sentiment suited to their tastes.

The older inscriptions are for the most part terse and emphatic protests against the utterances of calumny. The imaginative character of the Scottish mind had devised this method of attack against those who had awakened unkindly feeling, and were otherwise incapable of assault. In dealing with the early annals the national historian has experienced much difficulty in separating the wheat of truth from the chaff of fiction. The patriot Wallace excited the invidious feelings of the nobility. His prowess was unassailable. The fervour and sincerity of his patriotism might not be challenged. The impugners therefore sought to arraign the honour of his private life. Marion Broadfoot, his lawful wife, they pronounced to be his mistress.

Robert II. espoused as his first queen the daughter of one of the lesser barons. The validity of his marriage was questioned. James III. adopted a life of literary and domestic seclusion; he was accused of incest. Queen Mary was imprudent, but she was most grossly slandered in the case of Rizzio.

The prevalence of calumny in ancient Scotland may account for the numerous indictments for witchcraft, and the testimony by which they were supported. When a poor widow or other aged and unprotected female had offended her neighbours by angry words and unguarded menaces, they were prepared to ascribe to her every family mishap and personal calamity. They traced her presence in every startled hare, and swore they had seen her gambolling with the devil on the mountain heath, and preparing by incantation instruments of destruction. During the sixteenth and seventeenth centuries, calumny was one of the vices which most frequently called for the discipline of the Church.

At the Reformation, the unequal division of the Church lands among the nobility invoked much hostile feeling on the part of the disappointed. Calumnies consequently arose against the fortunate. The Earl Marischal got the rich temporalities of the Abbey of Deer, and therewith a proportionate share of envy and detraction. He built a tower at Deer, on which he caused these words to be inscribed:—

> "They haif said—
> Quhat say thay?
> Let them say."

The Regent Mar was even more defiant. He had received the temporalities of Cambuskenneth. He caused stones from the dilapidated structure to be removed to the Castle hill of Stirling, where he commenced to erect a superb mansion. To indicate his contempt for calumny and criticism, he caused metrical challenges to be sculptured above each of his three doorways. These are still legible. They proceed thus:—

> "I pray at lukaris* on this luging,†
> With gentil e to give thair juging."
>
> "The moir I stand on opin hitht ‡
> My faults moir subject are to sicht."
>
> "Espy,§ speik furth and spair notht,
> Considder veil I cair nocht."

---

* Onlookers.   † Lodging.   ‡ Height.   § See.

Robert Pitcairn, Secretary of State in the reign of James VI., and Commendator of the Abbey of Dunfermline, had been assailed by calumny. He built a new residence at Dunfermline, and in allusion to the rumours which he knew to be circulated to his disadvantage, he caused these lines to be inscribed in the front wall:—

> "Sin' verd* is thral and thocht is free,
> Keip veill thy tonge, I counsel thee."

Over the entrance of an old house at Forglen, Banffshire, is the following:—

> "Do veil and dovpt † nocht
>   Althoch thov be spyit;
> He is lytil gvid vorth
>   That is nocht envyit;
> Tak thov no tent
>   Qvht everie man tels;
> Gyve thov vald leive ondemit ‡
>   Gang qvhair na man dvels."

In allusion to the invidious feelings engendered by success, the lady of Pringle, of Smailholm, caused these lines to be inscribed over the doorway of a mansion which she reared at Galashiels. The date is 1457:—

> "Elspeth Dishington builted me
>   In syne lye not;
> The thyngs thou canst not gette
>   Desyre not."

The front wall of the old village inn at Darnick, Roxburghshire, exhibits the following:—

* Word.   † Despair.   ‡ Unenvied.

> "This is a good world to live in,
>   To lend, to spend, and to give in;
> But to get, or to borrow, or keep what's one's own,
>   'Tis the very worst world that ever was known."

On the death of Lord President Dundas, the house in which he resided was converted into a smithy. These lines were found on a piece of paper attached to the door:—

> "This house a lawyer once enjoyed
>   A smith does now possess;
> How naturally the *iron age*
>   Succeeds the *age of brass!*"

A trader in Stirling had formed the design of erecting an elegant residence in the principal street. He caused the escutcheon of his family arms to be displayed on the front wall. But his means failed, and he was necessitated to dispose of the walls to discharge the builder's charges. A neighbour some time after reared a lesser dwelling immediately adjoining. As a hit to the unfortunate trader, he caused the following lines to be inscribed on a large stone in the front wall of his house:—

> "Here I forbeare
>   My name or armes to fix,
> Lest I or myne should sell
>   Those stones and sticks."

Many of the older tombstones in the rural churchyards bear inscriptions sufficiently quaint. These lines were sculptured on a plain memorial stone at Leslie, Fifeshire:—

> "Here lyes the dust of Charles Brown,
> Some time a wright in London town.
> When coming home parents to see,
> And of his years being twenty-three,
> Of a decay with a bad host *
> He dyed upon the Yorkshire coast."

Larbert churchyard, Stirlingshire, contained the following:—

> "Here lyes interred within this urn
> The corpse of honest good John Burn,
> Who was the eight John of that name
> That lived with love and dyed with fame."

At Largs, the tombstone of a blacksmith bears these lines:—

> "Of all mechanics we have renown,
> Above the hammer we wear the crown."

The churchyard of Urquhart contains the following:—

> "Here lies father and son
> Goodsire and grand,
> Who liv'd and died
> Upon a poor twelfth of land."

A magistrate of Montrose was commemorated in his parish churchyard by these lines:—

> "The pious, noble Bailie Scott,
> Montrose's honour high,
> Beside this pretty monument
> Interrèd here doth lie."

In the same place of tombs the gravestone of a handloom weaver bears these lines:—

> "The weaver's art renowned is so
> That poor nor rich without it cannot go."

---

* Cough.

These lines were sculptured on a tombstone in the cathedral churchyard of St. Andrews :—

"Here lyes James Brown, of old extract;
In fifty-five God did exact
From him the debt that all must pay
Who mortal are and made of clay."

A ploughman's tombstone in the parish churchyard of North Berwick is inscribed thus:—

"Oft have I till'd the fertile soil,
Which was my destined lot;
But here, beneath this towering elm,
I lie to be forgot."

The honours of the village doctor are thus recorded in the churchyard of Saltoun, East Lothian :—

"Reader, here lyes good Robert Henderson,
Physician, gardener, surgeon,—all in one;
In all which three such success he did have,
That now, when gone, his virtues do require
A monument more ample than is here."

These lines are from the churchyard of Melrose :—

"The earth goeth on the earth,
Glistening like gold;
The earth goeth to the earth
Sooner than it wold.
The earth builds on the earth
Castles and towers;
The earth says to the earth,
All shall be ours."

A burgh magistrate of Annan is thus commemorated :—

> "He thought it honour, with all his might,
> To pursue the ancient burgh's right;
> No man with bribes would, for his blood,
> Tempt him to hurt the common good:
> Let every one that him succeeds
> Think on his faithful words and deeds."

A minister of Kirkpatrick-Juxta is, in the churchyard of that parish, thus commemorated:—

> "The Rev. Dr. Stewart's call to Mousewald
> Was turned into a call to another land."

The following couplet is from a churchyard at Lockerbie:—

> "Praises on tombs are trifles vainly spent,
> A man's good name is his best monument."

A plain couple have their unpretending virtues thus set forth on their gravestone at Torthorwald:—

> "They aimed at no titles,
> But honest and unstained characters;
> None of them were rich,
> Neither were they poor."

The following inscription from the churchyard of Kells, Kirkcudbrightshire, is sufficiently quaint. It commemorates a prolific matron:—

> "Here lyes the corps of Agnes Harris,
> Spouse of Robert Cornon, also Mary,
> Agnes, Marion, Margaret in one birth,
> Robert, Andrew, James at one birth."

In the churchyard of Wigton, a village merchant is commemorated in prose, and his son in these lines of verse:—

> " And his son John, of honest fame,
> Of stature small, and a leg lame,
> Content he was with portion small,
> Kept shop in Wigton, and that's all."

In the old churchyard of Hamilton the epitaph of a seaman has this commencement :—

> " The seas he ploughed for twenty years,
> Without the smallest dread or fears ;
> And all that time was never known
> To strike upon a bank or stone."

A miller's tombstone at Campsie is thus inscribed :—

> " Eternity is
> A wheel that turns,
> A wheel that turned ever,
> A wheel that turns,
> And will leave turning never."

The following is from the churchyard of Cults, Fifeshire :—

> " Here lies, retired from mortal strife,
> A man who lived a happy life ;
> A happy life, and sober too,
> A thing that all men ought to do."

The following inscription adorned the tombstone of a noble lord at Kilmarnock :—

> " Here lies yat godly, noble, wise Lord Boyd,
> Who Kirk and King and Commons all eccor'd,
> Which were, while they this jewel all enjoy'd,
> Maintain'd, govern'd, and counsell'd by that Lord.
> His antient House so oft peril'd he restor'd,
> Twice six, and sixty years he liv'd ; and fine,
> By death the third of January devor'd
> In anno thrice five hundred, eighty-nine."

In the churchyard of Alves, Morayshire, a tombstone, bearing date 1590, is thus inscribed:—

> "Here lies
> Anderson of Pittensere,
> Maire of the Earldom of Moray,
> With his wife Marjory,
> Whilk him never displiscit!"

During a pestilence which visited Scotland in 1644, many persons perished. One of the sufferers is commemorated in the churchyard of Brechin in these lines:—

> "Here lies John Erskine,
> Who died of the affliction;
> No one must disturb his bones
> Until the Resurrection."

The Howff, or old burial-ground of Dundee, formerly contained many curious inscriptions. A number of these were obliterated when this old place of sepulture remained in a condition of neglect. About forty years ago Mr. Charles Roger, an ingenious antiquary, induced the authorities of the burgh to level the ground and arrange the tombstones. Since that period the Howff has been appropriately enclosed and carefully kept.

In the south-east corner of the Howff a tombstone is inscribed thus:—

> "The time will come when all must fall,
> Like Robert Paris—dead;
> And may all meet the solemn call
> As we think Robert did."

The tombstone of a Mr. Yeaman bears this couplet:—

"To honor ye sepultor ve may be bald:
Ve lerne of Abraham ovr father avld."

Bailie William Watson is thus commemorated:—

"Approach and read not with your hats on,
For here lies Bailie William Watson
Inclosed within a grave that's narrow.
The earth scarce ever saw his marrow
For piety and painful thinking,
And moderation in his drinking;
And finding him both wise and witty
The Town of him did make a Bailie."

The tombstone of Patrick Gourlay, town clerk of Dundee, who died in 1666, bears these lines:—

"This Clerk was calm and kind to persons all,
His Goodness and his candour were not small;
His Life prov'd this unto the very end,
When trembling joints his quill could not extend.
Painful and wise, meek, faithful; and his days
Closed in honour and immortal praise.
Son, in his Father's steps, and loving Spouse
Built up this Tomb for the dear defunct's use."

Captain Alexander Baxter thus inscribed the gravestone of his daughter Katherine, who died in 1632, in her seventeenth year:—

"Stay, Passenger; no more for Marvels seek,
  Among these many Monuments of Death;
For, here a Demi-scot, a Demi-greek
  Doth lie, to whom the Cretan Isle gave Birth.
And is it not a wonder? Is it not?
Her Birth and Burial to be so remote.
So falls, by Winter-blasts, a Virgin-rose;

> For blotless, spotless, blameless did she die :
> As many Virtues Nature did disclose
> In her, as oft in greatest Age we see.
> Ne're Jason glor'd more in the golden Fleece
> Than her brave Sire in bringing her from Greece."

Robert Davidson of Balgay, an ancestor of the writer, who died in 1663, was commemorated by his widow in these words :—

> "Here you behold great Davidson in Dust
> In charges all, was faithful to his trust;
> A famous Bailie, greatest was his Praise,
> He sober, wise and harmless in his ways ;
> Sharp Wit and Cheerful Countenance, yea he
> A noble Pattern of all Honestie.
> To whom his dearest wife caus'd cut this Stone,
> For his Memorial lasting and her own."

In the Howff of Dundee, William Playfair, another connexion of the writer, is celebrated thus :—

> "Beneath this Stone survivors did inter
> The Breathless Corps of William Playfair,
> He was not fully eighteen years of age
> When he, of flow'ring worth, quit the stage;
> Some Golden Beams of Heavenly virtues strove
> To hold his life unstain'd—His thoughts on things above."

The Howff formerly contained a gravestone with the following inscription :—

> "Here, in this urne, good Andrew Cochran lies,
> Sober and painful, harmless in his ways.
> Here also Eupham Couper his dear spouse,
> Of good Report, a Monument did chuse.
> Both void of Guile; Pairs in Sobriety;
> Both loving virtue, with Integrity.
> Lastly, who equal were, in holy Life,
> Here sleep together, godly Man and Wife."

The memory of Andrew Schippert, baxter burgess of Dundee, who died in 1641, is thus celebrated:—

"Nathaniel's Heart, Bezaleel's Hand,
 If ever any had;
Then boldly may ye say, had he
 Who lieth in this Bed."

A marble monument which marked the last resting-place of Bailie Andrew Forrester, of Dundee, bore these lines:—

"My Soul to Heav'n is gone;
 My Body made of Clay,
Lies rotting here under this Stone,
 Till the uprising day."

A skipper's gravestone was inscribed thus:—

"Here, underneath this Stone,
Lies Skipper George Adamson,
Who died Anno Eighty-four,
And was of age Three and threescore."

In 1819, a tombstone bearing the following inscription, with the date 1628, was found in the Howff:—

"Epyte Pie,
 Here ly I,
My twentie bairnes,
My good man & I."

Captain Henry Lyell, of Blackness, was thus celebrated on a tablet in one of the Dundee churches:—

"To Solomon's temple, king Hiram sent from Tyre
Fine cedar-wood; but upon great desire,
This church, thou Henry Lyell, to repair,
Didst freely give all that was necessar;
Tho' th' Syrian king gave Sol'mon towns twice ten,
Thou greater than these all, and best of men."

David Kinloch, a physician, and the descendant of an ancient family, is in the churchyard of Arbroath thus celebrated. He died in 1617 :—

> "Gallant Kinloch! his famous ancient Race
> Appear by this erected on this place;
> This Honour great indeed! His Art and skill
> And famous Name both sides o' the pole do fill."

A country farmer is thus commemorated on his tombstone in the churchyard of Newtyle :—

> "Here lies the dust of Robert Small,
> Who when in life was thick, not tall;
> But what's of greater consequence,
> He was endowèd with good sense."

Gilbert Quittet, town clerk of Forfar, who died in 1594, was commemorated in the following couplet:—

> "Hier Sleeps unto the Secund Lyfe
> A Faithful man to Friend and Wyfe."

John Randal, a publican, was celebrated thus :—

> "Here old John Randal lies, who telling of his Tale,
> Liv'd threescore years and ten, such Virtue was in ale.
> Ale was his meat, ale was his drink, ale did his heart revive;
> And if he could have drunk his ale, he still had been alive."

These quaint lines were inscribed on the tombstone of Alexander Speid in a churchyard in Forfarshire:—

> "Time flies with speed; With speed Speid's fled
> To the Dark Regions of the dead.
> With Speed Consumption's Sorrows flew,
> And stopt Speid's speed, for Speid it slew.
> Miss Speid beheld with Frantic woe,
> Poor Speid with Speed turned pale as snow;

And beat her breast, and tore her hair,
For Speid, Poor Speid was all her care.
Yet learn of Speid with speed to flee
From Sin, since we like Speid must die."

Two unamiable characters have been thus described in their epitaphs:—

"Here he lies, beside a Witch,
Hated both by Poor and Rich.
Where he is, or how he fares,
No-body knows, no-body cares."

"Here fast asleep lies Saunders Scott,
Lang may he snort and snore;
His bains are now in Gorman's pot,
That us'd to strut the streets before.
He liv'd a lude and tastrel Life,
For gude he nae regarded;
His perjur'd clack rais'd mickle strife,
For whilk belike he'll be rewarded.
Ill temper'd Loon, that us'd to snort
When ilk his Neighbour fell in trouble,
His gybes do now lie in the dirt,
To satisfy his brethren double."

Above the gateway of Footdee churchyard, Aberdeen, is the following inscription:—

"George Davidson, elder, civis Aberdonensis,
Bigged thir churchyard dykes upon his own expenses."

A similar inscription is placed on the tombstone of a sailor at Deckford, near Cullen.

Marjery Scott died at Dunkeld in 1728, at the age of an hundred. An epitaph was composed for her by the poet, Alexander Pennecuik. It proceeds thus:—

"Stop, passenger, until my life you read,
The living may get knowledge from the dead.
Five times five years I led a virgin life;
Five times five years I was a virtuous wife;
Ten times five years I lived a widow chaste;
Now tired of this mortal life I rest.
Betwixt my cradle and my grave have been
Eight mighty kings of Scotland and a queen.
Full twice five years the Commonwealth I saw;
Ten times the subjects rise against the law;
And, which is worse than any civil war,
A king arraigned before the subjects' bar;
Swarms of sectarians, hot with hellish rage,
Cut off his royal head upon the stage.
Twice did I see old prelacy pulled down,
And twice the cloak did sing beneath the gown.
I saw the Stuart race thrust out; nay, more,
I saw our country sold for English ore;
Our numerous nobles, who have famous been,
Sunk to the lowly number of sixteen.
Such desolation in my days have been,
I have an end of all perfection seen."

Some other instances of longevity may be quoted. Robert Bain died at Lochee in April, 1867, at the age of 108. At the same age, Charles Craig, a weaver, died at Dundee in 1817. There was living at Glasgow in 1731 one Robert Lyon, aged 109. He had obtained a new set of teeth, and had recovered his sight in a wonderful manner. The newspaper obituary of the period records the death, on the 19th November, 1731, of William Eadie, sexton of the Canongate, Edinburgh, who had reached his 120th year. He had been a freeman of the city for ninety years, had buried three generations of parishioners, and had married his second wife, a young woman, after he had attained his hundredth year. Peter Garden died at Auchterless, Aberdeenshire, about the year 1780. In his 120th year he married his second wife, and danced gleefully on the occasion. He remembered having seen the Marquis of Montrose, whom he described as "a little black man, who wore a ruff, as the ladies do now-a-days."

The sign-boards and finger-posts of the past generation often exhibited much absurdity of diction. At the entrance of a lane in the Canongate, Edinburgh, a sign-board was inscribed, "Deafness cured down this close every morning between six and eight." At the foot of Candlemaker Row, Edinburgh, a board was exhibited, stating that down the close "ass's milk from the cow" would be had three times a day. On the wall of Newbattle Park a board contained this serious intimation,—"Any person entering these enclosures without permission will be *shot* and *prosecuted.*" At a spot where several roads branched off from the turnpike, a finger-post contained some directions for tourists, with this addition, "If you cannot read, ask at the blacksmith's shop."

Of the numerous provincial rhymes, the more curious are subjoined. The following eight are connected with the state of the weather:—

"February fills the dyke
Either with black or white."

"April showers
Mak May flowers."

"March dust and May sun
　Mak corn white and maidens dun."

"Till May be oot,
　Change na a cloot." *

"Mist in May and heat in June
　Mak the harvest richt soon."

"As the day lengthens
　The cold strengthens."

"A rainbow in the morning,—sailors, take warning;
A rainbow at night is the sailor's delight."

"The evening red and the morning gray
Are the certain signs o' a beautiful day."

There are rhymes descriptive of certain localities. These are specimens:—

"Glasgow for bells,
　Lithgow for wells,
　Falkirk for beans an' peas."

"Carrick for a man,
　Kyle for a coo,
　Cunningham for corn an' bere, †
　And Galloway for woo." ‡

"Ordweil's a bonny place,
　Stands upon the water;
　Drakemyre's a scaw'd § place,
　Rotten tripe and butter."

"Hutton for auld wives,
　Broadmeadows for swine;
　Paxton for drunken wives
　And saumon sae fine."

---

* Change no clothes.　　† Barley.　　‡ Wool.　　§ Faded.

> "Gowkscroft and Barnside,
> Windy-wallets fu' o' pride;
> Monynut and Laikyshiel,
> Plenty milk, plenty meal;
> Straphunton mill and Bankend,
> Green cheese as rough as bend;
> Shannabank and Blackerstane,
> Pike the flesh to the bane;
> Quixwood and Butterdean,
> Fu' o' parritch to the een."

A well-known rhyme is connected with Tintock Hill, in Lanarkshire :—

> "On Tintock Tap there is a mist,
> And in that mist there is a kist,*
> And in the kist there is a caup,†
> And in the caup there is a drap;
> Tak up the caup, drink off the drap,
> And set the caup on Tintock Tap."

The more remarkable rivers have been associated with rhymes. These are three specimens :—

> "A crook o' the Forth
> Is worth an earldom o' the north."

> "Annan, Tweed, an' Clyde,
> Rise a' out o' ae hill-side."

> "Prosin, Esk, and Carity,
> Meet a' at the birken buss o' Inverarity."

Certain bridges are thus celebrated :—

> "Lochtie, Lothrie, Leven, and Orr,
> Rin a' through Cameron brig bore."

> "The new brig o' Doon, and the auld brig o' Callander,
> Four-and-twenty bows in the auld brig o' Callander."

---

* Chest.   † Cup.

"Brig o' Balgownie, black's your wa',
Wi' a wife's ae son an' a mear's ae foal
Doun ye shall fa'."

With respect to the prophecy embodied in the last of these rhymes, Lord Byron records that, as the only son of his mother, he was deeply impressed by it in boyhood. An Earl of Aberdeen, also the only son of his mother, always dismounted from his horse and walked across Balgownie Bridge, causing the animal to be brought up by his servant.

Prophetic rhymes have maintained a powerful influence on the popular mind. One of those connected with Craig Clatchart, in Fife, predicted that a massive basaltic column, which rose up in front of that rock, would fall upon a nobleman riding on a white horse. About twenty years ago it was found necessary to remove the column during the construction of a line of railway. Before the commencement of operations the late Earl of Leven rode on a white horse in front of the column, with the view of dissipating the popular credulity. It has been stated that an episcopal clergyman at St. Andrews, of the last century, conceived he was the subject of a metrical "saw" to the effect that the ancient wall of the abbey would fall upon the wisest man of the place. He could on no account be persuaded to approach within range of the erection.

The most celebrated prophetic rhyme connected with family concerns is the following relating to an old family in Roxburghshire:—

"Tide, tide, whate'er betide,
There'll aye be Haigs in Bemersyde."

Certain localities have been celebrated in connection with their staple trades, their physical condition, or the habits of their inhabitants. The following are examples:—

"The sutors o' Selkirk,
The Kilmarnock wabsters,*
The lang toun o' Kirkcaldy,
Bonny Dundee,
Lousie Lauder,
Drucken Dunblane,
Brosie Forfar."

The common saying applied to those who affected gentility, "They're queer folk no to be Falkland folk," bore reference to the superior manners of the people of Falkland, owing to their residing in the immediate vicinity of a royal palace, which was a frequent residence of the sovereign and his court. A person supposed to be overreaching his neighbour was addressed, "Go to Freuchie." The saying seems to have originated from the practice of offending courtiers being dismissed from the neighbourhood of the palace at Falkland to a hamlet several miles off which bears the name.

The inhabitants of different districts are characterized by such expressions as "The men o' the Merse," "The folk o' Fife," and "The bairns o' Falkirk." "Jethart or Jeddart justice" was a proverbial phrase, having reference to the border thieves

* Weavers.

being frequently hanged by the municipal authorities of Jedburgh without receiving the benefit of a trial.

Some Scottish families have been described with reference to the qualities of their more conspicuous members. The following list has been arranged alphabetically:—

> The Sturdy Armstrongs,
> The trusty Boyds,
> The greedy Campbells,
> The dirty Dalrymples,
> The lying Dicks,
> The famous Dicksons,
> The lucky Duffs,
> The bauld Frasers,
> The gallant Grahams,
> The haughty Hamiltons,
> The handsome Hays,
> The muckle-backit Hendersons,
> The jingling Jardines,
> The gentle Johnstones,
> The angry Kerrs,
> The light Lindsays,
> The black Macraes,
> The wild Macraws,
> The brave Macdonalds,
> The fiery Macintoshes,
> The proud Macneils,
> The false Monteiths,
> The manly Morrisons,
> The gentle Neilsons,
> The bauld Rutherfords,
> The saucy Scotts,
> The proud Setons,
> The puddling Somervilles,
> The worthy Watsons.

Notable persons in country districts have been celebrated with reference to their real or supposed qualities. A farmer's wife in the parish of Foulden, Berwickshire, has been celebrated in these lines:—

" The trusty gudewife o' Whitecornlees,
　She never faikit *—she never faikit;
　She milked the ewes, the bannas † she bakit;
　She darn'd, she span, she sewed, she shapit;
　She kirn'd the kirn, she made the cheese;
　She mucked the byre, she riddled the corn;
　She carded the woo, she redd up the barn;
　She fother'd the pigs and the hens i' the morn,
　And ne'er took a minute o' rest or ease;
　She made the parritch in hay-time and hairst,
　And boilt the kail for the shearers' dinner;
　Ye ne'er could wrang her at ony birst, ‡
　She was foremost ay, and ay was a winner,
　The trusty gudewife o' Whitecornlees."

One Mrs. Christian Bell, who lived somewhere in the Merse, received quite an opposite character from the "gudewife o' Whitecornlees." Thus proceeds the rhyme:—

" Clarty Kirstan's cheese and butter
　Wad gie a Hielandman the scunner; §
　Clarty Kirstan's brose and kail
　Wad mak a sow to turn her tail;
　Clarty Kirstan's milk and whey
　Wad mak you scunner ilka day,
　Lapper'd ‖ milk and singit ¶ sowens, **
　Mauky †† kail wi' mony stowens;
　Rampan ‡‡ bread and parritch muddy,
　Stinkin' braxy, teugh as wuddy,

---

* Stopped.　　† Bannocks.　　‡ Undertaking.　　§ Disgust.
‖ Coagulated.　¶ Burnt.　　　** Pottage of meal seeds.
　　†† Full of maggots.　　‡‡ Sour.

Wad staw * the deil, or Simon Sivis,
Clarty † Kirstan, midden mavis,
Rub your gruntle ‡ wi' a docken,
An we'll away and hae our yoken."

The lasses of various parishes in the Merse are thus described :—

"The lasses o' Lauder are mim § and meek,
The lasses o' the Fanns smell o' peat reek,
The lasses o' Gordon canna sew a steek,
The lasses o' Earlstoun are bonny and braw,
The lasses o' Greenlaw are black as a craw,
The lasses o' Polwarth are the best o' them a'."

Certain farm homesteads in the parishes of Buncle and Chirnside are also celebrated for their fair maidens :—

"Little Billy, Billy Mill,
Billy Mains, and Billy-hill,
Ashfield, and Auchinoraw,
Butterhead, and Pefferlaw,
There's bonnie lasses in them a'."

There is an old rhyme, which obtains in many districts, descriptive of the marvellous activities of Sir William Wallace :—

"Wallace wight, upon a nicht,
Coost ‖ in a stack o' bere,
An' in the morn at fair daylight
It was meltit ¶ for his meare."

Some of the older toasts were sufficiently quaint. "Horn, corn, wool, and yarn," was abundantly comprehensive. "May ne'er waur be amang us;" "Health, wealth, and wit;" "May the moose ne'er leave our meal pock wi' the tear in its e'e," were

* Surfeit or disgust.   † Dirty.   ‡ Face.   § Prudish.
‖ Cast or took.   ¶ Thrashed.

quaint sentiments which delighted rustic assemblies. Some metrical toasts may be quoted:—

"The deil rock them in a creel
Wha dinna wish us a' weel.

"May we a' be canty and cosy,
May each hae a wife in his bosie;
A cosie but an' a cantie ben
To couthie * women and trusty men."

A Scottish author relates that three maiden ladies met annually on the tenth of June to celebrate the birthday of the old Pretender. On the glasses being charged the lady president opened with—

"Here's the king, oor *nain* † king."

The second lady gave—

"Here's to him that has the right,
And yet received the wrang,
Has five shillings in his pouch,
And yet he wants a crown."

Then followed the third, the most thoroughly Jacobite of the triad:—

"Here's to him that's out,
And no to him that pits him out;
And deil turn a' their insides out
That disna drink this toast aboot."

Mr. Reid, of the well-known publishing firm of Bell and Brash, Glasgow, had a remarkable gift of impromptu rhyming. During the agitation consequent on the proceedings of the Addington Administration in regard to the corn laws, he addressed to

* Affectionate.   † Own.

the Prime Minister an expressive epistle in these lines :—

"I entreat you, Mr. Addington,
Look to the prices at Haddington."

Among Mr. Reid's papers a parcel was found with this docquet,—

"Anent the hobble
With Joshua Noble."

Messrs. Dewar and Scott were two rhyming shopkeepers in Edinburgh. They frequently afforded to each other proofs of their mutual predilections. Mr. Scott called on his neighbour, Mr. Dewar, to ask change for a bank note. He said,—

"Mister Scott,
Can you change a note?"

Mr. Scott, proceeding to his money-drawer, replied :—

"I'm not quite sure, but I'll see;
Indeed, Mr. Dewar,
It's out of my power,
For my wife's away with the key."

Hugo Arnot, the historian of Edinburgh, was the most emaciated specimen of mankind. He published an "Essay on Nothing," which led the Hon. Andrew Erskine (brother of Lord Kellie) to compose, at his expense, the following epigram :—

"To find out where the bent of one's genius lies
Oft puzzles the witty and sometimes the wise.
Your discernment in this all true critics must find,
Since the subject's so pat to your body and mind."

There is a schoolboy game in Berwickshire in which these lines are repeated:—

> "I, Willie Wastle,
> Stand firm in my castle,
> And a' the dougs in your toun
> Can no ding Willie Wastle doun."

According to tradition, this *rhyme* was sent by Cockburn, the governor of Home Castle, in answer to a summons of surrender sent by Fenwick, who commanded a party of Cromwell's soldiers.

Mr. John Ross, minister of Blairgowrie, was remarkable for his quaint utterances in the pulpit. A portion of his parishioners, from a highland and outlying portion of his parish, came to church armed, much to the annoyance of Mr. Ross, who frequently heard of affairs of bloodshed on their homeward journeys. In order to induce them to abandon their weapons, as well as to lower their self-esteem, he used these expressions in the course of a sermon:—

> "Ye men o' Mause,
> Ye come down wi' dirks an' wi' spears,
> But when the mouse in yer tubs drakes her diblet,*
> Poor beastie, her een fa' in tears."

When tea was first introduced into Scotland, the proper application of the leaf was misunderstood. There are many anecdotes related of farmers' wives boiling the leaves and presenting them to their guests to be eaten with bread and butter. A farmer

* Places her mouth.

is thus represented as having had his gift of a pound of tea to his wife most ungratefully received:—

> "I coft * my wife a pund o' tea,
> And boiled it weel as weel could be,
> Then chopt it up wi' butter fine,
> And made it sweet as saps o' wine;
> But still she gloom'd as black's a craw,
> And wasna pleas'd wi't after a'."

Bees were formerly reared extensively in Scotland, the produce of the hives constituting an important article of cottage merchandise. Mr. James Playfair, minister of Bendochy, formed the benevolent design of preparing a work on the management of the apiary, which he conceived would prove of essential service to the cottage population. In order that he might dedicate his entire energies to the preparation of the work, he devolved his parochial duties on a substitute, and, regardless of cost, sought everywhere for such information as might elucidate his subject. His volume was at length prepared, and it was about to be issued under the auspices of an eminent publishing house in the metropolis. But an accidental conflagration in the printing office destroyed every portion of the manuscript; and as the reverend author had destroyed his notes, the loss was irreparable. A facetious neighbour, to whom Mr. Playfair had read a portion of his work, said he could so far help him to recall the contents of the consumed manuscript. He remembered the motto:—

* Purchased.

"The todler tyke has a very gude byke,
  And sae has the gairy bee;
But leeze me on the little red-doup,
  The best o' a' the three."

Some juvenile rhymes may be quoted. When children mount on each other's backs in the playground they are wont to say,—

"Cripple Dick upon a stick,
  Sandy on a sow,
Ride awa' to Gallowa'
  To buy a pund o' woo."

Herds and shepherds sing these rhymes:—

"Fish guts and stinkin' herrin'
Are bread and milk for an Eyemouth bairn."

"Tweed said to Till,
  What gars ye rin sae still?
Till said to Tweed,
  Though ye rin wi' speed,
    An' I rin slaw,
Where ye droun ae man
  I droun twa."

"Sunny, sunny shower,
  Come an' fa' half an hour;
Gar a' the hens cour,
Gar a' the hares clap,
Gar ilka wife o' Lammermoor,
  Put on her kail-pat."

"Rainbow, rainbow, haud away hame,
A' your bairns are dead but ane,
And it is sick at yon grey stane,
And will be dead ere ye win hame;

Gang owre the Drumaw,* and yont the lea,
And down by the side o' yonder sea,
Your. bairn lies greetin' like to die,
And the big tear-drap is in his e'e."

A strong tendency on the part of provincial poets to indulge a vein of sarcasm, at the cost of public persons or obnoxious neighbours, has led to the production of some powerful verses, which, however, cannot be reproduced on account of the private feelings which they have outraged. This unfortunate bent of the Scottish mind should be repressed; it has enkindled the worst resentments, provoked duels, excited litigation, and laid the foundation of bitter and lasting animosities.

* A hill in Berwickshire.

CHAPTER VIII.

SOME SCOTTISH ADVENTURERS.

" The man who consecrates his hours
By vigorous effort and an honest aim,
At once he draws the sting of life and death;
He walks with nature, and his paths are peace."
                                            YOUNG.

AN adventurous spirit is characteristic of a Scotsman. The Celts and the Cymbri celebrated liberty in their songs, but were unable to cope with those who pressed upon their soil. The lowland Scots, like their adventurous ancestors of Scandinavia, bid defiance to the invader, and maintained their independence. Galgacus resisted and drove back the Roman legions. Kenneth Macalpine checked the inferior races, and, rendering them obedient to his rule, established the permanent supremacy of the Scottish sceptre. The valiant Wallace restored the national liberties by the arms of a few vigorous compatriots, and a band of unskilled but resolute followers. Robert Bruce established his sovereignty by the force of a determined will, and

SOME SCOTTISH ADVENTURERS. 259

by inspiring his troops with a share of his own courage.

Scottish national enterprise has in recent times been represented by such men as William Paterson, who projected the Darien scheme, and founded the Bank of England; James Bruce, who discovered the sources of the Nile; Mungo Park, the African explorer; and the illustrious David Livingstone. "You are no doubt proud of your son," said the author of this work to the aged mother of the last-named traveller. "I am thankful for him," said the venerable matron.

The congratulatory odes addressed to King James on his accession to the English throne were legion. They were composed in Latin, English, and the Scottish vernacular. A panegyric in Latin hexameters particularly attracted the attention of the monarch. He was alike gratified by its complimentary character, and by the elegant language in which the compliments were conveyed. He invited the author to his court. His name was Robert Aytoun, the younger son of a Fife laird, who had prosecuted classical study at St. Andrews, and had lately returned from following literary pursuits in France. Aytoun presented an agreeable exterior, and his manners were courtly. The king was much attracted towards him, and at once attached him to the court. He appointed him private secretary to the Queen, and afterwards bestowed upon him a succession of honourable and lucrative offices. He was nominated a Gentleman of the Bedchamber, Master of Requests, and Master of Ceremonies. He received the honour of knighthood, and was raised to the dignity of a Privy Councillor. When James published his "Apology for the Oath of Allegiance," which he dedicated to Rodolph II., Emperor of Germany, and to the other princes of the German states, Sir Robert Aytoun was entrusted with the duty of bearing copies of the royal work to those illustrious personages. On the decease of his royal patron, Aytoun found another friend in his successor. He was continued in all his offices, and was appointed Private Secretary to Queen Henrietta Maria. On the death of Sir Julius Cæsar, in 1636, he was appointed by his royal mistress to the Mastership of St. Catherine. He attained other honours and emoluments. Having amassed a considerable fortune, he purchased an estate in Perthshire. He died in March, 1638, and was interred in Westminster Abbey, where a handsome monument, with an encomiastic Latin elegy has been erected to his memory.

Sir Robert Aytoun was an elegant writer of English verse. He composed numerous short poems, songs, and sonnets. These he presented to his friends, without being careful to retain copies. They were, after his death, partially collected by his ingenious friend, Sir James Balfour. Two MS. collections of his verses are extant, one being in the library of the British Museum, and the other in the possession of the present writer.

Early in the last century, Mrs. Douglas, widow of

Mr. Archibald Douglas, minister of Saltoun, rented a small cottage in the burgh of Pittenweem, on the south coast of Fifeshire. Her only son engaged in trade, and when he attained manhood became a shopkeeper, or general merchant. But the sphere of business at Pittenweem was too limited for his energies, and in the hope of improving his circumstances he removed to London, where he opened the British Coffee-house in Cockspur Street. His family consisted of a son and daughter. The daughter assisted in the house; the son studied at Oxford and took orders in the Church. In his twenty-third year the youth was appointed Chaplain of the 3rd Foot Guards, whom he attended in Flanders; he afterwards obtained a curacy in the neighbourhood of Oxford. Many of the nobility frequented the coffee-house of Cockspur Street. Miss Douglas, who was now the landlady, was respected for her intelligence and her extreme attention to the comfort of her patrons. One day the Earl of Bath, who was an occasional visitor, remarked to Miss Douglas that he was much concerned about securing a proper travelling companion for his son. The landlady modestly suggested her brother, and the Earl said he would inquire about his qualifications. A favourable account was obtained, and the young clergyman was offered by Lord Bath the appointment of companion to his son, Lord Pulteney. Mr. John Douglas performed the duties assigned him so satisfactorily, that Lord Bath became his personal friend. Through his lordship's influence he procured a succession of ecclesiastical appointments, and at length attained the mitre. Dr. Douglas, Bishop of Salisbury, son of the Scottish coffee-house keeper, is known as one of the most learned and accomplished prelates of the Church of England. His lordship died in May, 1807.

In the summer of 1759, John Home, author of "Douglas," was spending some weeks at the Moffat mineral Springs. In his peregrinations he met a Highland schoolmaster who had accompanied a pupil to the Wells. Home was much pleased by the intelligence of his northern acquaintance. His regard was increased when he found that his new friend cherished poetical tastes, and had produced some respectable verses. The conversation turned on the poetry of the Highlands—Home expressing the opinion that the Gaels had always been an unlettered people. The Highlander dissented, and quoted some fragments of Highland minstrelsy which he said were translations from Celtic originals. Home was much interested, and requested his new acquaintance to supply him with some translations in MS., that he might show them to his literary friends in the capital. The translator complied. The Edinburgh *savans* were delighted and surprised, and Home was entreated not to lose sight of the ingenious Highlander.

Mr. James Macpherson now presented himself in the capital, and was introduced by Home to the literary circles. Dr. Blair especially interested himself in promoting the work of translation. Fragments of Gaelic poetry collected by Macpherson were published under his auspices in 1760. Soon after a literary dinner was held at Edinburgh, to which Macpherson was invited. Subscriptions were laid on the table to enable him to proceed on a tour through the Highlands to collect all the fragments of ancient poetry which might be procured. The result of these researches was published in two quarto volumes. Thus were the poems of Ossian given to the world.

The discussion which arose as to the genuineness of these Ossianic poems was unprecedented. Persons of the greatest ability and learning were arrayed on both sides, and much angry feeling was expended on the part of the combatants. Meanwhile, the ingenious schoolmaster who had published them was not forgotten. He was appointed private secretary to Captain Johnston, governor of Pensacola; an office from the duties of which he soon retired with a handsome pension. He established his residence in London, and devoted himself to literary pursuits. Two pamphlets from his pen in support of the Government, and against the claims of the American Colonies, were conducive to his further success. He was constituted agent to the Nabob of Arcot. In 1780 he entered Parliament as member for Camelford. His death took place in his mansion of Belleville, Inverness-shire, in 1796, and his remains were interred in Westminster Abbey. Macpherson attained great opulence, and purchased a handsome estate

The city of St. Andrews has long been celebrated for its educational advantages. About the year 1768 a hairdresser of the place sent his son to the university, in the hope that he might be induced to study for the Church. The youth evinced an abundant aptitude for learning, but was withal wilful and headstrong. He quarrelled with a companion, and challenged him to mortal combat. The juvenile duellists borrowed two old firelocks, and therewith proceeded to a sequestered spot to justify their mutual honour. The seconds arranged that the party who should first fire should be chosen by lot. The priority fell to Mr. Bell, who discharged his weapon but missed his antagonist. Realizing what might be the consequences of the encounter, the seconds interfered, and further conflict was prevented. The affair, however, became known, and Bell, who possessed an extraordinary spirit of adventure, abandoned his college studies, and proceeded to Virginia. There he attracted the notice of a planter, who, perceiving his scholarship, placed two sons under his care, and gave him permission to travel with them to Scotland. Bell returned to his native city. The intervals in which he was not engaged with his American pupils he devoted to the study of medicine, which he prosecuted so successfully as to qualify himself for a degree. He next thought of taking orders in the Church of England, as affording a wider field for preferment than the Church of his native country. Through the influence of Mr. Dempster, Member of Parliament, he was appointed chaplain to Fort St. George, Madras; he accordingly proceeded to India.

At Madras, Dr. Bell originated the Monitorial method of instruction which has become associated with his name. The development and extension of his system, together with the acquisition of money, became henceforth the main object of his life. His latter years were spent in England. He became founder of an educational institution in his native city, towards the erection and endowment of which, and the support of some kindred institutions, he bequeathed his fortune of £120,000. Dr. Bell died in 1832.

In the closing year of the last century, a young Scotsman who had taught the parochial schools of Dunino and Kettle, in Fifeshire, proceeded to North America in the hope of procuring educational employment. He reached Kingston, Canada West, where he discovered that certain hopes of preferment which he had cherished could not be realized. Without a single acquaintance to recommend his efforts, he opened a school. The venture was only partially successful. He taught at Kingston about four years, when he took orders in the Episcopal Church. He now accepted the mission at Cornwall, where he founded an academy which he successfully conducted for nine years. In 1812 he received a clerical appointment at Toronto, where he likewise planted a seminary.

From the outset of his American career, Mr. John

Strachan, the Fifeshire schoolmaster, had formed the conception of a Canadian university. Aided by many of his former pupils, now in situations of influence, he continued to advocate his scheme till 1827, when King's College, Toronto, was founded by royal charter. Religious differences prevailed, which led to the retirement of the founder from the institution. In 1851 he founded a new college at Toronto in connection with the Church of England. In 1839 he became Bishop of Toronto. Bishop Strachan still lives; he has attained his ninety-third year.

Lord Gardenstone, a judge of the Court of Session, was a promoter of learning. He occupied a residence in the parish of Fordoun, Kincardineshire. The village schoolmaster, a young man lately appointed, was represented to him as a learned person, but as possessing an eccentricity which bordered on derangement. Gardenstone wished much to see him, but hesitated to make the acquaintance of one who might prove troublesome. Walking one afternoon in a beautiful glen in the neighbourhood of his residence, he observed a young man writing with a pencil. He drew near to the stranger, who seemed in a profound reverie. Having indicated his presence, his lordship proceeded to hail the stranger with a kindly greeting. The stranger, awakened from his fantasy, respectfully saluted his lordship, and announced himself as the village schoolmaster. Lord Gardenstone was much pleased with the appearance and manner of his new acquaintance. After a short walk with him he invited him to spend an evening at Gardenstone. When Lord Gardenstone had received several visits from his new friend without detecting any oddity, or other token of mental aberration, he ventured to inform him of the popular belief. The schoolmaster proceeded to explain that he was in the habit of composing poetry in the glen where his lordship had met him, and that he frequently repeated his compositions aloud. Besides, when meditating on his verses, he had repeatedly found himself to have been so engaged as to be unconscious of surrounding objects. This must have originated the report of his insanity. His explanation was most satisfactory to the benevolent judge, who resolved forthwith to befriend one whose talents so evidently entitled him to preferment. His lordship introduced the poet to Lord Monboddo, who was equally attracted by his ingenuity and learning.

In a few years, Mr. James Beattie, schoolmaster of Fordoun, was, under the strong recommendation of the Lords Gardenstone and Monboddo, promoted to a professorship in Marischal College, Aberdeen. Few Scottish professors have been more distinguished than the ingenious author of " The Minstrel."

It was a subject of deep concern to the Rev. David Wilkie, minister of Cults, that his son, who bore his own Christian name, was so neglectful of his lessons. Three schools had been tried—Pitlessie, Kettle, and the Academy of Cupar; but David was incorrigibly bent on ignoring scholastic knowledge. The walls, the kitchen pavement, the uncarpeted floors of his father's manse, and other places, bore evidence of his propensity to indulge in what seemed a perpetual pastime. Figures of men and brutes in all descriptions of attitude were scrawled, daubed, and delineated everywhere. Even in church, when his father was preaching, would the young rogue, unmindful of the sacredness of the place, be depicting on the blank leaves of his Psalm-book the more remarkable faces in the flock. Every sleeper was sure to find a place in his portfolio.

The case was hopeless. The youth could never become a scholar. He might be a painter. He was recommended as a pupil in the Trustees' Academy at Edinburgh. The application for his admission was rejected. George Thomson, the Trustees' secretary, and the promoter of genius in the person of Robert Burns, saw no genius in young David Wilkie. He pronounced an opinion that the lad was incapable of receiving instruction even in the most ordinary branches of his art. This was very discouraging to the worthy parson of Cults. His son was evidently unfitted for the pulpit, and by one who ruled the Scottish world of art the boy's best drawings were pronounced worthless.

The sequel may be related in a few sentences. Private influence overcame the hostile adjudication of the Trustees' secretary. Young Wilkie became a pupil in the Trustees' Academy, and obtained a prize. At the age of twenty he proceeded to London, and painted vigorously for his support. His paintings soon became known, and brought him fame and emolument. He became, in the words of Hayden, "the Raffaele of domestic art." He was at length elected a Royal Academician, and received the honour of knighthood. The name of Sir David Wilkie is familiar to every Scotsman. This distinguished painter died in 1841, in his fifty-fifth year.

John Campbell, son of the minister of Cupar, refused to study for the Church. Having obtained some acquaintance with the classics at St. Andrews University, he proceeded to London. He became a parliamentary reporter, and theatrical critic to the *Morning Chronicle*. Having saved a little money, he entered one of the Inns of Court, and was called to the bar. He became king's counsel. He entered Parliament, was chosen Solicitor-General, and afterwards Attorney-General. The adventurous student of St. Andrews, who turned his back on the humbler aspirations of his forefathers, was raised to the peerage, and became Lord Chancellor. Lord Campbell died in 1861.

When Robert Burns visited Ellisland, a young man, employed as a farm labourer in the neighbourhood, procured books from the poet's library. The youth's taste for learning increased; he sought employment in a joiner's workshop, and having saved a little money from his earnings, went to college. He studied medicine, and practised as a surgeon, first in Paisley and afterwards in Glasgow. This individual was Dr. Robert Watt, author of the "Bibliotheca

Britannica," the most remarkable work of the kind which has appeared in any country or age. Dr. Watt died at Glasgow in 1819, at the age of forty-five.

We now present some illustrations of Scottish enterprise not generally known. About the year 1684, an agricultural labourer, named Macrae, died at Ochiltree, Ayrshire. He left a widow and two children— a boy and girl. The widow removed to a suburb of the town of Ayr, where she obtained employment as a washerwoman. The son, James Macrae, was sometime a message-boy, and afterwards a cowherd. During his evening hours he received lessons in reading and other elementary branches from Hugh M'Guire, a maker of spinning-wheels, but who was better known as fiddler at the district merry-makings. This boy possessed a restless spirit, and was always getting into scrapes. At length he disappeared. He had run off to sea. Forty years passed. In 1731, James Macrae, Esq., late Governor of Madras, arrived in the town of Ayr, and proceeded to make inquiry about Mrs. Macrae, the poor washerwoman, and the fiddler M'Guire. The former had long been dead, but M'Guire had married the widow's daughter, and four handsome girls had been born to them. Governor Macrae announced himself as M'Guire's old protégé, now his brother-in-law, and the uncle of his daughters. He handed a sum of money to the fiddler, and promised to attend to the education of his girls. The fiddler procured a loaf of sugar and a bottle of brandy, and scooping a hole into the loaf, and pouring in brandy, he and his helpmate supped the sweetened liquor. Thus they felicitated themselves on their unexpected good fortune.

The career of James Macrae, up to the period of his reappearance at Ayr, must be sketched. After a short seafaring career, he enlisted as a soldier, and was sent to India. By his good conduct he obtained a commission, and in due time obtained a field officer's rank. He was subsequently employed in the commissariat. Being in the service of the East India Company, he was sent by the Directors on a special mission to an English settlement on the west coast of Sumatra. There his services proved efficient, and he was appointed by the Directors to the governorship of Fort St. David. On the 18th January, 1725, he became Governor of Madras. He returned to Britain in 1731, with a fortune of one hundred thousand pounds.

Governor Macrae now devoted himself to the welfare of his sister's family. He presented her husband with a farm, and sent the daughters to an approved place of education. They were educated in all the accomplishments of the time, and brought out in the first society. In 1744 the eldest married William, thirteenth Earl of Glencairn. On this occasion Governor Macrae presented his niece with the barony of Ochiltree, which he had purchased for £25,000. He bestowed on her diamonds to the value of £45,000. The Governor's second niece married Mr. James Erskine, advocate, afterwards

Lord Alva. She received the estate of Alva as her dower. The third daughter married her cousin, an illegitimate son of the Governor, and received the barony of Houston. Her husband is, as Captain Macrae, represented in "Kay's Edinburgh Portraits." He was a notorious duellist, and, having shot Sir George Ramsay in "an affair of honour," escaped from the country. The youngest niece succeeded to her uncle's estate of Orangefield, and married Mr. Charles Dalrymple, Sheriff Clerk of Ayr.

Two public acts of Governor Macrae evince his patriotism. He erected an equestrian statue of William III. at the Cross of Glasgow, at the cost of £3,000; and lent to the corporation of that city the sum of £5,000, to pay the amount levied upon them by Prince Charles Edward in 1745. He died about the year 1746, and was interred in the churchyard of Prestwick.

James, Earl of Glencairn, the Governor's grand-nephew, was one of the first and most attached patrons of Robert Burns. The Earl died in 1791, when the great poet lamented his departure in a touching ode. These are the concluding verses:—

> "The bridegroom may forget the bride
>   Was made his wedded wife yestreen;
> The monarch may forget the crown
>   That on his head an hour has been;
>
> "The mither may forget the bairn
>   That smiles sae sweetly on her knee:
> But I'll remember thee, Glencairn,
>   And a' that thou hast done for me."

SOME SCOTTISH ADVENTURERS. 273

The loftiest mountain of the Ochils is Ben Cleugh. In the clefts of its elevated summit falcons were wont to build. In a sporting expedition in quest of those royal birds, James VI. met William Alexander, the young laird of Menstry, who had already made the tour of Europe, and acquired reputation both as a scholar and poet. He was a sprightly youth, and possessed elegant manners. The king invited him to Stirling Castle. His Majesty and young Alexander became fast friends. Alexander obtained honours and immunities from his royal patron. Having filled the minor offices of state, he obtained higher posts. He was ultimately created Earl of Stirling, and had conferred on him, for colonizing purposes, the territories of Canada and Nova Scotia, with the right of creating baronets. No subject obtained such privileges before or since. The Earl died at London in 1640, and was interred, with much pomp, in the High Church of Stirling.

Robert Menteith, minister of Duddingston, professed Arminian doctrines, and gave occasion for scandal in his private life. He resigned his charge, and, proceeding to France, sought and obtained admission into the Catholic Church. He attached himself to the service of M. de la Porte, Grand Prior of France, and afterwards obtained the friendship of Cardinal de Retz, who bestowed upon him a canonry in Notre Dame. He cultivated the society of men of letters, and obtained a high position among the *literati* of Paris. Having been requested to name the Scottish family to which he belonged, he ingeniously styled himself one of the Menteiths of Salmonet, his father having been a salmon fisher at Stirling. Menteith is author of a posthumous work, entitled "Histoire des Troubles de la Grande Bretagne depuis l'an 1633 jusqu'en 1649. Paris, 1661." An English translation of this work was published in 1735 by Captain James Ogilvie.

About the year 1570 the elders of the parish church of Stirling discovered that a bodle * had been removed from the collecting-plate. Inquiry was instituted, and the offender proved to be a small boy, the son of a respectable "baxter," or baker in the place. The young delinquent acknowledged his misdemeanour, and was so ashamed of what he had done that he suddenly left the place. His parents made every inquiry after him, but failed to obtain any information of his movements. After a time they concluded that he had perished.

One Sunday in the spring of 1603, a military officer presented himself at a meeting of the Stirling kirk-session. He had come, he said, to offer some reparation for an offence which he had committed many years before, and which had weighed heavily on his conscience. He had taken a bodle from the collection-plate at the church door, and he now proposed by way of reparation to erect a manse for the first minister. His name was Colonel Edmond.

* A coin, value the third part of an English halfpenny.

The history of his career the colonel afterwards related. He was so stung with the disgrace he had brought upon his parents by his act of plunder, that he resolved to absent himself from his country till he should be able to wipe out his offence by some deed of liberality. Soon after leaving Stirling he had worked his passage to the Continent in a trading vessel. He afterwards joined the army of Maurice, Prince of Orange. By his prudent behaviour he rose in the service. He had attained a colonelcy, and was enabled to retire from military service with a handsome fortune.

The colonel had the satisfaction to find both his parents alive after his long absence. He endowed them liberally, and proceeded to live under their roof. Whatever honours were offered him, he insisted that these should be shared by them. He presented a pair of colours to the corporation, which were used upwards of a century. When his parents were both dead, he formed a matrimonial connection. His family consisted of two daughters, one of whom married Sir Thomas Livingston, of Jerviswood, a cadet of the noble families of Callendar, Linlithgow, and Kilsyth. The eldest son of the marriage was commander-in-chief of the forces in Scotland, and was afterwards created Viscount Teviot.

When Colonel Edmond was still in the service of the Prince of Orange, a native of Scotland, desirous of obtaining his favour, made up to him in presence of some of his brother officers, and saying he had just come from Scotland, added, "Your cousin, my Lord ———, is very well, and your cousin Sir John." "Get you gone, you sycophant," said the colonel; " I have no relations either lords or knights. My father is an honest baker in the town of Stirling."

About the close of the Rebellion of 1745-6, a Highland regiment was stationed in the town of Elgin. A private soldier of the regiment, named Anderson, married one Marjery Gilzean, a native of the place. The young woman's friends were much opposed to the match, and when it took place they deserted her. She left Elgin with her husband for some other military station, but returned to her native place about a year after, a widow, and with a little son in her arms. She was entirely destitute, and sought refuge for herself and her infant in the sacristy of the cathedral. An old font in the corner of the apartment was the child's bed. Marjery received with thankfulness the gifts of the benevolent, and devoted herself, with unceasing solicitude, to the care of her infant.

The boy, whose name was Andrew Anderson, having attained a suitable age, was received as pauper pupil in the grammar school. In lieu of his services in lighting the fires and sweeping out the rooms, he received his education. He was afterwards apprenticed to an uncle on the father's side, a staymaker, at St. Andrews Llanbride, the adjoining parish. Being harshly treated by this relative, he escaped from his service, and found his way to Leith. There he procured employment as clerk in the workshop of a merchant tailor. Having been sent with a suit of clothes to the residence of a military officer, that gentleman was struck by his intelligent aspect, and inquired as to his prospects. Finding that he had no definite views, the officer advised him to enlist in his own regiment, promising in that event to take him into his service. Anderson took the officer's counsel, and proceeded to India as a recruit.

In 1811 an elderly gentleman arrived at the Gordon Arms Hotel, Elgin. Next morning he proceeded to the cathedral ruins. He asked the sexton whether he knew where a poor woman, Marjery Gilzean, was interred? "Na, I dinna ken," replied the gravedigger; "she was a puir worthless craitur, naebody kens where she was buriet." "Unfortunate I know she was," said the gentleman, "but I never heard that she was worthless." The stranger was her son—now Lieutenant-General Anderson. Possessing the faculty of readily acquiring languages, he had obtained employment as an interpreter. He received a commission, and rose step by step to the rank of a general officer. At the taking of Seringapatam in 1799 he greatly distinguished himself.

Having retired from the army, General Anderson settled in the neighbourhood of Elgin, his winters being spent in London. He died at London on the 16th September, 1824. By a trust disposition executed in November, 1815, he assigned the whole of his heritable and moveable property to certain gentlemen in Elgin, for the purpose of founding and endowing an hospital in that town for indigent men and women, and likewise for establishing a School of Industry for the maintenance and education of male and female children of the labouring classes. Consequent on the provisions of the testamentary deed, an elegant building has been constructed at Elgin, in which three hundred persons, old and young, are now reaping the benefit of the General's munificence.

The palace of James V. in the castle of Stirling has its principal windows protected by interlaced iron gratings. These were executed at the instance of the Queen Dowager, Mary of Guise, owing to the unsettled condition of the country after the death of her royal husband, James V. The artificer was one Callander, a blacksmith of the town. He and his successors were constituted blacksmiths to the Royal Family; but beyond this nominal distinction they seem for several generations to have received no recompence for their services. There is a story that the son of Callander who constructed the gratings of the castle proceeded to London after the accession of James VI. to the English throne, and obtaining the royal mandate for payment of his account, presented it to the English treasury, and so obtained payment in sterling instead of Scottish money, whereby he was enriched. This tradition seems to be fabulous, for many years after, John Callander of Stirling is found making application to the Privy Council for payment of charges for work

SOME SCOTTISH ADVENTURERS. 279

executed at Stirling and Edinburgh castles, of which "he had never yet received payment of a sixpence." The Privy Council ordered him to be paid £6,567 17s. 2d., Scots money. This sum he made loan of on a wadset, or mortgage, to the proprietor of the estate of Craigforth. As the mortgage was not redeemed by the proprietor, John Callander afterwards took possession of the property. His grandson, John Callander of Craigforth, was an eminent scholar and ingenious antiquary. Two granddaughters of this gentleman obtained important marriages. One became the wife of Tom Sheridan; the other married Sir James Graham of Netherby, the late distinguished statesman.

In the middle of the last century there flourished in "the East Neuk" of Fife a retired general and county gentleman, who was the greatest man of his time in one department—that of card-playing. General Scott of Balcomie, for such were his name and title, received challenges to play from all parts of the kingdom. When his competitors were rich, he would have hazarded his own estates against theirs. He always came off winner. He amassed an immense fortune, and got possession of estates in various parts of the kingdom.

The facility with which young noblemen hazarded their fortunes led the General to conceive a strong aversion to their order. He executed a singular will. His family consisted of three daughters, and he divided his wealth among them equally, with the provision that should any of them marry a person of noble rank, she should lose her portion. This stipulation was cancelled by Act of Parliament, and the ladies were left a free choice of partners. They all became allied to persons of noble rank. Henrietta, the eldest, married the Marquis of Titchfield, subsequently fourth Duke of Portland. She brought her husband a fortune of £300,000. Lucy, the second daughter, married Francis, Earl of Moray. Joan, the youngest, became wife of Mr. Canning, the distinguished statesman, and on his decease was, in acknowledgment of his services, created a viscountess.

William Forbes, a tinsmith's apprentice in Aberdeen, and a native of the place, proceeded to London in the hope of bettering his circumstances. In the metropolis he worked at his trade for some years, and with his savings began a little business on his own account. He was a very sagacious person, and those who came in contact with him liked his conversation and manners. Admiral Byron, grandfather of Lord Byron, the celebrated poet, was one of his customers. The Admiral chanced to remark to him that he had obtained private information that the Admiralty had resolved to sheathe the bottoms of ships of war with copper, instead of continuing the old method of coal-tarring. The information did not pass unheeded by the acute Aberdonian. He immediately purchased all the copper which could be found. When the order was publicly given for the coppering of the ships, the naval authorities were compelled to apply to him for metal. Subsequently he obtained the exclusive privilege of coppering the vessels of the navy. In the course of twenty years he realized a large fortune. In 1786, when the fine estate of Callander, in Stirlingshire, was exposed for sale, William Forbes became the purchaser. He now retired from business, and took up his abode in the ancient demesne of the Earls of Callander. He became a zealous agriculturist, and one of the most enterprising county gentlemen of his neighbourhood. He died on the 21st June, 1815, and was succeeded in his princely possessions by his eldest son, the late William Forbes, Esq., who was long parliamentary representative of the county of Stirling.

An Argyleshire tailor, named Campbell, opened a shop in London. The Duke of Argyle, his hereditary chief, had promised to do him any service which lay in his power. On the death of George I., which took place abroad, the Duke received early intelligence of the event, which he concealed several hours from the public, but communicated at once to his clansman. The tailor, on the Duke's security, obtained money, and at once bought up all the fine black cloth in the city. The public, therefore, came to him for mourning, and he supplied them on his own terms. He realized a splendid fortune, with which he built Argyle Square, so named by him in honour of his patron.

A sister of the celebrated Dr. Cullen was waiting-maid to the Duchess of Hamilton. She married the

Duke's valet, whose name was Macall. Both were favourites of the family, and the Duke and Duchess resolved to establish them comfortably in life. They selected the business of hotel-keeping, and the Duke secured them premises in an eligible locality of the metropolis. The name of Macall was deemed unsuitable for a London landlord, and by the Duke's suggestion it was changed to Almack. So originated *Almack's Hotel*, so long the resort of fashionable life in London.

Rose, the usher of the National Assembly, and a principal actor in the first French Revolution, was a native of Scotland. By his prudent behaviour he attained an influence among many leading persons in France. Mirabeau entertained a high opinion of him, and on his death-bed appointed him to negotiate his affairs. He warned Louis XVI. of the danger which threatened him; he sheltered many leading persons during the Reign of Terror, and with his own hand arrested Robespierre. Rose held office in the Council of the Ancients, and afterwards was attached to the Chamber of Peers. He died at Paris, in March, 1841, in his eighty-fourth year.

Alexander Selkirk, the prototype of Robinson Crusoe, may be included in the list of Scottish adventurers. He was the son of a respectable shoemaker at Largo, Fifeshire. In his youth he was remarkable not more for his roving disposition than for an ungovernable temper, which led him into frequent scrapes. In his nineteenth year he was brought before the kirk-session for "indecent behaviour in church." Two years after, he was again cited before that tribunal, on account of promoting a disturbance at home. His brother Andrew had brought into the house "a can full of salt water," which Alexander, on coming in, drank off through mistake. On this his brother smiled, when the future navigator beat the offender with his staff. He further challenged him to "a combat of neiffells." Alexander acknowledged his perversity, and submitted to a public rebuke.

The spirit of enterprise which is so largely inherent in the Scottish mind, and which, under the regulation of sound judgment and correct principle, leads to success and honour, is, when unrestrained by proper safeguards, repellent and dangerous. The murders perpetrated by Burke and Hare, in order to obtain the reward of providing bodies to the dissecting-room, exceeded in number and deliberate heartlessness those which have been committed in the other divisions of the empire. Angria, the noted pirate of Indian seas, was born in Dundee. An anecdote, illustrative of his generosity to a townsman, may be admissible.

In the year 1750, a vessel commanded by one Captain Crichton, of Dundee, was captured by Angria. When he had boarded his prize, Angria proceeded to address the master of the captured ship in the Scottish accent. These questions were put and answers given :—

Pirate. Where do you come from?

Captain. From Dundee.

P. Ay, from Dundee. Where does the Cross of Dundee stand?

C. Near the west end of the large square, opposite the new Town House.

P. How many steps are in it?

C. Six; and all go round about it.

P. Quite right. Where stands Monk's holm?

C. On the south side of the Nethergate, and east from the hospital, opposite to Girzy Gourlay's stable.

P. Right again. Where stands the Machlin Tower?

C. Just at the west end of the broad of the Murraygate, on the north side, where they have lately erected a public well, to be called the Dog Well, from Archibald Doig, a merchant, who has been at the expense of erecting a dog upon the top of it cut out of solid stone.

P. I am much obliged for the information, being news to me. But pray where stands St. Paul's?

C. On the south side of Murraygate, immediately opposite the Machlin Tower.

P. Do you know St. Roche?

C. We call it Semmirookie. It is at the east end of Cowgate, on the north side, near the Den burn.

Angria was moved to tears on recalling scenes familiar to him at a period when he did not contemplate a course of crime. He shook hands with

Captain Crichton, and said feelingly, "You have your liberty and your ship."

The history of Scottish smuggling, which yet remains to be written, would reveal many remarkable illustrations of ingenuity and enterprise, which, employed in honourable merchandise, would have doubtless conduced to distinction and affluence. The desire of vending contraband liquor was deeply inherent in the national mind. The stalwart yeoman abandoned the tillage of his fields to engage in secretly converting his barley into whisky. The peasant derived better remuneration by watching the still than in following the plough. The country laird loved whisky which tasted of the *peat reek*. Its manufacture by his tenants enabled them to pay better rents. Thus encouraged, the smuggling system, demoralizing as it was, long lingered in highland and also in some of the lowland districts.

One smuggling story we are enabled to relate. It is a narrative of probably the last adventure of the kind connected with Scotland. In boldness of conception and skill of execution it is unique. In relating it we would emphatically express our detestation of the proceedings which it involves. The particulars were communicated to us by one who became intimately conversant with the circumstances.

William IV. rejoiced in the society of a Scottish gentleman connected with his household. The gentleman was frequently honoured with a place at the royal table. The king drank Hollands gin. The

Scotsman informed his Majesty that he knew how the best description of that liquor could be procured. He afterwards produced a specimen of the gin, which he recommended. It was cordially approved by the king, who requested his courtier to procure a supply for the royal table.

The Scotsman did not communicate with Holland, but proceeded to a well-known seaport on the east coast of Scotland. An agency was there constituted to procure the liquor from a distillery in a central district, then celebrated for the manufacture of a species of gin. On being received from the distillery, the liquor was deposited in a cellar, when a process of preparation for its shipment was secretly enacted.

That process must be described. The liquor was placed in bottles manufactured to the Holland pattern. The corking was an important affair. A slit was cut in the lower part of each cork, so that the motion of the liquor might not reveal its existence in the packing-cases. These cases consisted of casks, which were either old or made to assume the aspect of antiquity. Both ends of the casks were stowed with portions of old iron, the bottles were carefully packed in the centre, while labels marked "old iron" were attached on the outside.

The casks were deposited during the night in the reception-yard of the London packet, and were uniformly shipped without any information concerning the sender. Each cask was inscribed with a fictitious name, and addressed to a particular office near the landing wharf. At this office a person waited for the reception of the casks, and paid the dues of transmission. Should an exciseman accompany the deliverer, the person in charge was authorized to refuse the goods, and protest his ignorance of any individual bearing the name attached to the casks. But no detection was ever made. From the place of consignment in the city, the bottles were conveyed under a different packing to the royal cellars. The profits of these strange transactions were very considerable. The utmost value of the liquor was nine shillings per gallon. The king was charged thirty shillings, the difference of one guinea being divided between the adventurous courtier at the palace and his active abettor at the northern port.

CHAPTER IX.

UNFORTUNATE MEN OF GENIUS.

"Man, whose heaven-erected face
 The smiles of love adorn,
Man's inhumanity to man
 Makes countless thousands mourn."
                                    BURNS.

"Neglect stings even more than scorn;
What can he do
But hang his lute on some lone tree and die?"
                                    L. E. LANDON.

CALUMNY has been the scourge of ingenious Scotsmen. Robert Fergusson was eccentric; he was pronounced a drunkard and died insane. Bruce, the Abyssinian traveller, was charged with imposture. Burns, pierced by the shafts of detraction, died at the age of thirty-seven. The genial and loving John Wilson, when a candidate for the University chair, was proclaimed a domestic and a social tyrant. The Ettrick Shepherd was charged with ingratitude, an offence of which he was incapable.

William Ged, the inventor of stereotyping, was a Scotsman. He was a jeweller in Edinburgh. So long as he adhered to his original vocation he was permitted to prosper. When he ventured to exercise his ingenuity by facilitating the printer's art, he was doomed. On his making known his discovery of block printing, the trade deemed their craft in danger, and formed a combination for his destruction. Master printers, journeymen, and apprentices united against him as a common enemy; they assailed him with insult; they loaded him with invectives; they reproached him with ignorance and assumption. The arrows of calumny hit him on all sides. Who could long withstand such an array of hostilities? Poor Ged, who ought to have made a fortune by his discovery, sunk under the load of persecution, and died of a broken heart.

Who invented the percussion cap—the application of detonating powder to the explosion of firearms? Few are aware that the inventor was a Scottish clergyman. Who has heard of Mr. A. J. Forsyth, minister of Belhelvie? His name is scarcely known even to men of science; in the catalogue of discoverers it is unrecorded. Modest and unpretending in his scientific pursuits, and abundantly faithful in discharging the duties of his sacred office, Mr. Forsyth escaped personal reproach, but was gently consigned to the Lethe of oblivion.

James Watt possessed an aspiring nature, which oppression might vex but could not subdue. When he commenced business as a constructor of mathematical instruments, the hammermen of Glasgow determined on thrusting him from the city. In his difficulty he obtained shelter within the walls of the university, where he prosecuted for a time his ingenious labours.

The personal history of Michael Stirling, a Scotsman who invented the method of thrashing corn by machinery, is unknown. When Patrick Bell, a student in theology, invented the reaping machine, he made his experiments by night. He rightly apprehended that should his name, as a candidate for orders, be associated with mechanism and the reaping-field, he would receive no call to a parish. But the discovery did become known, and Mr. Bell was compelled to seek his first professional advancement on the opposite shores of the Atlantic.

Dr. James Anderson, commonly distinguished as editor of the *Bee*, possessed extraordinary ingenuity. Early directing his attention to social economy, he was one of the first who studied Agriculture as a science. He discovered an efficient method of draining wet lands, and demonstrated the utility of the two-horse plough. He studied Ocean husbandry, and under the direction of the Treasury surveyed the West coast. He abandoned his country farm, and proceeded to Edinburgh, where he expected to obtain the sympathy of the learned and the patronage of the nobility. He was disappointed, and afterwards removed to London, where he died.

James Smith, commonly styled of Deanston, from his long connection with the cotton-mills established at that place, was one of the ill-rewarded of modern

UNFORTUNATE MEN OF GENIUS. 291

Scotsmen. His modes of thorough drainage, and of economizing sewage manure, revolutionized the system of Scottish husbandry. His inventions connected with the mechanism of power-looms have likewise proved of important value. Mr. Smith received public entertainments and agricultural medals, but obtained no more substantial recompence for a long career devoted to the public service.

The constructor of the first steamboat was Henry Bell, a Scottish wheelwright. Abandoning his trade, he devoted himself for many years to the fabrication of a steam-vessel. The entire work of its formation was conducted under his personal superintendence, and chiefly with his own hands. He was then resident at Helensburgh, on the Clyde, and the numerous visitors at that watering-place regarded him with pity or contempt. He was pronounced a species of enthusiast, who might properly be entrusted to the care of his friends. Shipbuilders who had heard the details of his scheme declared his system to be impracticable.

At length, after the anxieties and labours of years, Henry Bell launched his little vessel on the Clyde. He styled his invention the *Comet*, a name which suggested to the abounding cavillers an opportunity for the indulgence of their rude wit respecting the alleged eccentricity of the mechanic, and the supposed ephemeral character of his discovery.

Contrary to all expectation, the little steamer moved steadily on the river. What the inventor had anticipated was fully realized. The possibility of steam navigation was established. Thereafter steamers were regularly constructed on the Clyde, and many merchants in Glasgow realized fortunes consequent on their use; but for years the inventor suffered from the pressure of abject poverty. At length some benevolent person brought his claims under the notice of the Clyde Trustees, who settled a small annuity upon him, and thus the discoverer of Steam Navigation was rescued from the workhouse.

William Playfair, brother of the better known professor of that name, was a person of remarkable ingenuity. He invented many important appliances for abridging manual labour in the decoration of silver plate, and a valuable rolling-machine for the use of silversmiths. A mode of telegraphing which he suggested was adopted by Government. He published many statistical and political works of great public utility. Yet this remarkable man had a constant struggle for existence, and died in circumstances of indigence.

The name of Dr. Tobias Smollett is familiar. Descended from an ancient and opulent family in Dumbartonshire, he studied medicine and passed as a physician. He served as surgeon's mate on board a man-of-war, but soon abandoned naval employment. For a period he attempted medical practice at Bath, but his attention becoming engrossed by literary concerns, he resolved to prosecute literature as a profession. He originated and became editor of the

Critical Review. He published a "History of England." A succession of novels proceeded from his pen, all of which at once became popular. But his constitution succumbed under the pressure of constant occupation. He tried the climate of Italy, hopeful of benefit from the change. There he died in 1774, at the age of fifty-three. The proceeds of a benefit in the Theatre Royal, Edinburgh, enabled his widow to return to Britain, and relieved her immediate necessities.

Mr. Smollett, cousin of the deceased, the opulent owner of Bonhill, had forgotten his relative while he lived, but rejoiced to share in his celebrity when he was gone. He reared a lofty column to his memory in a conspicuous locality of his estate, and was careful to intimate that he had thus honoured the memory of his ingenious kinsman.

Robert Mudie, author of the interesting volumes on the "Seasons," was a teacher in the academy of Dundee. Being an active politician, he joined the town council of the burgh, and there sought to advance the cause of local reform. His efforts were not appreciated by his fellow-councillors, who regarded him as an intermeddler. Those who were more strongly opposed to his views endeavoured to cause him annoyance in the performance of his scholastic duties. This was accomplished. Mr. Mudie resigned his office, and proceeded to London. There he employed his pen with a diligence which has never been surpassed. He laboured at the desk twelve and fourteen hours daily. At length the exertion overcame a constitution originally robust. Death relieved him from the chilling hand of poverty at the age of sixty-four.

The works of no Scottish writer have been more useful or popular than those of Dr. Thomas Dick, author of "The Christian Philosopher." Dr. Dick attained his eighty-third year. His long career was attended with unceasing privations. He informed the writer that for upwards of half a century his principal meal consisted of bread and milk. The pressure of poverty compelled him to part with his copyrights. He obtained a small civil list pension in his eightieth year.

Scottish poets have been especially discouraged. The Scottish Parliament classed "bards, minstrels, and players," with "strolling vagabonds," and ordered their vocation to be suppressed. Within a comparatively recent period, some of the most gifted song-writers have been left to subsist on charity. William Thom, the Inverury poet, died at Dundee in 1848, in circumstances of the deepest poverty. John Younger, author of the Prize Essay on the Sabbath, and an ingenious poet, was, when unable to work at his trade of shoemaking, left to endure the bitterness of poverty and neglect. Younger died at St. Boswell's, in 1860, at the age of seventy-five. In this same neighbourhood, a brother of Dr. John Leyden, the distinguished poet and orientalist, has, at the age of fourscore, to seek subsistence as a farm labourer, with the prospect of the workhouse.

Mary Pyper, one of the best of living hymn-writers, is, at the age of seventy-two, dependent on the benevolence of a few gentlemen for her support. She is a native of the West of Scotland, but has long resided in Edinburgh.

The authors of two celebrated Scottish ballads, "Symon and Janet" and "The Brownie of Blednock," shared the usual fate of Scottish bards. For Andrew Scott, author of the former ballad, the office of parish sexton was provided. William Nicholson, author of "The Brownie," experienced a worse fate. When he was unable to earn his bread as a travelling musician, he was thrust into the workhouse.

To natives of Scotland in every part of the world the songs beginning "Ca' the yowes to the knowes" and "Owre the muir amang the heather" are abundantly familiar. These simple ditties have awakened in thousands the associations of youth, and enkindled delightful reminiscences. The authors, Isobel Pagan and Stuart Lewis, were compelled to subsist by mendicancy.

Every Scotsman knows the song of "Kelvin Grove;" and those who can appreciate the air are entranced by it. In 1859, Thomas Lyle, author of this delightful composition, and of a valuable work on "Ancient Ballads," passed to his rest in a condition of poverty.

Who has not been moved by the plaintive song of "Wae's me for Prince Charlie"? William Glen, the writer of this and other songs, died in indigence, at the age of thirty-seven. His widow and daughters live at Aberfoyle, utterly uncared for.

"My ain dear Nell" is one of the best esteemed of modern songs. Both the words and air were composed by Alexander Hume, another of the unfortunate bards. He died in 1859, in the deepest penury.

Two of the most accomplished collectors of Scottish song and ballad may be named together. They were brothers in misfortune. Peter Buchan is well known. His services in collecting northern minstrelsy were warmly commended by Sir Walter Scott. He also composed original songs, and published works in general literature. But his country did nothing for him, and he died poor. John Struthers, author of "The Poor Man's Sabbath," an admirable poem, and editor of "The Harp of Caledonia," shared the usual lot. He commenced life as a shoemaker, and like John Younger, laboured hard to overcome the necessity of pursuing this irksome occupation. For a period he obtained literary employment; but when he became old and infirm he was compelled to resume his original calling. He struggled with poverty to the last, and died in 1850, at the age of seventy-seven.

Three poets have lately passed away, whose genius would probably in any other country save that in which they were born—which they loved so well, and celebrated in impassioned strains—have redeemed them from the pressure of continual poverty and constant suffering. Elliot Aitchison died at Hawick in 1858. He was employed in a stocking factory when he was able to work, but possessing a feeble constitution, he was unable to prosecute his vocation continuously. He composed verses of remarkable power and classic elegance, which, had he been encouraged to publish, would have attracted attention and brought him both emolument and fame. But the bard was diffident, and shrunk from soliciting that patronage which none were found willing to bestow unasked.

Though not more ingenious than the former, Andrew Park is better known. His poem of "Silent Love" is one of the noblest compositions in the language. Published anonymously, it was ascribed to the more celebrated poets of the time. But the genius of Park only secured from his fellow-countrymen a coffin and a gravestone.

James Macfarlane has not obtained even the latter. His poetry is of the loftiest order—deep, sententious, chaste, and highly ornate. His ode, entitled "The Lords of Labour," is, as an incentive to industry, without a parallel in ancient or modern verse. Macfarlane led a life of poverty from the cradle to the grave. He often passed days without food, and occasionally lacked a home. His verses were admired, but the writer was unsought. A few generous persons soothed his last hours. He died in 1862, in his thirtieth year.

The catalogue of neglected genius is closed for the present, and it is hoped that no other name may be added. Some years since, the writer endeavoured to establish an institution for the relief of ingenious Scotsmen who suffered from temporary misfortune. He obtained the support of several influential persons; Lord Campbell became president, and Lord Brougham afforded his ready support. But the administration fell into inefficient hands; the fundamentals of the institution were changed, and the labour attending its formation was lost.

Scotland has been privileged as the birthplace of men of genius, but it has been destined that these should develop on other soils. The Scottish clergyman is expected to attend solely to the duties of his parish. Should he become an author, defects will be sought for in his discourses. The Edinburgh barrister who possesses the love of literature is careful to conceal his tastes till his professional reputation has been secured. The country lawyer who is frequently seen in the village library is not entrusted with the care of provincial suits. A Scottish surgeon who writes books may not obtain patients. No Scottish merchant will employ as clerk one who is known to compose verses, or to indulge in literary aspirations. These restrictions imply narrow views and a short-sighted policy. But a lesson is thereby taught that Scottish enterprise ought not to circumscribe the sphere of its development. Literary and other ingenious Scotsmen, when they betake themselves early in life to other lands, seldom fail to be successful. They reach the highest honours, not only as authors and men of science, but as statesmen, military commanders, and colonial governors. And with all the defects which attach to their native land, they are proud to acknowledge their northern origin. Amidst the prairies of South America, in the steppes of Africa, and on the burning plains of Hindostan, the Scotsman delights to recall the scenes and the customs of the dear old country. As he remembers its mountains and valleys, holms and haughs, carses and corries, and the old folks at home, with " the big ha' Bible," and the decent parish church, he is ready to exclaim, in an outburst of affection, " If I forget thee, O Jerusalem! let my right hand forget her cunning; if I do not remember thee, let my tongue cleave to the roof of my mouth."

CHAPTER X.

BIOGRAPHICAL AND HISTORICAL GLEANINGS.

"Great Julius, on the mountains bred,
A flock perhaps or herd had led;
He that the world subdued, had been
But the best wrestler on the green."
                                    WALLER.

"Dear I lo'e the wild war strains
    Our langsyne minstrels sung;
They rouse wi' patriotic fires
    The hearts of auld and young;
And even the dowie dirge that wails
    Some brave but ruined band,
Inspires us wi' a warmer love
    For hame and fatherland."
                          ARCHIBALD MACKAY.

IN the early part of the present century, a lively little Highland boy, named Colin Macliver, led the sports of his juvenile companions on Glasgow Green. His father came from one of the Western Isles, and had obtained employment in a carpenter's shop. He was a sober and industrious tradesman, and used his best efforts to provide for his wife and their two children, a boy and girl. He had been rather good-looking, for it was whispered that a Highland damsel had stooped from a higher social position to become his wife.

The Crimean war, which proved so disastrous to military reputations, revealed the qualities hitherto imperfectly known of a veteran officer of Scottish origin and name. Newspaper reports and military despatches teemed with the praises of Brigadier-General Sir Colin Campbell. His gallantry as leader of the Highland brigade at the Alma, and his remarkable resistance of the Russian charge at Balaklava, established his reputation. When tidings of the Indian insurrection of 1857 reached this country, every eye was fixed on Sir Colin Campbell as one equal to the terrible emergency. When he had assented to the royal wish that he would undertake the Indian command, he was asked when he would be ready. "To-morrow!" was his prompt reply. Under his victorious arms the Insurrection was speedily suppressed. He was ennobled, and took his place in the first Assembly of the nation. He chose as his title in the Peerage the name of the old river on the banks of which he had played at Glasgow Green. Colin Macliver, to please a maternal uncle, entered the army under his mother's name of Campbell. He rose step by step till he attained those honours which a grateful country rejoices to bestow on the deserving. His old father survived to rejoice in the prosperity of his son, and he was long supported by his bounty.

A gentleman of artistic tastes happened in the year 1805 to step into the cottage of a working shoemaker at Stockbridge, a suburb of Edinburgh. On the whitewashed wall of the apartment he observed a number of well-executed representations of animals drawn with keel* and charcoal. He examined the drawings, which he proceeded to commend highly. "Hoot," said the shoemaker's wife, "these are bits o' drawings o' oor Davie; he was seein' some wild beasts at a show, and he's caulked them there to let me see them." "Indeed," said the gentleman, "and what are you to make of the boy?" "Deed," said the honest woman, "he'll jist need to sit down on the stool aside his father, and learn to mak and mend shoon."† "That will never do," said the gentleman; "he is quite a genius, and you must make him a painter." Through the gentleman's intervention, the shoemaker's son was soon after apprenticed to a house-painter.

The youth proved industrious, and indicated uncommon genius in his art. He became a painter of dramatic scenery,—a department which he eminently adorned. He bestowed attention on Gothic architecture, and produced some admirable paintings of the ruins of his native country. He sought subjects for his pencil in the ancient structures of Normandy and of Northern Europe. Proceeding to Spain, he brought home noble representations of the architecture of the Moors. He visited the

---

* Red chalk. † Shoes.

HISTORICAL GLEANINGS. 303

Holy Land, and delineated scenes endeared to Christians of every country by early and hallowed associations.

This artist was David Roberts,—one of the most gifted of British painters, and a man endowed with the purest virtues. He lived to befriend the visitor at his father's cottage, who, discovering his artistic talent, had placed him on the first step of the ladder of fortune. Mr. Roberts died at London, on the 25th November, 1864, in his sixty-eighth year. His Memoirs have been published by his ingenious friend, Mr. James Ballantine.

In the year 1800, James, only child of Sergeant Nisbet, of the Royal Artillery, entered himself as apprentice to a solicitor at Kelso. After a trial of three years, he found that the prospect of following the business of a country attorney was intolerable. He recovered his indenture and proceeded to London, where he engaged himself as clerk to a West India merchant. He was now eighteen. His salary was at first £50; but it was periodically increased. He lived moderately, and saved a portion of his income every year. In 1809 he opened a bookseller's shop in Castle Street. He was attentive to business, and prospered. He purchased premises in Berners Street, and began to publish religious works. James Nisbet soon became widely known. Every work which bore his imprint was received with confidence by those who rejoiced to promote the circulation of evangelical literature. Mr. Nisbet died in 1854, full of years and honours. The publishing house originated by his enterprise is one of the most important in the kingdom.

The churchyard of Lochmaben, Dumfriesshire, contains a monumental obelisk without any inscription. It is associated with a curious history. James Mounsey, a native of the district, and grand-nephew of William Paterson, who founded the Bank of England, was physician to the Emperor Paul of Russia. When that unfortunate monarch was assassinated, a report arose that Dr. Mounsey was concerned in the massacre, and to prevent his becoming the victim of popular vengeance his death was reported. A mock funeral took place in Lochmaben churchyard, and the obelisk was reared to denote the grave.

When the Grand Duke Nicholas, afterwards Emperor of Russia, was on a visit to Britain, he evinced a particular interest in the cause of education. During his visit to Edinburgh the Duke expressed a wish that he might be conducted to the more celebrated schools. When visiting an academy in one of the suburbs, he requested the head-master to examine in his presence a few of his smartest pupils. The teacher remarked that his most promising scholar was a boy named Patterson. On the youth being examined before him the Duke expressed his surprise at his remarkable precocity. "If he will proceed to Russia I will make him a nobleman," said the Duke. The schoolmaster consulted the boy's mother on the Duke's proposal, but her consent could not be obtained. The youth studied for the Scottish Church. His career was short, but peculiarly brilliant. The name of John Brown Patterson, author of the Prize Essay on the "National Character of the Athenians," is familiar. He became minister of Falkirk, and died in 1835.

Alexander Peden, the celebrated Covenanter, enjoyed the reputation of being gifted as a prophet. The ascription of supernatural powers to those eminent for their sagacity and piety was not uncommon in ancient Scotland. The prophecies assigned to Peden are generally unimportant, or such as a shrewd person might readily vaticinate without supernatural assistance. One of his prophecies was sufficiently remarkable. Discoursing to his people from Amos vii. 8, he used these words,—"I'll tell you good news. Our Lord will take a feather out of Antichrist's wing which shall bring down the Duke of York, and banish him out of these kingdoms. And there shall never a man of the House of Stuart sit upon the throne of Britain after the Duke of York, whose reign is now short." Peden died in 1686, two years before the dethronement of James VII., and the event of the Revolution.

One of the tales included by Professor Wilson in his "Lights and Shadows of Scottish Life" is entitled "The Covenanter's Marriage Day." It is founded on an occurrence of real life, the tradition of which still obtains in Ettrick Forest. William Laidlaw, a shepherd at Chapelhope, had won the hand of Mary

Stewart, a beautiful shepherdess. It was the period of the religious persecutions, and the marriage was celebrated in a lonely retreat among the hills. As the couple were returning home from the celebration of their union, a party of soldiers marched towards them. "You are a Presbyterian, an attender of conventicles, and a harbourer of field-preachers," said the leader. Laidlaw was silent. "Prepare to die," added the commander. In a few seconds the lifeblood of the hapless bridegroom crimsoned the moor. The bride had fallen into a swoon, but she was aroused by the report of firearms. She threw herself upon the corpse of her beloved husband. In that hour her reason took flight, and she became a maniac. She gathered withered flowers, and went about singing a melancholy air, with the sad chorus, " The grave, the grave for me."

During the month of August 1859 the author of this work was residing at the village of Darnick, near Abbotsford. Having undertaken to conduct Divine service in a neighbouring parish, he was proceeding on the Sunday morning to the scene of duty. In the course of his journey he found an aged female lying on the side of the turnpike. He was about to assist her, when he was informed by his conductor that the woman was intoxicated. This was an error. The hapless woman was dying,—she died that day. The next person who came up recognised her, and, conveying her to a cottage, comforted her last hours. This was Elizabeth Graham, one of the two prototypes of *Madge Wildfire,* celebrated by Sir Walter Scott in his "Heart of Mid Lothian." Her sister prototype was *Feckless Fannie* of Ayrshire. Elizabeth Graham was the daughter of a respectable farmer, but having been seduced by a false lover, she lost her reason, and became a constant wanderer.

The old and popular song of "Jenny Nettles" celebrates a rustic beauty of Fife, whose melancholy fate might have been depicted in more plaintive strains. Jenny was disowned by a faithless lover, and unable to bear the scorn of society, she terminated her existence. Her remains were interred between two lairds' lands near the Lomond Hills, where a cairn was placed to denote the spot. About forty years ago the grave was examined, when the skull of the unhappy maiden was discovered, along with her earrings and necklace. The skull is now in the museum of Mr. Joseph Paton of Dunfermline.

Mr. John Home's tragedy of "Douglas" is founded on the old ballad of "Gil Morice." The hero of the ballad, Gil Morice, an earl's son, is represented as sending a message to the wife of Lord Barnard to meet him in the "green wood." His page delivered the message to the dame in the hearing of her lord. His lordship's jealousy was excited, and he proceeded to the "green wood" to encounter one whom he supposed to be the paramour of his faithless spouse. He found Gil Morice, whom he complimented on his manly beauty, and then stabbed to the heart. The baron's spouse, when she saw the lifeless remains of the youth, announced to her lord that Gil Morice was her son. She had built for him a bower in the "green wood," that she might occasionally see him, while shame had prevented her acknowledging the existence of one to whom before wedlock she had given birth. The baron expressed his deep concern for his rashness, and joined his lamentations with those of his spouse. He said,—

> "I'll aye lament for Gil Morice
> As gin he were my ain,
> I'll ne'er forget the driery day
> On which the youth was slain."

The romantic character of the story led the collectors of the older ballads to hazard an opinion that the story was a creation of romance. Tradition had, however, assigned a particular spot on the banks of the Carron river as the burying-place of the youth. During the course of the present century the proprietor of the estate resolved to erect a cottage at the spot, and in digging for the foundation, the workmen discovered an ancient grave, containing bones. These mouldered into dust on exposure to the air, but several of the teeth were found to be perfectly entire. They were inserted in a glass case, which has been attached to the wall of the cottage vestibule. The writer has inspected the relics.

The old ballad of "Johnny Faa, or the Gypsie Laddie," describes the elopement of a Countess of Cassilis with a gipsy. The story is thus represented in the tradition. Faa was a gentleman of good family, in the county of Haddington, and was an attached lover of the Countess before her marriage. She had married the Earl to gratify her kinsfolk, but contrary to her own inclinations. Though the lady was wedded to another, Faa had resolved to make an attempt to secure her person. Accordingly he proceeded to her residence during her lord's absence, accompanied by eight retainers, all being disguised as gipsies.

Having procured an interview with the Countess, Faa made himself known to her, and induced her to elope with him. When Lord Cassilis returned home, he assembled his vassals and proceeded in quest of the fugitives. He overtook them somewhere on the borders of England, and at a pitched battle slew Faa and seven of his followers. Having recovered his wife, he built a tower for her reception in the village of Maybole, where he caused her to be kept a close prisoner during the remainder of her life. This story has been often related in connection with the ballad, but the genealogical accounts of the family do not afford any evidence as to its accuracy.

In the parish churchyard of Kirkconnell, Dumfriesshire, a flat tombstone exhibits two sculptured swords, and is inscribed with these words:—"*Hic jacet Adamus Fleming.*" The stone is associated with the touching old ballad of "Fair Helen of Kirkconnell." Some time in the seventeenth century, Helen Irving, a celebrated beauty, and daughter of the Laird of Kirkconnell, was beloved by two young gentlemen of the neighbourhood. The favoured lover was Adam Fleming. The rejected suitor, Bell of Blacket House, vowed to sacrifice his successful rival on the first opportunity. One evening Helen was seated with her accepted lover on a romantic spot, by the margin of the river Kirtle, when Bell suddenly appeared on the other side of the stream, in the act of presenting a musket at his rival. The maiden, perceiving the imminent danger of her lover, threw herself between him and his assassin. Pierced with the bullet intended for her admirer, she fell into his arms and immediately expired. Fleming pursued the murderer and slew him. He afterwards proceeded to Spain, where he fought against the infidels. Returning to Kirkconnell, he went to the parish churchyard, and stretched himself on the grave of the hapless maid, who, to preserve his life, had sacrificed her own. His feelings so overcame him, that he burst a blood vessel and died. His remains were deposited beside those of the gentle Helen.

The story of Bessy Bell and Mary Gray, celebrated in ballad, is, though partaking of a romantic character, founded on truth. Two young ladies in Perthshire were attached friends. One of them, Miss Elizabeth Bell, was the daughter of Mr. Bell of Kinvaid; the other, Miss Mary Gray, was daughter of Mr. Gray, proprietor of Lynedoch. They both were beautiful and of engaging manners, and had each attracted the affection of a young gentleman in the neighbourhood. The plague of 1645 was raging with terrible severity, and the maidens left their paternal homes, and took shelter in a bower at Burn Braes, on the banks of the Lednoch. They determined to receive no visitors save the youth whom they held in mutual esteem. He paid daily visits to the bower, and having caught the infection unconsciously carried it to Burn Braes. The maidens died, and, as they had requested, were both interred at the spot where they had sought unavailing shelter. In the words of the ballad,—

> "They wadna lie in Methven kirkyard
> Amang their gentle kin;
> But they wad lie on Dronach haugh
> To beak fornent* the sun."

Some years ago the writer made a pilgrimage to the grave of the loving maidens; he found the spot enclosed by a railing. This was erected through the liberality and kindly sentiment of Major Berry, the late proprietor of Lynedoch.

Lynedoch became the property of Thomas Graham of Balgowan, the hero of Barossa, who, on his elevation to the peerage, chose it as his title. Mr. Graham lived many years on his estate of Balgowan in Perthshire, attending to the duties of a country landowner. In his forty-second year, his wife, a daughter of Lord Cathcart, died somewhat suddenly, and having been extremely attached to her, the shock of her removal severely depressed him. He entered the army, and,

* To rest together in a sunny spot.

regardless of his life, fought with desperate courage. He became one of the most distinguished of the Peninsular heroes.

The sudden death of a young lady to whom he was about to be married led William Drummond of Hawthornden to betake himself to literary seclusion. To the event of his bereavement the world is indebted for the production of those works, in prose and verse, which reflect so much credit on his country and age.

There is an anecdote illustrative of strong family affection during the political troubles of the seventeenth century. In 1646, several noble persons were tried at St. Andrews for bearing arms in the royal army. Among those sentenced to death was Lord Ogilvie, eldest son of the Earl of Airlie. The noble convict, having pretended sickness, was allowed to receive a visit from the members of his family. When his wife, mother, and sisters entered his cell, the guards retired for a short period. In the interval one of his lordship's sisters arrayed him in her gown, while she threw herself into the bed, and put his night-cap on her head. When the guards entered, an affectionate parting ensued, and the visitors, including the disguised nobleman, were conducted to their carriage. On the escape of Lord Ogilvie being made known, some of the nobility would have wreaked vengeance on the ladies, but more merciful counsels prevailed.

Charles, sixth Earl of Strathmore, was killed in 1728 from an accidental wound received in a scuffle.

He had married, three years before, Lady Susan Cochrane, second daughter of the Earl of Dundonald, who was then in her fifteenth year. Left a widow at eighteen, Lady Strathmore received many advantageous offers of marriage, all of which she chose to reject. When she had reached the mature age of thirty-six she took a fancy for her groom, George Forbes, to whom she offered herself in marriage. The groom at first thought that the Countess had become mentally disordered, but when he perceived that she was serious, he gladly embraced the good fortune which had so unexpectedly fallen in his way. The marriage took place, and the Countess, who had no children by her first union, gave birth to a daughter. Her husband proved most unworthy of his elevation, and rendered himself so obnoxious by his low tastes and intemperate habits, that the Countess left him and proceeded to reside in France. She placed the child in a convent at Rouen. Lady Strathmore died in 1754, and it was found that, having lived expensively, she had left nothing for the support of her child. Some years after, George Forbes, who had set up as a keeper of livery stables at Leith, married a girl of his own rank, and became the father of a family. He now sent to Rouen for his daughter by the Countess, who had reached her fifteenth year. On her arrival in her father's house she was treated most cruelly by her stepmother, and so made an abrupt departure from the family. She crossed the Forth at the Kinghorn ferry, probably with a view of proceeding to the seat of the Strathmore family in Forfarshire. In her journey through Fife she became exhausted, and sought rest and a night's lodging at a farmhouse occupied by a family of the name of Lauder. She narrated to the family her remarkable story, with which they were so interested that they asked her to reside with them. Soon after, Miss Forbes married the farmer's son, who proved an affectionate husband. But the Lauder family suffered reverses, and the daughter of Lady Strathmore, now a widow, was found in 1821 residing in a small cottage near Stirling. When her history became known, several influential persons in the district appealed on her behalf to her noble relatives. Her claims were acknowledged, and an annuity of one hundred pounds was settled on her. Her latter years were spent in comparative comfort.

Lord Dalmeny, eldest son of James, second Earl of Roseberry, met in London a most fascinating lady, whom he persuaded to marry him. After marriage the parties proceeded to the Continent, where they lived together with much concord. At length the lady was seized with a severe illness, which the physicians assured her she could not long survive. She called for a slip of paper, and wrote upon it these words:—" I am the wife of the Rev. Mr. Gough, rector of Thorpe, in Essex. My maiden name was C. Cannon, and my last request is to be buried at Thorpe." Lord Dalmeny was deeply grieved at the loss of his wife, and was inclined to believe that the writing she had left had been caused by her ailment affecting her brain, and producing delusion. He caused, however, the body to be removed to England, and on his arrival sent for the Rev. Mr. Gough to consult with him on the subject of the writing. The clergyman recognised in the corpse the features of his wife. She had left him for some years, and he had been unable to obtain any trace of her movements. Lord Dalmeny and the clergyman compassionated with each other on the strange occurrence which had brought them together. The funeral took place at Thorpe, and both the husbands of the deceased lady were mourners at her grave.

Towards the end of the sixteenth century, Mr. Chisholm, the young laird of Cromlix, became enamoured of Miss Helen Murray, daughter of the laird of Ardoch, a lady much celebrated for her beauty. Miss Murray reciprocated the affection of her admirer, and it was agreed that, during his absence on some business in France, their correspondence should be conducted through the intervention of a gentleman in Dunblane. This person proved untrue. He secreted the letters on both sides, and sought to prejudice the lady against her admirer. Protracted silence and false representations at length succeeded in overcoming Miss Murray's affection for young Chisholm, and his unworthy confidant now sought to win the lady's affection for himself. By the strong importunities of her friends, she was persuaded to assent to his proposals. Their marriage was solemnized; but the event had just taken place when Chisholm unexpectedly returned. The villany of the treacherous friend was exposed, and the marriage was annulled. Helen was now united to her faithful admirer. A song, composed by the lover during the period of the supposed desertion of his mistress, was long popular. It is known as "Cromlet's Lilt." A similar story in connection with the courtship and marriage of the gallant Sir Robert Munro, Bart., of Foulis, is related by Mr. Hugh Miller, in his "Scenes and Legends of the North of Scotland."

Dr. Abernethy, the celebrated physician, carried his well-known abruptness of manner even into his courting his wife. He had been professionally attending a widow lady for several weeks, when he was struck with the prudent conduct of her daughter, and formed the opinion that she might suit as his helpmate. Taking leave of his patient on a Saturday, he said to her, "Madam, you are now so well that I will make my farewell visit on Monday. Meanwhile I wish you and your daughter seriously to consider the proposal I am about to make. It is abrupt and unceremonious, I am aware; but the excessive occupation of my time by my professional duties affords me no leisure to accomplish what I desire by the more ordinary course of solicitation. My annual receipts amount to £——, and I can settle £—— on my wife. My character is generally known. I have seen in your daughter an affectionate child, a careful nurse, and a ladylike member of a family. Such a person is all a husband could covet. I offer her my hand. On Monday I shall receive your determination, for I have no time for courtship." The answer was an acceptance of the offered hand. The marriage proved a happy one.

Few persons are aware that the popular song "The Boatie rows," was composed by John Ewen, an ironmonger in Aberdeen, who died in 1821. Ewen was a person of miserly habits, and a sort of domestic tyrant. His only child, Miss Ewen, married in 1787 a person of her own rank and of most respectable character, but he would make no proper provision on the occasion. He afterwards ignored the existence of his daughter and her family, and bequeathed his fortune of £16,000 for the establishment of an hospital at Aberdeen. Much to the satisfaction of the public, the settlement, which was challenged by the daughter, was pronounced invalid by the House of Lords, and the money restored to the descendants of the ill-conditioned poet.

Another unamiable Scottish poet was David Mallet. His original family name was Malloch; his father kept a small public-house at Crieff, and he held in his younger years the humble situation of janitor of the Edinburgh High School. When he rose to a position of affluence, and mixed in the literary society of London, Malloch was most desirous of concealing all particulars of his origin and early history. With this view he changed his name to Mallet. The immediate cause of the change has been assigned to the circumstance that he had received from some wit the soubriquet of *Moloch*, on account of his habit of declaiming against the Christian Religion. Mallet composed " The Birks of Invermay," and the ballad of " William and Margaret."

One of the parties celebrated by Burns in his well-known festive song beginning—

> " O Willie brewed a peck o' maut,
> And Rob and Allan cam to pree,"

was Mr. Allan Masterton, writing-master in Edinburgh. The author's father enjoyed the acquaintance of Mr. Masterton, and was informed by him of the following remarkable occurrence in his own personal history. Having been on a visit to London, he had arranged to return home in a passenger vessel bound for Leith. He had paid his passage-money, and a porter had brought his luggage to the place of embarkation. Just as he was on the point of stepping on board, he was seized with a strong presentiment that the vessel would not reach her destination. He therefore determined of a sudden to forego his original intention, and to proceed homewards by land. When he reached Edinburgh, he learned that the ship in which he had proposed to sail had foundered at sea, and that all the passengers had perished.

HISTORICAL GLEANINGS. 319

These are a few gleanings from a field of biographical and historical Lore, in which much remains to be collected and gathered up. What has been accomplished by the author of this Work, and by those who have preceded him in such inquiries, may prompt others to prosecute similar researches.

Such investigations have a salutary tendency. The untravelled Scotsman who plumes himself on his ancient pedigree, and on the moralities of his sires, may be led to discover that the credit of the family tree may have chiefly to rest on his own good deeds, since the virtues of one portion of his progenitors may be more than counterbalanced by the misdemeanours of another.

The country which produced Wallace and Bruce, Knox and Chalmers, Napier and Watt, Abercromby, Moore, and Lord Clyde, teemed with highland reivers, border thieves, and lazy islanders. The most inhuman monsters who ever disgraced civilization were not greater offenders than Cardinal Beaton, Thomas Dalyell, Robert Grierson, John Graham, and Archbishop Sharpe.

On the other hand, in gleaning from his country's Annals, the Scotsman finds examples prompting him to virtuous enterprise. He discovers that he belongs to a country in which the footprint of the invader was extinguished in his blood, and in which thousands of a God-fearing population consented to die rather than renounce their religion. Those who prove unworthy of the better deeds of such a country incur a responsibility from which the virtuous would instinctively shrink.

Let the glory of Scotland be upheld by a discreet reverence of the past and an earnest improvement of the present. In rearing Memorial Stones to our illustrious departed, let us strive to imitate their patient self-denial and Christian earnestness. Let us seek to be governed by those principles of honour, truth, and justice, which guided our old heroes, and the possession of which will best evidence that we represent them worthily.

THE END.

J. AND W. RIDER, PRINTERS, LONDON.

www.ingramcontent.com/pod-product-compliance
Lightning Source LLC
Chambersburg PA
CBHW022020240426

43667CB00042B/993